BAUDELAIRE, MAN OF HIS TIME

WITHDRAWN

WITHDRAWN

PQ 2191 .Z5 H9
Hyslop, Lois Boe, 1908-
Baudelaire, man of his time

BAUDELAIRE

MAN OF HIS TIME

LOIS BOE HYSLOP

YALE UNIVERSITY PRESS   NEW HAVEN AND LONDON

Copyright © 1980 by Yale University.
All rights reserved. This book may not be
reproduced, in whole or in part, in any form
(beyond that copying permitted by Sections 107
and 108 of the U.S. Copyright Law and except by
reviewers for the public press), without written
permission from the publishers.

Designed by James J. Johnson
and set in VIP Sabon type.
Printed in the United States of America by
Vail-Ballou Press, Binghamton, N.Y.

Library of Congress Cataloging in Publication Data

Hyslop, Lois Boe, 1908–
    Baudelaire, man of his time.

    Includes bibliographical references and index.
    1. Baudelaire, Charles Pierre, 1821–1867—
Contemporaries.   2. Poets, French—19th century—
Biography.   I. Title.
PQ2191.Z5H9   841'.8 [B]   80–145
ISBN 0-300-02513-0
10   9   8   7   6   5   4   3   2   1

IN MEMORY OF
FRANCIS—A TRIBUTE OF LOVE AND ESTEEM

Contents

Preface

SO MUCH HAS BEEN WRITTEN ABOUT THE
emotional and spiritual life of Baudelaire, about his torments
and despair, about his relationship with his mother, with Jeanne
Duval, Madame Sabatier, and Marie Daubrun that the reader
tends to think of him as a lonely, tormented genius who, especially in later years, longed to flee "the horror of the human
face" and seek, in moments of deepest gloom, only "emptiness,
blackness, and starkness" ("*le vide, le noir, et le nu*").

It is easy to forget that in happier days he had been full of
enthusiasm for life, curious about all its aspects, and deeply re-
sponsive to its beauty, its ugliness, its intriguing mysteries. One
tends to overlook the fact that, very much caught up in the world
about him, he was truly a man of his time.

A brilliant conversationalist, Baudelaire deliberately sought
the company of gifted people with whom he could exchange
ideas or engage in stimulating discussions. Though his emotional
and spiritual life may be largely explained in terms of his temperament and psychological makeup, his intellectual life was
necessarily determined to a great extent by his associations with
the men and women of his day.

The informed reader of Baudelaire is not unaware of the
poet's participation in the intellectual, artistic, and political life
of his time. Nevertheless, it comes as something of a surprise to
note both the large number of his contacts and the wide diversity
of his interests. Artists, musicians, sculptors, men of letters, ac-
tors, social reformers, all aroused in him an inquisitiveness and a
desire to learn more about their creative activity and their aesthetic and philosophical beliefs. Throughout his life he associated

with people from all professions and from almost all walks of life—from Nadar, the famous photographer and balloonist, to Charles Meryon, the gifted and mentally unbalanced printmaker; from the squint-eyed Sarah, a common prostitute, to the charming Madame Meurice, a cultivated and kindhearted society woman who quickly learned to see through the saturnine pose of the poet and grew to be as fond of him as he was of her.

Throughout the years, Baudelaire was to continue to be a man of his age, observing and sometimes participating in its changing, chaotic events, exchanging ideas with its most brilliant representatives, while developing and elaborating his own aesthetic beliefs. The development of these ideas was in large part a result of his endless discussions with his friends and acquaintances as well as of his voluminous reading. In a few instances, as in the case of Delacroix, he adopted certain of the artistic conceptions of an associate. In other cases, like that of Paul Chenavard, he clarified his own thinking by analyzing and arguing against concepts which seemed to him false or unsound.

What he wrote of Pierre Dupont is equally applicable to Baudelaire himself: "I prefer the poet who is in continuous communication with the men of his time and exchanges with them thoughts and emotions translated into a noble language that is sufficiently correct." Though Baudelaire was referring specifically to the poetry of Dupont, he could scarcely have described in more accurate fashion his own way of life. Some saw in his visits to art galleries, studios, and cafés, and in his love of frequent and prolonged conversations with his companions a tendency to fritter away his time, to "flâner et de vagabonder, même en esprit," as Jules Troubat, Sainte-Beuve's secretary, wrote somewhat disapprovingly.

In certain respects, Troubat was right. And Baudelaire knew it. He himself often acknowledged with a feeling of remorse his proclivity to pleasure, his proneness to put intellectual or artistic diversions before creative activity. Yet at least once in his life he seemed to realize the importance and value of those moments of leisure:

It is partly through leisure that I grew. To my great detriment; for leisure, without money, increases debts and results in disrespect. But to my great advantage as far as sensibility, meditation, and the possibility of dandyism and dilettantism are concerned. Other men of letters are, for the most part, disgusting, ignorant grinds. [*OC*, I:697]

There can be little doubt that the poet's association with men like Manet, Daumier, Liszt, Sainte-Beuve, and Gautier did much to broaden his horizon and contribute to his storehouse of knowledge. At the same time, his friendship with persons of lesser stature, like Champfleury, Chenavard, Jean-Jacques Pradier, Charles Asselineau, and Auguste Poulet-Malassis, may have proved equally effective. To criticize Baudelaire, as has been done, for having had among his closest friends a number of minor figures is to forget that brilliance of idea and thought is not limited to the creative genius. In fact, the ideas of a Champfleury may well have been more bracing and stimulating than those of a Hugo.

To detail exhaustively all those with whom Baudelaire came in contact or to seek the exact nature of their relationship would be an exercise in futility and monotony. I have had to exclude many with whom his association was either transient or more or less insignificant. There was Whistler, whose Thames etchings (done in 1858 and shown in Paris in 1861) were glowingly described by the poet-critic in his *Salon de 1859;* there was Alphonse Legros, painter and etcher, who did a little-known etching of the poet as well as a number based on the stories of Poe; there was more importantly Fantin-Latour, whose *Hommage à Delacroix* depicts a sad and strangely gentle Baudelaire seated among a group of Delacroix's admirers that included Whistler, Manet, Legros, and Champfleury. And there were too many others to mention.

It is our hope that by seeing the author of *Les Fleurs du Mal* in the context of his day, among his friends and acquaintances, we may better understand his intellectual and artistic growth and better appreciate the complexity of his genius. If Baudelaire offers us a penetrating insight into the art and culture of his day, it was largely because he was so completely a man of his time. Fortunately, for the reader of today, his work—"a vessel favored by a strong north wind" ("vaisseau favorisé par un grand aquilon")—has lost none of its relevance and appeal and has made its author a man of our own time as well.

ABBREVIATIONS

I have cited primary sources in the text, using the following abbreviations:

> *Corr.*   *Baudelaire, Correspondance.* 2 vols. Pléiade Edition, edited by Claude Pichois. Paris: Gallimard, 1973.
>
> *OC*   Charles Baudelaire, *Oeuvres complètes.* 2 vols. Edited by Claude Pichois. Paris: Gallimard, 1975.
>
> *PLB*   *Lettres à Baudelaire.* Compiled and edited by Claude Pichois and Vincenette Pichois. Neuchâtel: A la Baconnière, 1973.
>
> *POC*   Pierre-Joseph Proudhon, *Oeuvres complètes.* 15 vols. Edited by C. Bouglé and H. Moysset. Paris: Marcel Rivière, 1923–59.

In quoting Baudelaire and his circle, I have generally given prose passages in English (my own translations) but have retained the original French for verse quotations.

ACKNOWLEDGMENTS

I should like to express my deep appreciation to the distinguished scholar W. T. Bandy, who kindly read the first two chapters of this book and encouraged me to continue my project. I also wish to thank the Pennsylvania State University Press, University Park, Pennsylvania, and London, for permission to reprint part of an essay from *Baudelaire as a Love Poet and Other Essays.*

Most of all I wish to acknowledge my great debt to my husband, Francis E. Hyslop, for his invaluable assistance and his unflagging support.

Chronology

1821   9 April: Birth of Charles Baudelaire in Paris.

1827   10 February: Death of François Baudelaire, Charles's father, at age of 68. Charles's mother was 34 years younger than her husband.

1828   8 November: Marriage of Charles's mother to Major (later General) Aupick.

1832   Charles and his mother go to Lyons, where his step-father had been sent to repress the uprisings, and where he attends the Collège royal.

1836   Returns with family to Paris. Attends the Lycée Louis-le-Grand.

1839–40 Registers periodically at the Ecole de Droit. Leads a carefree life in the Latin Quarter. Contracts a venereal disease in the autumn of 1839.

1841   9 June: Alarmed by the Bohemian life of Charles, his family sends him on a sea voyage. He embarks on the *Paquebot-des-Mers-du-Sud* destined to sail to Calcutta, but goes only as far as the islands of Mauritius and Réunion.

1842   18 February: Returns to France on the *Alcide*.

           9 April: Comes of age and receives an inheritance of 100,000 gold francs left him by his father. Moves to the Ile Saint-Louis where for a time he lives in the Hôtel Pimodan (Hôtel de Lauzun). Becomes a close friend of the painter Emile Deroy.

1844   To prevent Charles from squandering his inheritance, Mme Aupick arranges the appointment of a legal guardian, M. Narcisse-Désiré Ancelle, who was to have complete control over the remaining capital and pay Charles the interest in monthly installments.

1845   May: *Le Salon de 1845*.

        30 June: Makes a feeble attempt at suicide.

1846   21 January: "Le Musée classique du bazar Bonne-Nouvelle" in *Le Corsaire-Satan*.
        May: *Le Salon de 1846*.

1847   January: A short novel, *La Fanfarlo*. Baudelaire's interest in Edgar Allan Poe is aroused by his reading of Isabelle Meunier's translation of *The Black Cat* in *La Démocratie pacifique*.

1848   24 February: Takes a small part in the revolution of 1848. Jules Buisson claims to have seen Baudelaire brandishing a new rifle and shouting, "We must go and shoot General Aupick."

        27 February, 1 & 2 March: Baudelaire, Champfleury, and Toubin publish two issues of an ephemeral newspaper, *Le Salut public*. Courbet draws a vignette for the second issue.

        10 April–6 May: Is associated with *La Tribune nationale*, a moderate socialist newspaper.

        June: Takes a small part in the June insurrection.

        21 August: Writes his first letter to Proudhon.

        October: For a brief period serves as editor in chief of the provincial newspaper *Le Représentant de l'Indre* in Châteauroux.

1851   7,8,11,12 March: Publication of "Du Vin et du hachisch" in *Le Messager de l'Assemblée*.

        9 April: Eleven poems in *Le Messager de l'Assemblée*.

September: Shows Asselineau a calligraphed manuscript of his poems.

27 November: "Les Drames et les Romans honnêtes" in the *Semaine théâtrale.*

2 December: Coup d'état of Louis Napoleon. Baudelaire's disillusionment.

1852   22 January: "L'Ecole païenne" in the *Semaine théâtrale.*

March and April: "Edgar Allan Poe, sa vie et ses ouvrages" in *La Revue de Paris.*

1855   A series of articles on the world's fair held in Paris, including articles on Delacroix and Ingres.

8 July: "De l'essence du rire et généralement du comique dans les arts plastiques" in *Le Portefeuille.*

1856   12 March: *Histoires extraordinaires,* The first volume of Baudelaire's translations of Poe's stories.

1857   8 March: *Nouvelles Histoires extraordinaires,* the second volume of his translations of Poe.

25 June: First edition of *Les Fleurs du Mal.*

20 August: Six poems of *Les Fleurs du Mal* are ordered by the court to be removed from the volume.

1 October: *Quelques caricaturistes français.*

15 October: *Quelques caricaturistes étrangers.*

1858   13 May: Translation from Poe: *Aventures d'Arthur Gordon Pym.*

30 September: "De l'Idéal artificiel—Le Hachisch" in the *Revue contemporaine.*

1859   10 & 20 June; 1 & 20 July: *Le Salon de 1859.*

26 November: *Théophile Gautier,* a pamphlet with a letter-preface by Victor Hugo.

1860   May: *Les Paradis artificiels.*

1861   February: Second edition of *Les Fleurs du Mal* containing thirty-five new poems.

4 May: *Richard Wagner et "Tannhäuser" à Paris.*

15 June–15 August: Nine of the ten critical essays which constitute "Réflexions sur quelques-uns de mes contemporains" in the *Revue fantaisiste.*

1862   2 August: Seven critical essays (Hugo, Desbordes-Valmore, Gautier, Banville, Dupont, Leconte de Lisle, Le Vavasseur) and seven poems in Eugène Crépet's anthology *Les Poètes français.*

1863   2 September; 14 & 22 November: "L'Oeuvre et la vie d'Eugène Delacroix" in *L'Opinion nationale.*

November: Translation of Poe's *Eureka.*

26 & 29 November; 3 December: "Le Peintre de la vie moderne" in *Le Figaro.*

1864   24 April: Baudelaire arrives in Brussels to give a series of lectures and to find a publisher for his collected works.

1865   16 March: *Histoires grotesques et sérieuses,* the fifth and final volume of Poe translations.

1866   ca. 15 March: Baudelaire suffers a slight stroke while visiting the church of Saint-Loup in Namur. Later his condition worsens and he becomes partially paralyzed and aphasic.

2 July: Baudelaire is brought back to Paris and enters the nursing home of Doctor Duval.

1867   31 August: Death of Baudelaire.

2 September: Burial at the Montparnasse cemetery.

1

Baudelaire and the World of Art

"GLORIFIER LE CULTE DES images (ma grande, mon unique, ma primitive passion)," Baudelaire wrote in *Mon Coeur mis à nu* (*OC*, I:701). Hardly an exaggeration on his part, since his first important published work was the *Salon de 1845*, in which he wrote with a sureness of judgment quite remarkable for a young man of twenty-four. In contrast to his vastly superior *Salon de 1846* and *Salon de 1859*, he followed the traditional format used by Diderot, whom he had read with the greatest admiration and whose *Salon de 1759* had just been republished when the Salon of 1845 opened.

Like Diderot, Baudelaire classified works by genres and considered the various artists within that genre. He even adopted the same tone as his illustrious predecessor—at times chatty, lively, and familiar; at other times uncompromising, scornful, and even harsh, particularly in his treatment of popular artists such as Victor Hugo's friend Louis Boulanger or the much admired Horace Vernet. He hailed the superiority of Corot and Rousseau as landscape painters, agreed with other contemporary critics in their admiration for Delacroix and Ingres, and—almost alone in his time and with extraordinary judgment and courage—singled out Daumier as the equal in draftsmanship of the two great artists. Finally, thinking undoubtedly of Balzac in the novel, he called on the artists of his day to "heed tomorrow's wind" and to portray the heroism of modern life. From his commentary on the various painters there emerged three key aesthetic principles that figured prominently in all his later criticism: the importance of

I

color, the necessity for "temperament" in artists as opposed to skill, and the use of subjects drawn from modern life.

The reader can only wonder how one so young and untrained could write with such authority. The answer lies in his self-education and in his close association with the artists and critics of his time. From them and from his reading Baudelaire learned all he could, took what he considered valid, and turned it into something more or less new.

Distinguished scholars—including among others Jean Pommier, Margaret Gilman, Jean Adhémar, René Huyghe, Lucie Horner, and Gita May—have discovered many of the sources of the aesthetic principles espoused by Baudelaire in his Salons of 1845 and 1846. There is no doubt that Diderot, Stendhal, Heine, and Delacroix—to mention only a few—played an important role in the formation of his aesthetic theories. But it is also true that many of their ideas could have come to him indirectly. As David Kelley points out in his brilliant study on the *Salon de 1846,* "Simply by listening, Baudelaire could have gleaned all that he needed in order to write the *Salon de 1846* without having read a single word of his 'sources'. . ."[1] Kelley reminds us that the "salonniers" of the middle of the nineteenth century were often well acquainted with each other, drew their knowledge from the same basic sources, and, what is even more important, engaged in long discussions of the same aesthetic problems.

That Baudelaire learned much from his association with the artists and critics of his day is undeniable. But despite his debt to others his originality and his superiority as a critic stemmed from his ability to formulate a unified and comprehensive whole from so many and, at times, such disparate ideas.

His interest had first been stimulated by his father, an art lover and mediocre amateur painter who had been named under the Empire "conservateur du Luxembourg," responsible for ordering pictures and statues for the palace. Yet Baudelaire's critical taste and acumen must have been formed later, for he was only six when his father died, and though he remembered him with love and respect he was aware, as he admitted to his mother, that the courtly old gentleman was "un détestable artiste" whose paintings nevertheless had for his son "une valeur morale" (*Corr.,* I:439).

Baudelaire continued to be interested in art and even to read art criticism, as is evident from a letter that he wrote to his step-father, Monsieur Aupick, on July 17, 1838, while he was a student at Louis-le-Grand. Following a visit to the art gallery at Versailles with his classmates, he expressed his distaste for the stereotyped pictures of the Empire and evinced his esteem for the paintings of Horace Vernet (by 1845 he had changed his mind completely), of Ary Scheffer, and especially of Delacroix. After apologizing for his temerity in criticizing the painting of the Empire, he added significantly: "Perhaps I'm speaking foolishly, but I'm only giving an account of my impressions; perhaps too it's the result of reading the articles in *La Presse* which praise Delacroix to the skies" (*Corr.,* I:58).

It was none other than Théophile Gautier who had written so favorably about Delacroix in *La Presse* and had praised *La Bataille de Taillebourg,* seen and admired by the young Baudelaire at Versailles. Gautier, who believed in the autonomy of a work of art, in its complete independence of any practical or moral usefulness, had also written about *La Mort de Sardanapale, Les Massacres de Scio,* and *Les Femmes d'Alger,* all of which were to become favorites of the future poet and writer. Baudelaire later became a close friend of Gautier, and though he sometimes deprecated his art criticism he continued to read his "feuilletons" on painting, literature, and music and to profit by what he learned. Moreover, he so valued his poetry that he dedicated *Les Fleurs du Mal* to the "poète impeccable," the "parfait magicien ès lettres françaises" and devoted two articles to his verse and short stories.

At the Pension Bailly, where, after earning his *baccalauréat,* he lived while ostensibly studying at the Ecole de Droit, and again on his return from the trip to the Indian Ocean imposed on him by his family, his enthusiasm for the plastic arts seemed, if anything, to intensify. He renewed his friendship with his former companions Ernest Prarond and Le Vavasseur from the Pension Bailly, spent much of his time visiting museums and studios, and was often seen with Jules Buisson, the painter and engraver, and with Philippe de Chennevières, the future director of the Beaux-Arts. Prarond recounts that between 1842 and 1845 Baudelaire was preoccupied more with painting than with poetry. He never passed the Louvre without entering, according to Prarond, and he was especially fond of Spanish painting and modern art.[2]

EMILE DEROY

In April 1842 Baudelaire moved to the Ile Saint-Louis (10, quai de Béthune). After the July revolution of 1830 the island had become a haven for a small colony of artists who lived with the greatest informality, not even bothering to change their working clothes whenever they paid a visit to their colleagues. Here Baudelaire had every opportunity to listen to discussions about art and to acquire the technical knowledge that he would otherwise have lacked. Of the many artists whom Baudelaire saw when he first moved to the Ile Saint-Louis, none influenced him more than his close neighbor, the painter Emile Deroy (1820–46), a young impoverished artist who was soon to die tragically at the age of twenty-six. The two became inseparable friends, visiting restaurants, cafés, studios, and museums together— "Baudelaire followed by *his* painter," as Champfleury, the novelist and critic, once remarked. Jean Ziegler argues that Deroy taught Baudelaire much about the technical problems of painting.[3] The very fact that the *Salon de 1845* is more concerned with technique than any of Baudelaire's other criticism seems evidence of their discussions with each other and with other members of their group.

Knowingly or unknowingly, Baudelaire was following the advice once given by Diderot: "Do you want to make certain progress in the knowledge, so difficult to acquire, of the technique of art? Go through a gallery with an artist and have him explain and point out to you on the canvases examples of technical expressions; unless you do that, you will never have anything but confused notions." The artist should accompany us on our visits to the Salons, Diderot added, and, after allowing us to look and talk as freely as we wish, make us "flatten our noses against the beautiful things that we would have disdained and the mediocre things over which we would have gone into raptures."[4]

Diderot himself had learned much from the painter Chardin, and Baudelaire and his close friends were to follow his example. He and the poet Théodore de Banville, as well as Charles Asselineau, a man of letters, had as their chief mentor Deroy, whereas Champfleury seems to have depended more on the painter Chintreuil for his initiation into art.

That Baudelaire had great respect for Deroy's knowledge and judgment is evident from the few references that the poet's friends made to them. Banville claims that Baudelaire loved Deroy "as much for his artistic talent as for his mind." And Auguste Vitu, in his "nouvelle" *Arnold,* which Claude Pichois discovered and recognized as the story of Deroy, wrote that the young artist had many new ideas which he didn't know how to develop and which only needed to be carried out with some reservations.[5] Baudelaire himself seems never to have mentioned Deroy in his works. Except for one short note addressed to a Monsieur Jaleau, who was asked to give the message to Deroy (*Corr.,* I:136), there exists no correspondence between the two friends, probably because they saw each other so regularly that there was no need to write.

Asselineau, who also did a review of the Salon of 1845 and who was to become Baudelaire's closest friend, tells in his *Notes sur Baudelaire* how he first met the poet in the company of Deroy at the exhibition in the Louvre.[6] On leaving the Louvre, the three went to a tavern on the rue du Carrousel and there drew up a list of the painters whom Baudelaire and Asselineau planned to discuss.

Not surprisingly, considering the consultation with Deroy, the Salons of the two young critics were in complete agreement, though Asselineau, who was more restricted in space, could mention only sixty-five names whereas Baudelaire referred to one hundred and two. Both scoffed at the work of Vernet and praised the paintings of Delacroix, Decamps, and Corot; and both acclaimed Delacroix as the most original artist of the past and present, particularly in his use of light and in his harmony of color. The technical precision of Baudelaire's analysis of the four paintings exhibited by Delacroix is somewhat unusual for him and suggests that he may have been aided by Deroy.

Unlike other critics of the salon, both Baudelaire and Asselineau eulogized the rather mediocre allegorical painting of William Hausoullier entitled *La Fontaine de Jouvence*. Their admiration may well have been partly a reflection of Deroy's opinion, since Hausoullier was a fellow student in the atelier of Delaroche. However, Baudelaire may have been influenced even more by his fondness for allegory and myth, and especially by the myth that René Galand has called "the realization of his dearest dreams, the return to the 'paradis parfumé' of childhood evoked in *Moesta et errabunda*."[7]

Baudelaire's praise of the painting was not without certain reservations, however. Referring to its "raw color," he expressed the hope that Hausoullier would some day become a "genuine colorist" and warned him against the danger of excessive erudition, which tends to repress an artist's spontaneity.

Deroy's influence also seems apparent in other aspects of Baudelaire's *Salon,* especially in his high regard for Rubens and Titian, whom the artist looked upon as his masters and of whose works he had made copies. Baudelaire himself knew little about the history of art at this time and what he knew was drawn mainly from others. Kelley maintains that his references to the old masters in the *Salon de 1846* were devoid of originality and that "the names of Raphael, Veronese, and even of Rubens are evoked as slogans."[8]

Moreover, Deroy was also a great admirer of the English, especially of Reynolds and Lawrence. Baudelaire refers twice to Lawrence—to his "urbane popularity" and to what he calls "the best in Lawrence." Deroy's influence, however, would not have been alone in inspiring Baudelaire's interest in English painting, for during this period British art was much in vogue. Delacroix himself—to mention only one case—had read and drawn heavily on Reynolds's *Discourses* for his aesthetic ideas and, in 1830, had written an article on Lawrence, whom he knew personally.

One is also tempted to believe that Baudelaire's liking for Corot may have been strengthened by Deroy, who himself did a number of landscape paintings and who loved "the open air, the fields, the trees, the water, and the sky, everything that gives light, everything that reflects it."[9] Baudelaire's attitude toward nature was more favorable in 1845 and 1846 than in later years, though, like most critics, he always considered landscape as lower in the hierarchy of painting than either historical or biblical subjects.

Baudelaire's concern in the *Salon* with the question of color and his avowed preference for color over line reflected, to a degree at least, Deroy's intense fascination with color and his belief that it had the power, as Asselineau recalled, "to express the soul, thought, the beyond, the mysterious attitude of the inner being." Banville, at whose apartment Baudelaire, Deroy, and the poet and songwriter Pierre Dupont used to meet regularly, tells how the artist would spend the evening seeking to obtain unusual color harmonies by working with bits of colored material fastened to a piece of string, just as Chevreul, the famous chemist, had used colored threads to devise his theories for the Gobelins. Ziegler suggests that Deroy may even have attended the course given by Chevreul three times a week in the amphitheater of the Gobelins as advertised at the entrance of the Louvre.[10] Whatever the case, according to all accounts Deroy was an excellent colorist filled with new ideas which he tried to put into practice. Asselineau characterized him as a "marvelous colorist, as well as an intelligent man and a shrewd judge," and Banville praised the "delicate" and "musical" colors which the young artist achieved and which he so much admired in English painting.[11] In his *Salon de 1845* Baudelaire also referred to the musical quality of color—to color as "a musical science" and to color that "sings on a canvas."

The close tie between Baudelaire and Deroy continued until the untimely death of the artist in May 1846, though the two saw less of each other during the last year of their friendship. Baudelaire left the Ile Saint-Louis after his attempt at suicide on June 30, 1845, and about a year later Deroy also changed quarters. In February 1846, Deroy presented his famous portrait of

Baudelaire to the Salon of 1846. Not until the opening of the Salon on March 15 did he learn of its rejection. In April he moved to the Montagne-Sainte-Geneviève, where he died, alone and saddened and embittered by his lack of success. Poverty and isolation had made him caustic and suspicious, according to Asselineau, and he had few friends among his confrères, who were intimidated by his blunt, forbidding manner.[12] His death went unnoticed even in journals to which his friends Banville and Asselineau were contributors.

Among the works which Deroy left is the famous portrait of Baudelaire as a young dandy that had been refused by the Salon of 1846 and that now hangs in the museum in Versailles. It had been done in Baudelaire's apartment at the Hôtel Pimodan, in four sittings, in the presence of Léon Fauré, a close friend of Deroy who worked in Delacroix's studio, Nadar, who was to become a famous photographer, and two other companions, all of whom doubtless offered their suggestions and opinions. Dressed all in black with only a bit of white showing at the neckline and at the cuffs, Baudelaire is portrayed in a studied, self-conscious pose, based on a portrait of Sterne, darkly handsome with long hair and a beard, his head leaning against one hand while the other grasps the arm of the chair. The intensity of his gaze, both meditative and quizzical, and the strange almost contorted position of the hands are fascinating. The overall effect is one of aristocratic distinction, a Titianesque quality such as that found in the Italian master's painting *Man with the Glove,* which Deroy could easily have seen in the Louvre. In 1844, Deroy had done a lithograph much like the painting, but with a stylistic mannerism so exaggerated that it takes on a caricatural quality.

Baudelaire kept the painting for some time, moving it from lodging to lodging until, as Asselineau recounts, he gave it to a friend saying, "I don't like daubs like this any more."[13] What he never ceased to prize, however, was Deroy's copy of Delacroix's *Femmes d'Alger,* which he had first displayed with great pride in his apartment at the Pimodan.

Among Deroy's best works is *La Mendiante rousse,* the portrait of an attractive young street singer who served as a subject for both artist and poet. She was often seen by Baudelaire and his friends in the cafés of the Champs-Elysées, accompanied by an older girl who played the guitar and who was believed to be the singer's Lesbian friend. The painting, which today hangs in the Louvre, shows a young girl with shoulder-length auburn hair, pale, creamy skin, red lips that seem half pouting, and eyes that reveal a sort of melancholy apathy.

Baudelaire, who was evidently working on his poem "*A une mendiante rousse*" (1845–46) at the same time that his friend was occupied in doing the portrait, adopted a somewhat different approach.[14] Like the poets of the Baroque period, for whom "la belle mendiante" was a favorite subject, he starts out in light, colorful verse, full of fantasy. Then, after suddenly switching from the real to the ideal as he imagines the young girl adorned like the queen of some romance, he returns to the harsh reality in which she found herself in everyday life. Banville, to whom Deroy gave the portrait, was likewise inspired to celebrate her beauty in a poem entitled "A une petite chanteuse des rues," which he published in *Les Stalactites* in 1846.

THÉOPHILE THORÉ

Baudelaire often went with Deroy to the Café Tabourey, near the Odéon, where they joined a group of artists and men of letters. Here they shared in lively discussions with friends that included Prarond, Dupont, Nadar, Champfleury, and the Republican journalist and critic Théophile Thoré, who, during his exile after the coup d'état of 1851, was to rediscover Vermeer and to exalt the merits of Dutch art.

Both Deroy and Baudelaire respected Thoré and listened with keen interest to the aesthetic ideas which he professed. As a democrat, Thoré, like other humanitarian critics, was convinced of society's need for the artist; yet he also understood and appreciated the artist's need for freedom of expression. Much of his criticism reveals an attempt to reconcile the two contradictory beliefs, as in his commentary on Delacroix, whose proud isolation he disapproved of but whose genius as a colorist and draftsman he acclaimed.

Though Baudelaire was not a Republican, he clearly shared many of Thoré's ideas. David Kelley believes that Thoré, together with Gautier, had a direct influence on the poet-critic's thought. Baudelaire, he suggests, seems to have adopted from the social and humanitarian critics certain aspects of their aesthetics that did not endanger the autonomy of art.[15] Frances Jowell, in her dissertation on Thoré, expresses much the same opinion and reminds us that, though Baudelaire and Thoré "agree[d] in many of their likes and dislikes, they disagree[d] on the grounds on which they made their judgments."[16] Unlike the early Thoré, for example, Baudelaire did not believe that art should have for its purpose social or moral reform, and in his *Salon de 1845* he did not hesitate to criticize Thoré—without mentioning his name—for his humanitarian interpretation of Delacroix's painting *Marc-Aurèle*.

By 1847 Thoré had modified his view, perhaps as a result of his conversations with Delacroix and his close friend Théodore Rousseau. The moral effect of a painting, he came to believe, should not be derived from a subject realistically treated but rather from beauty of form, from the artist's idea or feeling embodied within the painting.

Both critics were likewise deeply concerned with the problem of color and line and believed that color could suggest form just as well, if not better, than line. In fact, Baudelaire made color as opposed to line one of the central themes of his *Salon de 1846*, basing his discussion on a comparison between Delacroix, the proponent of color, and Ingres, the proponent of line. The admiration that both critics had for Delacroix and especially for his use of color was one of the things they had most in common. In a number of articles and reviews Thoré rose to the defense of Delacroix and the colorists in general. And on March 29, 1845, not long after the opening of the Salon of that year, he boldly affirmed in the *Constitutionnel* that Delacroix ranked not only with the great French artists of all time but also with those of the Italian, Spanish, and Flemish schools. In his brochure on the

Salon, which appeared on May 13, 1845, Baudelaire showed himself equally fervent in his praise of the great Romantic artist and maintained that Delacroix was "decidedly the most original painter of ancient and of modern times" (*OC*, II:353).

Thoré was not alone in sharing Baudelaire's passion for color. Deroy, Gautier, Charles Blanc, Laverdant, not to mention Delacroix, the greatest colorist of his time, were among those who held the same opinion. Even Balzac broached the problem of color and line in his 1837 edition of *Un Chef-d'oeuvre inconnu*. Baudelaire must have noted with interest the words of Frenhofer which so strangely paralleled the sentiments expressed by Delacroix in his *Journal*: "Strictly speaking, drawing does not exist. . . . There are not any lines in nature. . . . It is in modeling that one draws."[17]

In their conversations together, Baudelaire and Thoré also found common ground in their conviction that mere formal skill was not sufficient in art, and that originality and invention were sadly lacking among modern artists. At the same time both agreed on the importance of thought or idea in great art. Thoré was firm in his belief that the critic as well as the artist should have "a philosophical idea, a *political* and social belief" (my italics) and that he should urge the artist to seek inspiration in the contemporary concerns of mankind.[18]

Interestingly, Asselineau recounts that in the Baudelaire of 1845 "the artist was at one and the same time a philosopher, and that the philosopher dominated."[19] One wonders if Baudelaire's strange use of the adjective "politique" in the definition of criticism that he cites in his *Salon de 1846* ("criticism must be partial, passionate, and political") was inspired by Thoré's convictions (*OC*, II:418).

Thoré and Baudelaire were also alike in their belief that artists should find inspiration in contemporary life—Thoré, largely because he felt that social art must necessarily and logically be contemporary; Baudelaire, because he believed that, in losing sight of modernity, art had become a sterile imitation of the past. In their conception of beauty the two were also strikingly similar. In his Salon of 1845, the elder critic maintains that beauty is the fundamental principle of art and distinguishes between an ideal, abstract, permanent beauty and what he calls "accidental, contingent beauty."[20] Baudelaire, in his *Salon de 1846,* likewise distinguished between "eternal and transitory" or "absolute and particular" beauty and insisted that both elements were inevitably present in all forms of beauty (*OC,* II:493).

Such a conception of beauty logically led both critics to condemn the Pagan School. As early as 1836 Thoré had argued that, in imitating the Greek ideal of beauty, the Pagan School was denying both time and space. In 1852 Baudelaire was also to criticize the writers of the Pagan School and to reproach its adherents for reproducing only the eternal element of beauty while neglecting the circumstantial element belonging to the present.

It would seem, as Kelley suggests, that in 1846 Baudelaire was already moving away from Gautier's influence and coming closer to the social optimism and the belief in progress that characterized Thoré and other humanitarian critics.[21] Between 1848 and 1852 his association with Thoré and the social reformers as well as his close friendship with the socialist poet Pierre Dupont were important factors in leading him to denounce the "puerile Utopia of the school of *art for art's sake*" and to declare that art was inseparable from morality and utility—a view which he was to repudiate after the coup d'état of Louis Napoleon in 1851 (*OC,* II:26, 27).

Following the revolutionary period Thoré was forced to leave France and go into exile. Many years later, while he was in Brussells, Baudelaire was to remember their talks in a letter that he sent to his former companion. "I don't know if you remember me and our discussions of long ago," he began. "The years fly by so quickly." But, he went on to add, "I have read assiduously everything that you write and I wish to thank you for the pleasure you have given me in coming to the defense of my friend Edouard Manet and in doing him a *little* justice" (*Corr.,* II:386).

In the *Indépendance belge,* Thoré, writing under the pseudonym William Bürger, had praised two paintings of Manet that had been exhibited in the Salon of 1864. He had, however, faulted them for being too much a pastiche of Velásquez, Goya, and Greco. It was to deny this allegation that Baudelaire wrote his old acquaintance, assuring him that Manet had not seen the works of either Goya or Greco, though, somewhere—he didn't know where—he had seen a few Velásquezes. Any resemblance between them, he wrote, was as much a coincidence as the similarity between his own writing and that of Edgar Allan Poe.

EUGÈNE DELACROIX

Of all the men of his time, Eugène Delacroix had the strongest and most enduring influence on Baudelaire, for it was he who furnished him with his most important aesthetic principles in addition to inspiring a number of his poems. Much of that influence, however, came indirectly through friends and acquaintances or from reading the articles that the artist published between 1829 and 1862. His critical essays begin and end with Delacroix and date from the *Salon de 1845* to the obituary article of 1863, in which he sums up his personal recollections as well as his critical impressions of the art of the celebrated Romantic painter.

Baudelaire seems to have met Delacroix in February or March 846, and though he liked to give the impression that he was a close personal friend the truth is that he saw very little of the artist during the twenty years of their acquaintance.[22] The controversial and aristocratic painter was grateful for the lavish praise contained in Baudelaire's critical essays, but continued nevertheless to be aloof and a bit wary of the extravagant notions of his eccentric admirer. Delacroix kept no journal during the first and third years (1846 and 1848) of their acquaintance, and references to the poet in the later journals are few: an ironic comment, dated February 1849, refers to a visit during which the poet talked of Proudhon and of the notion of progress; others, between April and May 1856, concern Baudelaire's translations of Poe. Delacroix mentions four visits which a Monsieur Dufaÿs paid him between March and May 1847. Until recently it was believed that the person in question was Gabriel-Alexandre

Dufaï, a man of letters who wrote for *l'Artiste.* Lloyd James Austin disagrees and suggests that the visitor was really Baudelaire, who between 1844 and 1848 used either the signature "Baudelaire-Dufaÿs" (Dufaÿs was his mother's maiden name) or the initials "B.D."[23] Armand Moss confirms Austin's theory and states categorically that the person was indeed Baudelaire.[24]

None of the entries in Delacroix's *Journal* offers any evidence of a close friendship between the two men, despite the fact that Baudelaire presented the artist with an inscribed copy of *Les Fleurs du Mal,* printed on special paper.[25] A note written on May 3, 1847, indicates even a decided coolness on the part of the painter: "I am wrong to express my opinions so freely with people who are not my friends."[26]

Evidently Delacroix was not always too pleased with Baudelaire's criticism of his art. Jules Buisson, a friend of both Baudelaire and Prarond, maintained that the artist complained of the poet's insistence on the morbid and "savage" elements of his work: "Delacroix thanked him warmly [for his articles]. But I know that he complained in private of the critic who saw fit to praise something sickly in his painting, something unhealthy, an insistent melancholy, a leaden feverishness, the strange and abnormal burning flow of illness.—'He really gets on my nerves,' he said . . ." (*Corr.,* II:997).

That Baudelaire was hurt by Delacroix's coolness is suggested in his letter to Jules Troubat, Sainte-Beuve's secretary, written on March 6, 1866. Sainte-Beuve's illness, he told Troubat, moved him as much as had that of Delacroix, "who was moreover a great egoist" (*Corr.,* II:627). In his obituary article on Delacroix, Baudelaire was probably speaking from firsthand experience when he mentioned the artist's "rigid and contemptuous wisdom," the "perpetual tension of will that gave an expression of cruelty to his face," his "bitter laugh filled with sarcastic pity," and the number of meanings to be found in his "twenty different ways of uttering the words 'mon cher Monsieur'" (*OC,* II:758, 760).

Despite any coolness on the part of the artist, however, Baudelaire never lost his enthusiasm for the Romantic turbulence, the brilliant use of color, and the spiritual content of Delacroix's art. He was equally impressed by the artist's aesthetic ideas, many of which he adopted. He mentions them frequently in his essay, and in a lecture on Delacroix, given in Brussells in 1864, he graciously admitted his debt to the artist "*who,*" he stressed, "*taught me so much*" (*OC,* II:774).

Both artist and poet gave equal importance to the creative imagination, and both believed that art could transform the ugly into the beautiful. Nothing could be more Baudelairean in tone than the comment made by Delacroix in his *Journal* (March 5, 1849) on Meissonier's drawing *La Barricade,* which he felt lacked "that indefinable quality which makes a work of art out of an odious object." And like Baudelaire after 1851 Delacroix ridiculed the notion of progress, both in his conversations and in a lengthy entry made by him in his *Journal* on April 23, 1849.[27] In fact, as we have seen, the ironic notation made by the artist after Baudelaire's visit in 1849 was directed at the poet's attraction to Proudhon and his acceptance (short-lived) of the idea of progress.

Baudelaire's intense admiration for Delacroix is usually thought to conflict with his ideas on modernity. On close examination, however, his views are not as contradictory as they might appear, for, rightly or wrongly, Baudelaire distinguished modernity achieved through execution and feeling from modernity achieved through choice of subject. In the *Salon de 1845,* his conception of modernity is made clear to the reader in his discussion of the drawings of Joseph Fay: "We should like to see this talent exercised in support of more modern ideas—or rather in support of a new way of seeing and understanding the arts. By this we do *not mean to speak of choice of subject;* in that respect, artists are not always free—but rather of the *manner* in which subjects are comprehended and depicted" (my italics) (*OC,* II:374).

It was precisely Delacroix's way of seeing and understanding, his manner of comprehending and depicting his subjects that revealed his modernity to Baudelaire in 1845. In his Salon of that year, where he was mainly concerned with technique—

perhaps largely because of Deroy's influence—the poet-critic devotes almost all his discussion to the problem of execution, especially to the problem of color. *La Madeleine dans le desert,* he maintains, shows an extraordinary amount of "intimate, mysterious, and romantic poetry," and reveals its creator to be "stronger than ever [as a harmonist], and on a path of progress that renews itself unendingly." The color in *Marc-Aurèle* is "incomparably scientific" and loses none of its "cruel originality in this new and more complete science." *Le Sultan du Maroc* shows not only an "advance in the science of harmony" but also a "musical seductiveness" and a "suggestivity" that is not to be found in the work of any other great colorist (*OC,* II:354–57).

In the last paragraph of the *Salon de 1845* Baudelaire mentions—almost as an afterthought, as if remembering his discussions at the Café Tabourey—the modernity that may be achieved through the choice of contemporary subjects: "The *painter,* the true painter, will be he who can seize the epic character of contemporary life and make us see and understand, through color or design, how great and poetic we are in our cravats and our patent-leather boots" (*OC,* II:407). But in this brief paragraph of 1845, which is further developed in the form of a short chapter in the *Salon de 1846,* he is obviously thinking not of Delacroix but of Balzac's heroes and of Balzac himself.

In the *Salon de 1846* Baudelaire stresses Delacroix's modernity by emphasizing his Romanticism, which he considered a form of modern art. "Romanticism is precisely neither in choice of subject nor in exact truth, but in a manner of feeling. . . . To say Romanticism is to say modern art—that is, intimacy, spirituality, color, aspiration toward the infinite, expressed by every means available to the arts" (*OC,* II:421, 422).

According to Baudelaire's definition, Delacroix, not Victor Hugo, was the veritable head of the Romantic School. And it was above all the "unique and persistent melancholy" that imbues the artist's work which made him "the *true* painter of the nineteenth century," even while remaining heir to the great tradition in the "breadth, nobility, and magnificence" of his compositions (my italics) (*OC,* II:430, 440, 441). Moreover, Baudelaire evidently saw in Delacroix some of the very qualities that make his own poetry completely modern: "nervous tension," "moral suffering," "lofty and serious melancholy," and finally, "human anguish."

Baudelaire's insistence that Delacroix's use of melancholy made him the "*true* painter of the nineteenth century" may seem inconsistent with his earlier claim that the true artist would be he who sought modernity through choice of subject. Though Baudelaire had no qualms about contradicting himself when the occasion warranted, it is evident that in this case he saw no inconsistency in his two statements. Obviously, he believed modernity could be attained in more than one way. Balzac had found it in his choice of subject—in his magnificent treatment of the problems of contemporary society. Delacroix had likewise found it in his manner of feeling, in his depiction through color and contour of universal and timeless emotions, whether spiritual or physical, natural or "surnaturel." And so, in 1846, Baudelaire could begin his chapter on Delacroix, after a preliminary discussion of Romanticism and color, by asserting: "Romanticism and color lead me straight to *Eugène Delacroix.* I do not know if he is proud of being designated romantic; but his place is here, because for a long time—from his first work in fact—the majority of the public has viewed him as the head of the *modern* school" (*OC,* II:427).

GUSTAVE COURBET

Among the artists with whom Baudelaire was on intimate terms, Gustave Courbet was one of the most controversial and outstanding. The son of a prosperous landowner in the Franche-Comté, he was as different temperamentally as physically from the dandy that was Baudelaire. Tall, vigorous, handsome (at least in his younger years), and self-confident, he loved to eat and drink prodigiously and to talk and laugh boisterously with the friends that gathered around him. In spite of their differences, however, artist and poet were fast friends for a number of years until, separated by events and by a growing divergence of ideologies, they drifted apart.

The two met about 1847 when Charles Toubin, one of Courbet's friends from the Franche-Comté, brought Baudelaire, as he himself tells us, to the Café de la Rotonde, where the artist and his friends used to meet. In a letter written in January 1848 to his family, Courbet speaks of being surrounded by people influential in the press and the arts—obviously a reference to Baudelaire and Champfleury—and of his intention to be the representative painter of a new school which was to be founded.

At the time of their meeting, Courbet was still an obscure artist. Despite the fact that he had been in Paris since 1840, he had had only three pictures accepted for exhibition in the Salon. Though one had been shown in 1845 and another in 1846, Baudelaire had not mentioned them in his Salons, either because he had not noticed them or because he considered them unworthy of comment.

During the revolution of 1848 the two evidently collaborated in their revolutionary activities, for Courbet drew the vignette for the short-lived newspaper, Le Salut public, which Toubin, Baudelaire, and Champfleury published jointly. Also about this time Courbet painted the well-known portrait of Baudelaire that now hangs in the museum in Montpellier. Critics disagree about the year in which the picture was done, mainly because, in the 1855 retrospective, it was incorrectly dated. The preponderance of evidence, however, indicates that the portrait was actually painted in 1848.[28] The fact that the date 1848 was included on the plate when Bracquemond etched the portrait lends credence to the belief.

The picture shows Baudelaire with closely cropped hair—in sharp contrast to the flowing locks of the Deroy portrait—seated at a writing table, pipe in mouth, and poring over a book. Courbet had had difficulty completing the picture, he told Champfleury, for Baudelaire's face kept changing every day. Neither the artist nor the subject was satisfied with the portrait and Baudelaire refused to accept it as a gift.

In 1848 and 1849 Baudelaire and Courbet were especially

close. In moments of financial need, the impecunious poet sometimes sought lodging in the studio of his friend. It is said that on
one occasion Courbet agreed to remain awake during the night
so that he could jot down the dreams and visions of the sleeping
poet. Baudelaire, in his turn, did favors for the artist. On May
12, 1849, he wrote a letter for him to the president of the Com-
mission charged with buying works for the "grande loterie," inviting him to view the artist's works either in his studio or in the
Salon. That same year he also wrote out in his own hand the
Notices that accompanied the pictures that were being sent to
the Salon of 1849. For one of them, *Les Communaux de Chas-
sagne,* he even wrote a short poem in blank verse and signed it G.
Courbet.

As Courbet became better known, his circle of friends increased. At the Brasserie Andler, only two doors from his studio
on the rue Hautefeuille, a group of artists and intellectuals
would gather around him every evening from six to eleven.
Thursdays were especially popular. A village tavern in style, the
brasserie with its barrels of sauerkraut, its hams hanging from
the ceiling, its piles of sausages and huge cheeses served as a sort
of club for Courbet and provided the setting for lively discussions, witty conversations, and for games, songs, and hearty
laughter.

Here, in what Champfleury called "le temple du réalisme,"
Baudelaire mingled with outstanding personalities including,
among many others, the artists Daumier, Chenavard, François
Bonvin, Alexandre Decamps; the animal sculptor Antoine Barye;
the art critics Théophile Silvestre and Gustave Planche; the
writers Champfleury, Philippe Duranty, Fernand Desnoyers; and
the social reformer Proudhon, who was to usurp Champfleury's
place as Courbet's chief mentor.

In the relationship of Courbet and Baudelaire, it was apparently the poet who influenced the artist. In an article on Courbet
and Baudelaire, Alan Bowness reminds us that in the Salons of
1845 and 1846 Baudelaire showed a marked taste both for allegory and modernity, and that in 1847 and 1848 Courbet
painted three allegorical pictures, including *Nuit classique de*

Walpurgis, which "appears to have been a rather naive attempt at a modern allegory according to the Baudelairean precept. . . ."[29] The other two paintings—now lost—were equally naive, according to Silvestre, the critic, friend, and first biographer of Courbet. The one known as *Le Char de l'Etat,* he dryly commented, "is amusing the rats in some attic."[30]

In 1850 Courbet painted his monumental *Un Enterrement à Ornans,* which most critics agree is strikingly Baudelairean in concept. As Bowness suggests, it is almost an answer to the lines in the *Salon de 1846* in which the poet-critic defends the use of modern dress. In fact, Champfleury actually made this very observation—as Bowness reminds us—in an article published in the *Messager de l'Assemblé* for February 25 and 26, 1851. In mentioning the fact that Courbet had painted his people in modern dress, Champfleury added: "The painter from Ornans has understood perfectly the ideas found in a rare and curious book (the *Salon de 1846* by M. Baudelaire) where are found these true lines: 'Great colorists know how to create color with a black coat, a white cravat and a grey background.'"[31] On republishing the essay in 1861, Champfleury was to drop entirely the direct reference to Baudelaire's *Salon de 1846* and to replace it with the line, "Our black and serious costume has its grounds. . . ."[32]

It is not known what Baudelaire thought about the picture, but obviously he was not too impressed, since he remained silent while Champfleury defended Courbet's painting in the press against the attacks of the public and the critics. The reason for Baudelaire's silence can be explained. Not only was he preparing *Du vin et du hachisch* as well as a group of eleven poems for publication, but also he was directing with Champfleury a short-lived magazine entitled *La Semaine Théâtrale* and planning a realist review which was to be called *Le Hibou Philosophe.* Even more important, he was undergoing a change of heart. For a short time around the revolution he seemed to be leaning toward Realism. But the antimaterialist in Baudelaire, strengthened by his reading of Joseph de Maistre and Edgar Allan Poe, soon reasserted itself, and he quickly renounced the

Realistic ideal, which he associated in his mind with Positivism and defined as the complete negation of the imagination, that "queen of faculties."

Baudelaire's dislike of Realism was shared by Thoré, who had complained bitterly in 1848 that many of the Salon pictures represented a misunderstood response to the call for an art of the day. Lacking "poésie" and creative originality, they were simply "coarse and contemptible imitations."[33]

In 1855, angered by the Salon's refusal to accept two such large paintings as *L'Enterrement* and *L'Atelier du peintre,* Courbet set up his own one-man show, facing the Salon in what he called the Pavilion of Realism. The *Atelier* found little favor with either the public or critics and left them puzzled as to its meaning. The subtitle given it by Courbet (*A Real Allegory Summing up Seven Years of my Life*) did little to clear up the mystery. Proudhon and Champfleury insisted that allegory and reality were mutually exclusive, and Baudelaire and Champfleury disliked the painting as a work of art.

Evidently Courbet was continuing the practice of using modern allegory, which he had attempted without success a few years earlier. In the center of the picture Courbet is seen seated before an easel on which rests a landscape painting. A nude model, who has been said to represent truth, leans against the back of his chair. A little boy looks on; to the right and left are grouped some thirty figures. While Courbet was working on the picture in Ornans, he wrote to Champfleury describing his intentions at great length: "It is the moral and physical history of my studio . . . my way of seeing society in its interests and passions." In the course of a long description he explains: "The picture is divided into two parts. I am in the centre, painting; on the right all the shareholders, that is my friends, the workers, the art collectors. On the left, the other world of trivialities—the common people, the misery, poverty, wealth, the exploited, the exploiter; those who thrive on death."[34] Among his friends he had given the most prominent positions to both Champfleury and Baudelaire, the former seated on a stool not far from the artist, the latter at the far right—apart from the others—seated at a table reading a book and oblivious to all about him. Courbet had used his 1848 portrait of Baudelaire as a basis for the figure of the poet, which explains why he looks younger than he actually was in 1855. Behind Baudelaire was a black woman—evidently Jeanne Duval—looking at herself in a mirror. The artist, who had been away from Paris much of the time between 1852 and 1855, evidently didn't know that Baudelaire had broken with Jeanne in 1852. Probably at the poet's request Courbet effaced her figure, although traces of it are still apparent.

Baudelaire was incensed at the thought that his inclusion in the picture would associate him in the eyes of the public with the Realist movement, which he had come to reject. His only published reference to Courbet was a passage in the *Exposition universelle,* where in his chapter on Ingres he unexpectedly compares the Idealist painter to the Realist Courbet: "In their war against the imagination they obey different motives; and their two opposing types of fanaticism lead them to the same immolation" (*OC,* II:586). The words "war against the imagination" are undoubtedly the key to Baudelaire's failure to appreciate the real greatness of Courbet. The artist's choice of subjects, not his manner of treatment is what he found disappointing. True, Baudelaire preferred urban subjects to those based on provincial or peasant life. But had Courbet treated these subjects with the same powerful emotion and the same dynamic and even melodramatic manner with which Balzac depicts his provincial characters, the poet-critic might have reacted differently. It was not "the heroism of modern life" that Courbet revealed; it was its unheroic aspects.

Baudelaire missed the "color, atmosphere, and movement" which he termed the chief preoccupation of Delacroix. Courbet's literal translation of reality and the lumbering effect of some of his less successful works contrasted sadly with the evocative power of the Romantic artist, who was able to suggest "the invisible, the impalpable, the dream, the soul." The static quality of *L'Enterrement* and *L'Atelier,* the photographic stillness and impersonality of the figures left the critic cold and angry.

Unfortunately, the absence of what he liked blinded him to

the virtues of Courbet's art, and he failed to note the sensitivity that the painter revealed in works such as his portraits of Berlioz, of Bruyas, and of himself (*L'Homme à la pipe*).

Delacroix, unlike his admirers, was one of the few to recognize the value of *L'Atelier*. On August 3 he noted in his *Journal:* "On leaving [the Salon], I went to see Courbet's exhibition; the admission was reduced to ten sous. I stayed there alone for almost an hour and I discovered a masterpiece in his picture which had been rejected. . . . They have refused one of the most singular pictures of this period."[35]

To make matters worse for Baudelaire, Champfleury published (September 2) in *L'Artiste* an open letter entitled "Sur Courbet, lettre à George Sand" which served both as a defense of the artist and as a sort of manifesto for the Realist movement. To divorce himself publicly from a movement that he had come to despise, Baudelaire began work on an article entitled "Puisque Réalisme il y a." The title itself was borrowed from a statement made by Courbet and quoted by Champfleury in his letter-manifesto. The essay was never finished, perhaps because Baudelaire hesitated to hurt his two old friends. From the notes, however, it was clearly intended to be a virulent attack on both Champfleury and Courbet, who, he believed, thought only of capturing external reality and of equating impression with expression. In a definition of poetry whose transcendental implications reveal the wide gap that separated his thinking from that of his former associates, the poet-critic can be seen moving toward his conception of imagination—one that enables the artist to interpret the "hieroglyphics" of this world and to discover "what is completely true only in another world" (*OC*, II:59).

For some time Baudelaire and Courbet had been seeing less and less of each other as they followed separate and divergent paths. In 1859 they met briefly in Honfleur and the artist dedicated to the poet his lovely *Bouquet d'astres*.[36] Several years later, on September 14, 1862, Baudelaire referred briefly and favorably to the artist in an article published in *Le Boulevard*. Courbet's paintings were, he wrote, "absolutely necessary" in a time of mediocrity in art. And he went on to add: "One must do

Courbet the justice to admit that he has contributed not a little to reestablishing a taste for simplicity and honesty and a disinterested, absolute love of painting" (OC, II:737).

Courbet was never to forget Baudelaire and his poetry. In 1863/64, Bowness reminds us, he attempted another allegorical painting, *La Source d'Hippocrène.* "The picture," he wrote the critic Castagnary, was "a satire on modern poets whom I portrayed in the act of drinking from the fount of Hippocrene in the sacred valley watered by the springs of Castalia and Permessus. Farewell Apolla; farewell Muses; farewell beautiful valley I had created; farewell Lamartine with wallet and lyre; farewell Baudelaire with notes in hand. . . ."[37]

Far more important, however, is the magnificent painting (1865–66) inspired by Baudelaire's poem "Les Femmes damnées" showing two Lesbian lovers asleep in each other's arms. One of the models was Whistler's beautiful Irish mistress, Joanna Heffernan. First known as *Paresse et Luxure,* the painting was later entitled *Le Sommeil.* Baudelaire never saw the picture. Because of its erotic character it was kept more or less out of sight until the exhibition of 1968 in the Petit Palais in Paris. It was, however, shown in a Courbet exhibition held in both Boston and Philadelphia in 1959–60.

PAUL CHENAVARD

With Paul Chenavard, the advocate of philosophic art, Baudelaire engaged in long and passionate discussions. A mediocre painter now forgotten but once known for his keen mind and brilliant conversation, Chenavard figured importantly in the intellectual life of the day and was on intimate terms with writers, artists, politicians, critics, and philosophers. The somewhat eccentric artist was one of the founders of the brilliant group which had as its center the Divan on the rue le Pelletier, where Baudelaire first met him in 1846. Other distinguished members of the circle included Gautier, Préault, and Henry Monnier.

Under the Second Republic, Chenavard proposed to decorate

the Pantheon with paintings in grisaille intended to represent the history of humanity (*La Palingénésie universelle*). Forced to abandon his grandiose scheme when, in 1851, the Pantheon was returned by the government to the Catholic church, he never completed the project. The cartoons which remain are preserved in the museum in Lyons.

In the 1850s Chenavard began to frequent the Brasserie Andler, where he was held in high regard by his companions and contributed much to the lively conversation. In his *Souvenirs* Champfleury recalls how on one occasion the artist and the poet engaged in a serious discussion on aesthetics, while near them Decamps, Courbet, Corot, and Champfleury played a game of billiards and Gustave Planche, the art critic, kept score.[38]

Despite important differences, Baudelaire and Chenavard had much in common, as Joseph Sloane points out in his study on the philosophical artist. Both held pessimistic views about the machine age, progress, and the rise of the common man to a position of importance. Observing the similarity of the passage from *Fusées* beginning "The world is going to come to an end" to the ideas of Chenavard, Sloane writes:

> The reversion to animality as a possibility, the grievous effects of American mechanization, the coming brutality were all painted in the now missing lower portion of his [Chenavard's] mosaic of *Social Palingenesis,* where brutish characters leaned on cotton bales, surrounded by the broken debris of the arts, while at the very bottom a fire consumed all except a rising Phoenix. The idea of republics acceptable and worthy of glory only if governed by dedicated men who were to be the aristocrats of communal states was one which the painter believed to be the only possible hope for the governments of the future. Above all, the prophecy in the first line, "The world is coming to an end," was the one on which both could agree.[39]

In matters of painting, however, the two were in almost complete disagreement. Baudelaire not only disapproved of his painting ("Chenavard is not a painter"), he also categorically rejected his belief that the purpose of the plastic arts was to teach history, morals, and philosophy (*OC,* II:601). Chenavard's brain, he wrote in the notes published posthumously under the title of *L'Art philosophique,* is as "foggy and sooty" as the city of Lyons itself. Yet paradoxically the poet-critic appreciated the artist's ability to reason and argue: "Chenavard knows how to read and reason, and has thus become the friend of all who like reasoning; he is remarkably learned and is experienced in the art of meditation" (*OC,* II:602).[40]

Evidently their discussions helped to clarify Baudelaire's own thinking. In *L'Art philosophique,* with its numerous references to Chenavard, the poet formulates his famous definition of pure art as "a suggestive magic containing both the object and the subject, the world exterior to the artist and the artist himself" (*OC,* II:598). It was this definition and its application in much of Baudelaire's verse that gave poetry a new impetus by encouraging writers to view poetry as suggestion or magic rather than as rhetoric or what Margaret Gilman has aptly called "embellished statement."[41]

Baudelaire did two drawings with Chenavard in mind: the one inscribed, "Sample of antique beauty dedicated to Chenavard"; the other, "Celestial vision for the use of Paul Chenavard." Despite Claude Pichois's objections, there is reason to believe that Chenavard in turn did a drawing of Baudelaire, probably about 1862. Sloane maintains that a sensitive portrait-sketch of a middle-aged man, hitherto unidentified, is actually a portrait of the poet done by the artist.[42] The drawing shows a Baudelaire quite unlike the one revealed in most of his photographs. Chenavard depicts an utterly different Baudelaire, a man lost in thought, who gives no suggestion of posing. However, the gentle, appealing expression is so much like that of the preparatory drawing done by Fantin-Latour for his portrait of the poet in the painting *Hommage à Delacroix* that Sloane's identification seems highly probable. Moreover, the description of Baudelaire made by his friend the sculptor Ernest Christophe lends further support to the conjecture, as we shall see.

AUGUSTE PRÉAULT

Another inspired conversationalist, who may have influenced Baudelaire's ideas on sculpture, was Auguste Préault. A friend of the entire generation of French Romantic poets and of Nerval in particular, he was also a former neighbor of Baudelaire on the Ile Saint-Louis. As a member of the group that met in the Divan, he often engaged the poet in long discussions and delighted his listeners with his biting wit.

Préault, according to the art historian Maurice Rheims, was "one of the most authentically Romantic artists of his generation" and the only Romantic sculptor who did not believe "that to be Romantic it sufficed to appear grandiloquent."[43] His rejection of conventional art won him the disfavor of the conservative juries that chose the works of art to be exhibited in the Salons. Although Romantic sculptors were admitted to the Salons in 1833, by 1834 Préault found himself barred once again. He was not able to resume showing until 1848, when, as a result of the revolution, juries were elected by the artists themselves.

Although Préault did not exhibit his work in the Salon of 1859, Baudelaire concludes his chapter on sculpture by praising the artist's talent: "For some years, people have been unduly criticizing one of our dearest friends; very well, I am one of those who confess without blushing that, whatever the skill that is displayed each year by our sculptors, I no longer discover in their works (since the death of David [d'Angers]) the ethereal pleasures which I have so often encountered in the tumultuous, though incomplete, dreams of Auguste Préault" (*OC*, II:680).

Baudelaire may well have been thinking of Préault's *Massacre*. Modeled in 1824 and cast in bronze in 1859, it was intended to resemble a fragment from a large bas-relief. Rheims calls it "one of the most beautiful Romantic and Symbolist works of the nineteenth century."[44] It is easy to understand why Baudelaire would have found it so admirable. In it can be seen the same sense of movement, of power, and of expressive emotions that characterize the paintings of Delacroix.

Pichois and Pommier have noticed a relationship between Préault's remarkable carved wooden statue of Christ on the cross (1840) and the crucified Christ described by Baudelaire in the fifth verse of his poem "Le Reniement de Saint Pierre." They tell how Préault is said to have succeeded in having his figure of Christ placed in the "Grande Sacristie" of Saint-Gervais et Saint Protais (where it is still to be found) after being refused acceptance by the parish priests of Saint-Germain l'Auxerrois and of Saint-Paul-Saint-Louis. Préault is supposed to have gained the consent of the ill and dying priest of Saint-Gervais by telling him: "Sir, your colleagues have twice driven out Our Lord; receive him, I beg of you; if not I shall become a Moslem."[45]

The baroque statue with its head thrown back in a convulsive movement, its arms distended by the weight of the body, its mouth gasping its last breath, does indeed suggest the gruesome vision evoked by Baudelaire in his poem. It would not be strange if the poet, drawn as he was to the plastic arts, had been influenced, consciously or unconsciously, in his choice of details by the memory of Preault's statue.

ERNEST CHRISTOPHE

With Ernest Christophe, another well-known sculptor of his day, Baudelaire was also on intimate terms. Christophe's two statuetts, *Le Squelette* and *La Comédie humaine,* both believed to have been influenced by a drawing of Grandville, inspired Baudelaire's poems "Danse macabre" and "Le Masque." In 1858 Baudelaire had seen *Le Squelette,* at that time not quite completed, and was deeply impressed by the subject, which appealed to his taste for the macabre. He wrote "Danse macabre" in December 1858 and was presented with a copy of the statuette shortly thereafter. Baudelaire insisted on dedicating his poem to Christophe ("The least I can do is to inscribe his name as a way of expressing my gratitude. . . .") despite the objection of Calonne, editor of the *Revue contemporaine,* in which it was published on November 30, 1859 (*Corr.,* I:546). That same year Baudelaire also wrote the poem "Le Masque," based on *La*

Comédie humaine, of which Christophe had also given him a cast. Though neither statuette appeared in the Salon of 1859, Baudelaire nevertheless described them in his *Salon,* using terms that suggested his poems and even quoting some verses from "Danse macabre."

In 1876, on doing a large-scale marble version of *La Comédie humaine,* Christophe changed its title to *Le Masque* in order to honor his friend who had died nine years before. The statue was awarded a medal by the Salon of that year, acquired by the state, and placed in the Jardin des Tuileries, where it is presently known under its original title.

Christophe was one of those who many years later helped dispel the false legends that had grown up around the name of Baudelaire. In a letter dated November 8, 1886, that was evidently intended to help Eugène Crépet document his biographical introduction to the *Oeuvres posthumes* of Baudelaire (1887) he wrote: "I knew Baudelaire very well indeed.... The Baudelaire I remember is very different from the legendary Baudelaire. The one I knew always gave me the impression of being simple as a child, often the victim of himself, a very good friend, and in short, all his life a dupe of himself" (*PLB,* p. 98).

Perhaps his friendship with Préault and Christophe as well as with Chenavard and Thoré explain the change in Baudelaire's attitude toward sculpture between 1845 and 1859. In his *Salon de 1845* he indicts French sculptors for their excessive preoccupation with technique and for the lack of taste, nobility, and grace shown in their work. Borrowing a term from Diderot's *Salon de 1767,* he scornfully refers to the unimaginative sculptors of his day as "*scultiers*" (which Jonathan Mayne effectively translates as "sculpturizers") and dismisses the work of the immensely popular Pradier as a tour de force and "a mixture of hidden borrowings" (*OC,* II:402, 404).

Baudelaire was not alone in his condemnation of contemporary French sculpture. His antipathy would surely have been reinforced by Thoré, to name only one, who undoubtedly reiterated in their meetings at the Café Tabourey much of what he had already written in his Salons. As early as 1836, in his Salon of that year, Thoré had characterized French sculpture of the Empire as a "miserable affair of cold pastiche or indecent eroticism," lacking "vitality, principles, invention, and decorum." One of the few artists whom he exempted from censure was Auguste Préault, whose art, the elder critic claimed, was "history incarnated in a palpitating and true form."[46]

In the *Salon de 1846*, Baudelaire intensifies his attack on contemporary sculpture in a chapter entitled "Why Sculpture is Boring." The reasons for his dislike are typical of his aesthetic taste in general. Sculpture comes close to nature, he maintains; it is "as brutal and positive as nature herself." Like Diderot, as critics have frequently pointed out, he considers it a complementary art—"a humble associate of painting and architecture"— and notes that because of its many surfaces it can be properly seen only from a single point of view. Moreover, like the great eighteenth-century critic, he objects strenuously to the lack of imagination and to the tendency to imitate the great art of the past. The fact that Pradier was considered "king" of contemporary sculpture was proof of its "pitiable state," for Pradier with his "cold and academic talent" was deficient both in graphic imagination and in "the imagination necessary for great compositions" (*OC*, II:489). Baudelaire's opinion was shared by Thoré and by Préault; the latter dryly remarked that Pradier "left every morning for Athens and returned every evening to the rue Bréda."[47]

Curiously, lack of color is one of the reasons that explains Baudelaire's early indifference to sculpture. If he accuses sculptors of being "prejudiced and half blind" and of having "judgment [which] is no more than half that of an architect," it is in part because he finds them unable to appreciate the color and movement so necessary to great art but so difficult and even impossible to obtain in sculpture (*OC*, II:434).

He frankly confesses, however, his approval of the "*painted* sculpture" (Baudelaire stresses the fact that he is speaking of *painted* sculpture) found in churches and cathedrals—sculpture whose "pure and simple colors, arranged according to a particular scale, harmonize with the rest and complete the poetic effect of the work as a whole" (*OC*, II:488). Even in the *Salon de 1859*, in which he radically changes his opinion of sculpture, he refers briefly to "the monotonous whiteness of all those great dolls" (*OC*, II:671).

Many years later when he was in Belgium, the ailing poet once again mentions his fondness for polychrome sculpture. Among the vituperative notes made for *Pauvre Belgique*—the never-realized book in which he had intended to express his loathing of the Belgians—he acknowledges the emotion he felt on viewing a colored image of the crucified Christ carried in a religious procession in Brussels. His brief notation, "Beauty of colored sculpture," is followed by a reference to the figure of Christ looming above the heads of the crowd and then by the simple words "My feeling of emotion" (*OC*, II:942). In still another note alluding to the polychrome crucifixes found in the churches of Belgium, he adds in parentheses the words "I adore colored sculpture" (*OC*, II:944).

Baudelaire came to be more and more interested in sculpture—the result probably of his connection with Préault, Christophe, and Chenavard. In 1847 he wrote his mother that he intended doing a book on sculpture, a project which, like so many others, never came to fruition. In his *Salon de 1859*, however, he seems to have included what would have been the core of his book.

By this time he had grown in knowledge, and his judgment had matured. He had come to see in sculpture the possibilities of a truly great art. Sculpture need no longer be boring; on the contrary, it can play "a divine role," for it has the power to make us "think of things which are not of this world." It demands perfect execution and an elevated spirituality; its beauty imprints itself on the memory more than that of any other medium. It bestows on everything human something of eternity. In lines reminiscent of his sonnet "La Beauté" he suggests the effect of great sculpture as opposed to the merely pretty: "Just as lyric poetry makes everything noble, even passion; so sculpture, true sculpture [Baudelaire had not changed his mind about the general mediocrity of his age] makes everything solemn, even movement" (*OC*, II:671).

Sculpture may assume various aspects. It may be mysterious and sacerdotal, charming and rational, scientifically precise, prodigious as a dream, heroic or frivolous. But in all these different manifestations, its power of expression and richness of feelings are the inevitable result of a profound imagination—an imagination which, Baudelaire notes, was too often lacking among contemporary artists. This imagination he found present, however, in the works of two great sculptors who had not exhibited in the Salon of 1859: in the mysterious beauty of Christophe's macabre subjects and in "the tumultuous though fragmentary dreams of Auguste Préault" (*OC*, II:680).

Imagination, Baudelaire maintained, made it possible for the sculptor, like the poet and the painter, to transform ugliness into beauty. In describing the courtesans portrayed by Constantin Guys, he noted that their poses often revealed "an audacity and nobility that would delight the most sensitive sculptor, provided he had the boldness and wit to seize upon nobility wherever it is to be found, even in the mire" (*OC*, II:721). That he believed Christophe possessed this "boldness and wit" is clearly revealed (*Salon de 1859*) in his praise of the sculptor's two statuettes *Le Squelette* and *La Comédie humaine*. The "flattened negroid face," "the lipless, gumless smile," the eyes that were but "shadowed holes," in short, "the horrible thing that had been a woman" were to the poet-critic sufficient proof that even ugliness could be transformed into art through "the sacred frenzy of the imagination" (*OC*, II:679).

Another reason for Baudelaire's change of attitude toward sculpture seems to have been his taste for the monumental, which, incidentally, is given expression in his poem "La Géante." In the *Salon de 1859*, where he admits that his "incorrigible passion for the *large*" had influenced his liking for Clésinger's *Eve*, he confesses: "In nature and in art, I prefer—other things being equal—what is *large* to all else: large animals, large landscapes, large ships, large men, large women, large churches; and transforming my tastes into principles, . . . I believe that size is no unimportant consideration in the eyes of the Muse" (*OC,* II:646).

In the fourteen years between 1845 and 1859, Baudelaire found himself no longer blinded by the mediocrity of his day and reversed his opinion of sculpture. Through his relationships with the men of his time and through his knowledge of their works and their ideas, he learned to seek and admire in sculpture what he sought and admired in painting: imagination, spirituality, powerful emotion, ugliness and the macabre transformed into beauty, movement, color, and, finally, perfection of execution.

It is interesting that Baudelaire, though usually concerned with contemporary painters and sculptors, shows the greatest respect for the work of Michelangelo. He not only mentions him frequently in his critical works but also gives him a place of honor in his poetry. One has only to think of his magnificent evocation of Michelangelo's art in "Les Phares" or of his sonnet "L'Idéal," in which he evokes the statue of Night found in the Medici Chapel.

In an article on Baudelaire and Michelangelo, Francis Hyslop points out that the poet had almost no first-hand knowledge of the work of the Italian master.[48] The two *Bound Slaves* in the Louvre were the only original works he knew; otherwise he had seen only reproductions and copies. Yet from the beginning of his career he was known to be "passionné pour Michel Ange," as Prarond wrote in an early poem. His companions, who had seen the original work of the Renaissance artist and had experienced directly its tragic grandeur and overwhelming power, no doubt stimulated Baudelaire's interest. Chenavard spent his entire life emulating the art of the great sixteenth-century sculptor; Préault claimed to be a connoisseur of Michelangelo and must often have spoken with customary eloquence of the glories of the Medici Chapel; Thoré maintained that Michelangelo was the "first sculptor to realize the great epic of the individual";[49] And finally, Delacroix was known to be an ardent admirer of Michelangelo and had written two laudatory articles about him (1830 and 1837).

As Hyslop points out, it was ironic that so great an enthusiast as Baudelaire should have failed to recognize the authenticity of the lovely *Bruges Madonna,* which he saw on a visit to the Church of Notre Dame—the only original work of Michelangelo, outside of the *Bound Slaves,* that he was ever to see.

HONORÉ DAUMIER

Of all the artists of his day, Baudelaire regarded Daumier almost as highly as he did Delacroix. He was among the first to recognize publicly that Daumier was not just a public entertainer but a true artist ranking with the greatest. Only Daumier and Ingres draw as well as Delacroix, he avowed in his *Salon de 1845,* and then added, no doubt to the consternation of most of his readers: "Daumier draws perhaps better than Delacroix, if you prefer healthy and robust qualities to the strange and astonishing power of a genius sick with genius" (*OC,* II:356).

Typically, the modest Daumier thought Baudelaire's compliment a "bizarre and embarrassing tribute," as he later confessed to Champfleury.[50] It is interesting that in 1853, the critic Hippolyte Castille, an acquaintance of Baudelaire, was to maintain that Daumier was "not only a greater painter than Ingres but also the greatest painter of the day" (*OC,* II:1357-58). Many years later Degas was to express much the same opinion and to declare the painter and caricaturist the equal of Delacroix.

An ardent Republican all his life—he was once imprisoned in Sainte-Pélagie for satirizing Louis-Philippe—Daumier earned the disfavor of Louis Napoleon through his vigorous caricature. He worked quietly in his simple attic studio above his apartment on the Ile Saint-Louis, where he was surrounded by a clutter of drawings, paintings, and lithographic tools. Baudelaire, Banville, Champfleury, and other friends came to watch the artist at work and to talk with him about various projects. Humble, retiring, and hampered by a slight speech defect, Daumier himself said little, being more interested in creative work than in aesthetic theories. But he admired the somewhat eccentric poet and is said to have remarked that his friend "could have become a great draftsman, had he not preferred to be a great poet."[51]

In 1857, even though Daumier was considered suspect by the government (his home had been searched for his subversive statuette *Ratapoil,* which had been adopted by the cartoonists and writers of *Le Charivari* as an emblem symbolizing Bonapartism), Baudelaire had the courage to praise him fervently in his *Quelques caricaturistes français.* Hailing him as one of the most important men not only in caricature but also "in all modern art," he pointed out Daumier's "sure hand," his ability to draw like the "great masters," his true sense of the comic, his remarkable ability to observe, and his "marvelous and, as it were, divine memory" (*OC,* II:556). But what made Daumier one of "the illustrious family of masters," Baudelaire claimed, was the fact that "he suggests color as he does thought—a true sign of a higher art (*OC,* II:557). In a footnote to the same article, the critic confessed that he had wanted to collaborate with Daumier on a catalogue of the artist's work, but that he had found the complex task too enormous to carry out.

Given Baudelaire's high opinion of Daumier and the fact that the artist was indeed a man of his time, it is strange that the poet-critic failed to write at greater length about this extraordinary painter of modern life. He seems, however, to have actually done so, for in his correspondence he alludes to a laudatory article on the artist which the editor Martinet had rejected and lost, despite Baudelaire's warning that he had failed to make a copy. In his letter to Martinet (July 1861) the poet wrote, "I am very sorry that a piece of criticism written with absolute admiration for our friend Daumier fails to please you in its totality" (*Corr.,* II:176). Martinet, of course, may have rejected the article out of fear of displeasing the government.

In Brussels, Baudelaire's belief in Daumier's excellence did not flag. Though he had written nothing about his friend's talents as a painter, he must have praised them highly to the artist Arthur Stevens, for in 1864 the latter wrote asking Daumier to send him *Le Wagon de troisième classe,* which, he said, Baudelaire had seen in his studio "some time ago."[52]

Moreover, in 1865 Champfleury, who was preparing his *Histoire de la caricature moderne,* wrote the ailing poet asking him to compose a poem introducing the Daumier section: "You are full of Daumier and his work, of the man and his pencil. The poetry applicable to this subject lies asleep in you and I am awakening it by writing you ..." (*PLB,* p. 83). The following day (May 25), Baudelaire sent his verses praising the genius of an artist whose ability to paint evil was only proof of "the beauty of his heart" and whose laughter was "a sign of his goodness." In the accompanying letter to Champfleury, Baudelaire explained: "I meant that the satiric genius of Daumier had nothing in common with satanic genius" (*Corr.,* II:502).

Baudelaire's approbation is hardly surprising, for Daumier was both an urban artist and a portrayer of modern life. Quick to note inauthenticity and hypocrisy in the political, social, and cultural life around him, he brilliantly satirized the rich and powerful, the smug and pompous, the vicious and arrogant, the sinister and grotesque. In his work, the whole city of Paris comes alive, especially the diverse and motley types of the urban bourgeoisie. At times, as in the work of the poet, satire gives way to compassion and the artist reveals the somber, tragic side of life.

The Baudelaire of 1848, whose sympathies were with the revolutionaries in their struggle against the government, must have experienced a special feeling of kinship with the Daumier of 1834, whose grim lithograph the *Rue Transnonain* served as a powerful protest against repressive government. "It is not exactly caricature, it is history, trivial and terrible reality," Baudelaire wrote in his *Quelques caricaturistes français.* "In that cold attic," where lie sprawled the dead bodies of a family awakened from their sleep and killed by government soldiers, "there is only silence and death" (*OC,* II:552).

Like Balzac, to whom Baudelaire compares him, Daumier created a veritable human comedy, inexhaustible in its range and power. "Glance through his work," Baudelaire noted, "and you will see parading before your eyes all that a great city contains of living monstrosities in all their fantastic and thrilling reality" (*OC,* II:554). The poet himself, inspired in part by Daumier, was attempting to do much the same thing in his *Tableaux parisiens* and in many of his prose poems.

Despite differences in personality and temperament, artist and poet had much in common and treated many themes and subjects in somewhat similar fashion. Both poked fun at the false antiquity of the Neo-Classicists—Baudelaire in his ironic essay on *L'Ecole païenne;* Daumier in his marvelous series of lithographs, *Histoire ancienne,* where classic heroes and heroines are irreverently portrayed as seedy Parisian nonentities, skinny or potbellied, chinless, scrawny-necked, smirking, and fatuous.

Baudelaire not only shared Daumier's taste for irony but also possessed the same ability to reveal beneath mere surface realism the tragic quality of the human condition. Nowhere are they more alike than in their treatment of the clown, to mention only one example. Though the myth of the clown was especially popular among the Romanticists, it was Baudelaire in literature and Daumier in art who were chiefly responsible for renewing the archetype of the tragic clown. In Baudelaire's prose poem "Le Vieux Saltimbanque," for example, an old clown, bent, worn, and decrepit, sadly watches a happy crowd who take no notice of him and seek entertainment elsewhere—the symbol of an old poet ignored by a fickle public.

Daumier's *Les Saltimbanques* is strongly reminiscent of Baudelaire's prose poem. Unlike the poet's protagonist, however, Daumier's clown, surrounded by his family, refuses to admit failure and beats his drum with a sad desperation, hoping to gain the attention of the crowd that ignores him. It is the wife who recalls the clown of the prose poem. The image of complete helplessness, she suggests weariness and dejection in every line of her body.

Equally poignant is Daumier's wash drawing *Le Déplacement des saltimbanques.* The three figures—father, mother, and son—moving their scanty equipment through the streets of Paris suggest the same sense of isolation and inescapable misery that characterize Baudelaire's prose poem. The overpowering sadness seen in the father's face, the blurred figure of the mother with her head turned to the wall, the emaciated child with a prematurely old expression, the crowd in the background, and the buildings looming beside them like a huge prison wall, all evoke the tragedy of the human condition.

Much the same sense of compassion and tough tenderness is revealed in the picture *Le Wagon de troisième classe,* which Baudelaire praised to Arthur Stevens. Its suggestive and symbolic power and the visionary realism with which the central figures are depicted remind us of Baudelaire. This is especially true of the grandmother. Weary, worn, and with a stoic dignity that commands respect, the old woman seems lost in thought, oblivious to all about her. Her astonishing eyes focus not outwardly—she is not looking at anyone or at anything—but rather inwardly, where she sees what no one else can see or guess. One is reminded of Baudelaire's "Les Petites Vieilles":

> —Ces yeux sont des puits faits d'un million de larmes,
> Des creusets qu'un métal refroidi pailleta . . .
> Ces yeux mystérieux ont d'invincibles charmes
> Pour celui que l'austère infortune allaita!

Works such as these explain why Baudelaire considered Daumier a great artist and a great moralist and why both artist and poet are so much alike in the physical and moral expression that they gave to the life of their time.

CHARLES MERYON

Among the struggling artists with whom Baudelaire came in contact, no one was more deserving of the compassion shown him by the poet-critic than Meryon (1821–68), the poor obscure printmaker who today is considered by many critics one of the greatest, if not the greatest, French etcher of all time. Charles Meryon was the illegitimate son of a dancer in the Paris Opera, who died insane, and of an English physician, Charles Lewis Meryon, of French Huguenot origin, better known today as the secretary-physician-companion to Lady Hester Stanhope and the author of her *Mémoires* "as related by Herself in a Conversation with her Physician."

After attending the naval school at Brest, Meryon embarked on a series of voyages that spanned a period of seven years and left him, as in the case of Baudelaire, with a love for the sea. Like Nerval, he was gentle, kind, overly sensitive, and deeply introspective. The knowledge of his illegitimacy troubled him greatly and may have hastened the insanity which became apparent after 1856.

Baudelaire, who met Meryon in 1859—probably after the latter's return from a stay in the asylum at Charenton—warmly praised the artist's genius for the first time in his *Salon de 1859*.[53] His tribute later prompted Victor Hugo, from whose "A l'Arc de Triomphe" Baudelaire had quoted a few lines and who, in the meantime, had seen some of the prints, to write the poet-critic (April 29, 1860) that he too had been "dazzled" by the etchings and that the artist well deserved "the profound and luminous page that he has inspired in you" (*PLB*, p. 191).

In an effort to aid Meryon, who "doesn't know how to sell or to find a publisher," Baudelaire suggested to Poulet-Malassis (March 9, 1860) that he publish a new edition of the *Eaux-Fortes sur Paris*. The poet had offered to write texts to accompany the etchings ("reveries of ten lines, of twenty or thirty lines ... the philosophical reveries of a strolling Parisian"), but the artist would have none of it (*Corr.*, I:670). His concern for Meryon's plight and his esteem for his art even led Baudelaire to express his willingness to write mere unsigned catalogue descriptions. For some unknown reason, however, the project was never carried out, and in 1861 the plates, after being retouched by the artist, were printed by Delâtre without any commentary by Baudelaire. The poet did, however, succeed in persuading the government to purchase several sets of Meryon's prints and acquired several for himself, including one for his mother and another for Madame Sabatier.

Meryon, who had been taken to Charenton in 1866 for the second time, died in February 1868, less than a year after the death of his ardent defender.

Meryon's preoccupation with the city and his refusal to allow Baudelaire to write the "reveries" which were to accompany his prints may have prompted the poet to go ahead on his own and to follow the advice he had given artists in the Salons of 1845 and 1846. During the years 1859–62 Baudelaire's concern with Parisian subjects was marked. Conceivably it was intensified by the urban art of Meryon, as well as that of Daumier, Guys, and even Manet, although there is no evidence of any direct influence on their part.

"Parisian life is rich in poetic and marvelous subjects," Baudelaire had written in the *Salon de 1846*. "The marvelous envelops us and permeates us like the atmosphere itself; but we do not see it." The words anticipate the etchings of Meryon, which contain a feeling both of the marvelous and of the poetic. In his comments on the artist's prints in 1859, Baudelaire noted this very fact and affirmed that he had "rarely seen the natural solemnity of an immense city more *poetically* reproduced" (my italics) (*OC*, II:666).

Baudelaire was quite right in his judgment. Meryon's *Eaux-Fortes sur Paris* differ sharply from the cartographic views characteristic of urban subjects in the first half of the nineteenth century. The artist loved the cityscape and shared with the poet a fondness for the older sections of Paris. One has only to think of Baudelaire's magnificent poem "Le Cygne" and of Meryon's sensitive rendering of medieval streets and buildings.

In its subjectivity and strange visionary quality, Meryon's art comes close to being a sort of visual equivalent of that of Baudelaire—of "Les Tableaux parisiens," in particular, and of certain of his prose poems. Both artist and poet mingled realism (in the case of Meryon a meticulous and accurate portrayal of objects) with the "surnaturel"; both gave the cityscape a personal interpretation often marked by a mysterious, somber, and even sinister spirit.

Moreover, Meryon's tendency to create in his etchings a small drama must have appealed strongly to Baudelaire. In an etching such as *La Morgue*, it is curious to note how this dramatic element results even more from the rendering of the building itself than from the movements of the minuscule figures depicted in the foreground. Meryon's friend Philippe Burty, who did a catalogue of the prints, maintains that it would be "impossible to extract a more moving treatment of a corner of houses."[54] He points out that the strange, superimposed roofs, the colliding angles, the blinding light, which form a striking contrast with the masses of shadows, suggest some ominous event about which the characters are talking. Of lesser importance visually is the action of the characters themselves. A crowd leaning over the parapet of the quay is watching the scene below. A corpse has just been dragged from the Seine; an anguished woman looks on; a little girl sobs, her head between her hands; and a policeman points out the Morgue to the men carrying the corpse.

The drama of the scene is intensified by some of the very things that Baudelaire had noted in the *Salon de 1859* as characteristic of Meryon's art: "majestic accumulations of stone ... obelisks of industry, spewing their conglomerations of smoke against the heavens ... tumultuous skies, charged with anger and spite" (*OC,* II:666–67). Finally, the lugubrious Morgue itself which, with its dark, gaping windows, takes on the menacing air of the "surnaturel" reminiscent of Baudelaire's description of his dismal lodging in the Spleen poem "Pluviôse, irrité contre la ville entière."

Meryon's evocation of the city has a parallel in the work of the poet-critic. In poems such as "Le Crépuscule du soir" and "Le Crépuscule du matin," he too evokes the city with a mixture of straightforward realism and the "surnaturel." By the use of sinister and even demonic images (the lamp like a bloody, palpitating eye, gaslights flickering in the wind, demons bumping against the shutters) the poet produces an effect somewhat similar to that achieved by the artist in his frequent portrayal of the black, ominous birds that fill the Parisian skies or of other seemingly mysterious and irrational elements that appear in his works. Baudelaire, too, often gives an almost demonic significance to the commonplace and evokes—though far more boldly than Meryon—the tragedy of human existence.

But where in Meryon the cityscape itself dominates over the elements of human tragedy, in Baudelaire urban atmosphere serves mainly as a sketchy but highly effective backdrop against which is played out the drama of the human condition. In their depiction of Parisian life—objective realism mingled with the "marvelous," the dramatic interplay of great forces behind the ordinary and trivial, a deep concern for the human condition—artist and poet rise above mere surface realism and succeed in giving a new dimension to their art by their transfiguration of commonplace reality.

CONSTANTIN GUYS

Sometime in 1859 Baudelaire seems to have made the acquaintance of an eccentric artist, Constantin Guys (1805–92), who, like Daumier, Meryon, and the poet himself, was fascinated by the life of the great city and found his inspiration in its streets and various haunts. Guys had been an art correspondent for the *Illustrated London News* and had made travel sketches in Spain, Turkey, and in the Crimea during the Crimean War. The last years of his long life were spent in Paris, where he did enchanting sketches, usually of the pageantry and pleasures of city life. Regiments of soldiers marching through the streets, dandies, aristocrats and wealthy bourgeois strolling through the parks or riding in elegant carriages, men and women riding horseback through the Bois de Boulogne, courtesans, and cheap prostitutes all are portrayed with consummate skill and spontaneity and offer a wonderfully accurate document of the time. In fact, a study of the hundreds of sketches Guys made during his years in Paris furnishes us with an authentic picture of the customs, the clothes, the preoccupations, and the amusements of the high and low echelons of Parisian society of that day.

Baudelaire was delighted to find in Guys the modernity which he had found lacking in the visual art of his contemporaries. In the artist's many sketches and watercolors he discovered a perfect pretext for the presentation of certain aesthetic ideas, particularly those pertaining to the sketch. The result was the famous essay *Le Peintre de la vie moderne* (published in 1863, but written between 1859 and 1860), probably the most important of all of Baudelaire's critical writings.

Baudelaire was not alone in praising Guys. The two had many friends in common. Delacroix admired his watercolors. Manet painted his portrait and owned a number of his sketches. Gautier, who had about sixty of his drawings, spoke well of him in his introduction to the Lévy edition of *Les Fleurs du Mal*. Nadar, to whom Guys bequeathed his portfolio in gratitude for his kindness and support during the last years of his life, was an especially close friend. In fact, it was after leaving the home of Nadar, where he had dined that evening, that Guys was struck by a carriage and left with injuries that resulted in his death.

Small and energetic, with a gray mustache and looking like an old soldier, Guys was almost neurotically modest and stubbornly refused to allow Baudelaire to use more than his initials in his essay. The critic was forced to comply and scrupulously avoided mentioning the artist by name. What he wrote, however, is less interesting for what it tells us about Guys than for what it reveals of Baudelaire's beliefs and aesthetic ideas.

Baudelaire has been widely criticized for choosing Guys as the subject of so important an essay. In a previous study (1969), we have already pointed out that nothing could be more unjust or incorrect.[55] A careful reading of Baudelaire's essay proves that he goes out of his way in the opening paragraphs to indirectly categorize Guys as one of the "poetae minores," one of the lesser great whose work nevertheless contains "du bon, du solide, et du délicieux"—hardly expressions of extravagant praise. Though he was cognizant of the many merits of Guys's work and is otherwise lavish with his praise, he by no means mistakes the sketches for masterpieces of the highest order. To compare his eulogy of Guys with that of Delacroix clarifies the nature and degree of his admiration. Whereas Baudelaire likens Guys to Devéria and to Gavarni, whose sketches of contemporary life make them what he calls "historians," Delacroix, on the other hand, is an "unrivaled artist without antecedents, without a precedent," who is on a par with Raphael and Veronese.

It was, then, Guy's portrayal of modern life, particularly the life of a great city, that caused Baudelaire to use him as the core of his great essay. Daumier, though a greater artist, would not have been representative of certain parts of the study—the chapter on dandyism, for example, as well as the chapters on makeup and on women. For there is little doubt that Baudelaire was utilizing in his article many pages which he had intended to publish as a general study on the painting of manners. Manet would have been equally unsuitable, for his production in 1859–60, as we shall see, was both too scanty and too lacking in authentic modern expression to have justified giving him the title "painter of modern life."

One of the things that Baudelaire most enjoyed in the work of Guys was his depiction of the crowd, whether found in the streets, at theaters, concerts, or the fair. In one of his prose poems, "Les Foules," the poet discusses from the aesthetic standpoint the importance of the crowd as a source of inspiration for the writer or artist. He maintains that "to enjoy the crowd is an art," that "the solitary and pensive walker draws a strange intoxication from this universal communion," and that he "enjoys the incomparable privilege of becoming himself or someone else at will" (*OC,* I:291). The reader of *Les Fleurs du Mal* and of the prose poems will recognize themes that have been inspired in this very way.

In *Le Peintre de la vie moderne,* Baudelaire labels Guys "a man of the crowds" and compares his healthy curiosity about life (curiosity, he maintains, is the mainspring of his genius) with the curiosity of the convalescent described by Poe in his story "The Man of the Crowd." Poe's hero, seated in the window of a coffeehouse, rapturously gazing at the passing crowd, suddenly rushes into the midst of the throng "in pursuit of an unknown, half-glimpsed face that has suddenly bewitched him" (*OC,* II:690).

Baudelaire was not only delighted by Guys's portrayal of the pageantry of life, whether military or social; he was also fascinated by the artist's ability to distill the "mysterious beauty" of modernity: "the transitory, the fugitive, the contingent, the half of art of which the other half is the eternal and immutable" (*OC,* II:695). Like a novelist or moralist, Guys was to Baudelaire "the painter of the passing moment with all its suggestions of eternity," for the poet-critic makes clear that in all beauty two elements must be present—the relative or circumstantial and the invariable or eternal: "I defy anyone to find a single scrap of beauty which does not contain these two elements" (*OC,* II:685).

Baudelaire was equally impressed by Guys's ability to portray women: complacent bourgeois wives, strolling arm in arm with their husbands; skinny little girls; elegantly dressed society women; provocative courtesans in ornate costume; and brazen or hapless prostitutes. But what especially intrigued Baudelaire in so many of these drawings was the artist's "moral fecundity," which reveals itself, he maintained, in his portrayal of "the special beauty of evil, the beautiful amid the horrible" (*OC,* II:722). Once again the reader is struck by the kinship between many of Baudelaire's poems and the artist's sketches depicting the "beauty which comes from Evil, always devoid of spirituality" (*OC,* II:720).

Baudelaire was also conscious of Guys's skill as a technician and praised the fluid lines, the spontaneity, the clever draftsmanship, and the suggestive and evocative aspects of his drawing. Like Daumier, Guys had the amazing ability to draw from memory rather than from models (a very important quality in the eyes of the poet-critic) and to do so with a rapidity, "a fire, an intoxication of the pencil or brush amounting almost to a frenzy" (*OC,* II:699).

Given Baudelaire's enthusiasm for the art of Guys, one wonders why he ranks him—though discreetly and indirectly—among the "*poetae minores.*" The answer is implicit both in this essay and in certain aesthetic ideas presented as early as 1845 and 1846. Of the heroic, epic, and poetic qualities of modern life which Baudelaire, in 1845 and 1846, had associated with the "true painter" of modernity, Guys seems to have portrayed only the poetic. The words *poetry, poem, poet,* and *poetic* occur at least seven times in Baudelaire's description of Guys's sketches; the adjective *heroic* but once. The passing of a regiment with its stirring music and glittering costumes is a "poem"; scenes of war itself are described as "the dreadful poetry of a battlefield"; and the multitude of drawings that make up the album of the Crimean War form "a vast and complicated poem." Moreover, with the exception of the scenes of war, the "poetry" of Guys is usually lighthearted, with little or no sense of the serious or tragic elements of life found in some of Daumier's work and in Baudelaire's own writing. Nor had Guys noted the "marvelous," which, according to the poet-critic, surrounds us everywhere in the city and which Meryon had so successfully suggested in his etchings.

Guys had displayed what Baudelaire calls "la pompe de la vie"—the pomp and circumstance of life which by its very nature is almost necessarily restricted to the outward appearance of people and of things. It should be remembered in passing that Baudelaire was primarily interested in the inward aspects of people and of things, or what he calls in Delacroix the soul, the dream, the impalpable. In the opening lines of chapter 8, Baudelaire explains: "To define once again the kind of subject preferred by our artist, we shall say that it is the pomp and circumstance of life such as is to be seen in the capitals of the civilized world: the pomp of military life, of elegant fashion and of love" (OC, II:707).

The definition clarifies what he had said in chapter 2: "Observer, flâneur, philosopher—call him what you will; but to characterize this artist you will certainly be led to bestow on him an adjective which you could not apply to the painter of eternal or at least more lasting things, of heroic or of religious subjects" (OC, II:687).

What Baudelaire found in Guys therefore and what he observes about his art pertain in general to the modernity that is revealed in a sketch as opposed to the modernity that may be found in a painting dealing with modern subjects in a more serious manner. As Claude Pichois observes, "Baudelaire has crystalized a new aesthetic, that of the sketch, of the fixation of the instantaneous impression, thanks to the precision and the rapidity of the execution" (OC, II:1418).

If then Baudelaire chose Guys as the subject of his essay, it was with full knowledge that he was dealing with an artist who was superb in a minor genre differing in its requirements from those of more serious genres such as history or religion. The closing paragraphs of the essay, like those of the beginning, leave no doubt in our minds. Guys's drawings, Baudelaire maintains, will take their place as "precious archives of civilized life" along with those of other "delightful artists" who are "no less serious historians." The artist, he concludes, "has deliberately fulfilled a function which other artists disdain and which require above all a man of the world to fulfill. He has everywhere sought the passing, fleeting beauty of present-day life... [which we] call *modernity*. Often strange, violent, and excessive, but always poetic, he has succeeded in concentrating within his drawings the bitter or heady bouquet of the wine of Life" (OC, II:724).

EDOUARD MANET

Baudelaire formed an even closer and more enduring friendship with Edouard Manet than he did with Guys. Various dates have been suggested as marking the beginning of their acquaintance. If we are to believe Antonin Proust, one of Manet's oldest and most intimate friends, they first met while Manet was studying (1850–56) under the direction of the well-known teacher and painter Thomas Couture. In his biography of the artist, Proust tells how he and Manet used to lunch during their student days at the Rôtisserie Pavard, rue Notre-Dame-de-Lorette in the company of Murger, Barbey d'Aurevilly, and Baudelaire.[56] Since Proust had not only attended the collège Rollin with Manet but had also studied with him under Couture, there is little reason to doubt the authenticity of his claim.

Though Proust maintains that it was the artist who influenced the poet—and to a certain extent he was of course right—there is much to indicate that the opposite was more true. Manet, who told Proust that Baudelaire had "tant de génie" beneath his bizarre appearance, must obviously have had a keen interest in the aesthetic ideas that the poet-critic had presented in his Salons of 1845 and 1846—ideas that they no doubt discussed in their many conversations together. There is reason to believe that Manet's wish to use models clothed in the costume of the day, despite Couture's objections, was encouraged and perhaps mainly inspired by Baudelaire's defense of modernity and of modern dress in particular. In fact, at the Rôtisserie Pavard, Proust tells us, Manet once inveighed against Couture after being reprimanded by him for using a clothed model.[57]

Artist and poet became inseparable friends and, according to Proust, were "constant companions," especially in the late 1850s and the early 1860s. Together with Proust, Baudelaire was in Manet's studio when word came that the *Buveur d'absinthe* had been rejected by the Salon of 1859. When the artist angrily accused Couture of having influenced the jury against him, Baudelaire put the blame directly on Manet himself: "The sum and substance of it all is that one must be oneself."[58] His remark may have been prompted by his objection to the fact that the artist had arbitrarily fitted a contemporary subject into the conventional design of an old master. (Curiously, one notes this same blend of the traditional and the innovative in Baudelaire's poetry.) Critics have often noted this tendency on the part of Manet—especially in his early work—and the artist himself frankly admitted his deliberate compositional borrowing in the case of *Le Buveur:* "I have made a Parisian type, observed in Paris, while putting into the execution the technical naiveté I had found in the painting by Velásquez. They do not understand. Perhaps they will understand better if I make a Spanish type."[59]

Couture, however, found other reasons to condemn his pupil's painting. Invited by the aspiring young artist to view the picture, he scornfully accused Manet of a lack of moral character for having painted such a subject. Anne Coffin Hanson is hesitant about accepting the story at face value, since the subject was a fairly common one and since Manet, presumably with the blessing of his teacher, had already made a copy of Adrian Brouwer's absinthe drinker. She believes that, if Couture objected to the painting, it was rather because he believed that Manet had been inspired by Baudelaire's "shocking *Les Fleurs du Mal.*"[60] Her explanation is all the more plausible since most critics point to the Baudelairean tone of Manet's early painting and have even associated *Le Buveur d'absinthe* with the poet's

"Le Vin de l'assassin." Hanson attests to the Baudelairean influence but suggests as a more appropriate source "Le Vin des
chiffonniers." Her suggestion seems well justified, since the
ragpicker of Baudelaire's poem was addicted to wine, if not to
absinthe.[61]

In 1859 or 1860 Manet's young model and assistant,
Alexandre, committed suicide in the artist's studio, much to the
horror of his master. The tragic event made a strong impression
on Baudelaire as well and led him to compose his prose poem
"La Corde," dedicated to Manet, in which the surprise ending
with its ironic twist attributes the mother's distress to greed and
avarice rather than maternal love.

Early in the 1860s, Proust recounts, Baudelaire used to accompany Manet on daily trips to the Tuileries Gardens, where
the artist was making studies in the open air of children playing
under the trees while watched over by their nurses.[62] The picture
in question is known as *Les Enfants aux Tuileries,* although
Proust seems to have been thinking of *La Musique aux Tuileries,*
since the plate reference he gives is to the latter. Both paintings
were done about the same time, however (*Les Enfants* in the
summer and *La Musique* completed in the fall of 1862), and
there is good reason to believe that Baudelaire may even have
suggested the subjects.[63] In fact, in one of his prose poems, "Les
Veuves," which is contemporaneous with the pictures, the poet
describes a scene very similar to that portrayed in *La Musique.*
One passage is particularly reminiscent of the painting:

> Through the darkness the orchestra sends forth festive,
> triumphant, or voluptuous songs. Shimmering gowns trail on
> the ground; glances cross each other; idlers, tiring from hav-
> ing done nothing, loll about, indolently pretending to enjoy
> the music. Here there is nothing but the rich, the happy;
> nothing which doesn't breathe and inspire nonchalance and
> the pleasure of taking life easily.

Poet and artist may have been deliberately vying with each
other in an effort to portray what Baudelaire had called "the
heroism of modern life." The abrupt change in Manet's style

from what Nils Sandblad calls "his paraphrases of Rubens and Velásquez" to the "realism of the flâneur" seems to indicate some such attempt on his part.[64] The composition of the painting, as Sandblad has shown, is based in part on a painting in the Louvre—incorrectly attributed at that time to Velásquez—which Manet had earlier copied in watercolor, in oil, and as an etching. The fact that Velásquez and Murillo appear to the far left in the picture undoubtedly gave Manet the idea of depicting himself and his artist friend Alfred de Balleroy in the very same position in his own work.

To give his picture even more immediacy, Manet also decided to include in the large crowd a number of friends and distinguished persons in the arts, much as Courbet had done in *L'Atelier*. Among them can be seen his brother Eugène, Baudelaire, Gautier, Baron Taylor, and Offenbach. The profile view of Baudelaire was later used by Manet as the basis for one of his well-known etchings of the writer.

Very possibly Manet was also influenced in his subject and treatment by several artists whom Baudelaire esteemed. *La Musique* bears a strong family resemblance to the engravings of two eighteenth-century artists, Debucourt and Saint-Aubin, whom Baudelaire had singled out for mention both at the beginning and the end of his study *Le Peintre de la vie moderne*. Manet, incidentally, owned two of Debucourt's engravings. An even closer resemblance may be noted between Manet's painting and a wood engraving entitled *Concert militaire dans le jardin des Tuileries,* much admired by Baudelaire, which appeared in *L'Illustration* on July 17, 1858.

Even more significant, *La Musique* has much in common with the drawings of Constantin Guys both in its subject and in its gray tonality, as Jean Adhémar has noted.[65] Nils Sandblad has pointed out the striking similarities between *La Musique* and Guys's wash drawing *Aux Champs-Elysées,* owned by none other than Baudelaire himself—a discovery we made independently and noted in our previous study on the poet and the painter.[66]

All in all, then, Baudelaire's influence was seemingly considerable, and the poet-critic may even have encouraged Manet to follow the example of Guys and to paint a similar subject in oil. Perhaps in thinking of *Concert militaire dans les jardins des Tuileries* (1858) he himself wrote his prose poem "Les Veuves" describing the lonely widow listening to the military band in the gardens. But there is an important difference between the poet's evocation of this urban scene and that of Manet or Guys. In the work of the latter, the crowd itself is the subject, and atmosphere is evoked for the sake of atmosphere. In the prose poem the central theme is the solitude of the proud, impoverished widow who, because she cannot afford the price of admission, is seated—a lonely, poignant figure—apart from the crowd. The contrast of her solitude with the gaiety of the multitude is characteristic of Baudelaire, as is his use of urban atmosphere which, as usual, remains subsidiary to the theme and serves either as background or as a symbol of his state of mind.

On April 24, 1864, Baudeliare went to Brussels ostensibly to lecture and to escape his creditors but mainly in hope of obtaining a publisher for his complete works. Before he left for Brussels it was to Manet that the poet turned for financial assistance, and during his stay in Belgium Manet often acted as his intermediary, whether to keep his eye on Baudelaire's literary agent or to intercede with some editor on his behalf. The artist even lent him five hundred francs in July 1865, though he had not yet been reimbursed for the one thousand francs he had lent him two years earlier.

After the poet suffered a stroke in Belgium and was brought back to a nursing home in Paris, Manet and his wife were among his most assiduous visitors. Madame Manet, an accomplished concert pianist, would often play for him his favorite passages from Wagner, and the artist was one of the group that used to take Baudelaire with them in the early days of his illness. The poet, weak and speechless, could do no more than listen and occasionally punctuate their conversation—or so the story goes—with the only word he could pronounce—*crénom, crénom* ("damn it, damn it"). On one occasion Manet failed to accompany them, and Nadar wrote to the artist telling how much

Baudelaire had missed him and how, to his great surprise, the poet had unexpectedly called from the back of the garden in a loud voice, "Manet! Manet!" "That took the place of the usual damn it," he added in his note.[67]

George Mauner believes that the painting *L'Enterrement* (ca. 1870), with its dark and somber sky, was inspired by memories of Baudelaire's funeral—and, in particular, by the small cortège that moved slowly on that hot oppressive day (September 2, 1867) to the cemetery of Montparnasse.[68] As Asselineau was pronouncing the eulogy in a voice choked with emotion, the rain began to fall, interrupting the speaker and dispersing the few mourners who had gathered at the graveside.

Of all Manet's paintings none is more Baudelairean in character than his famous *Olympia,* which was shown in the Salon of 1865. In it the artist had made a deliberate attempt to paint a contemporary version of Titian's *Venus of Urbino.* Instead of the languorous goddess reclining seductively against the pillows of her bed with a small dog lying at her feet, Manet depicts a slight young girl propped stiffly against huge pillows. The figure in the background of Titian's painting is replaced by a Negro servant holding a bouquet of dazzling flowers, obviously offered by an unseen admirer, and the small dog curled up cozily at the foot of the bed is replaced by a small black cat arching its back and glaring in alarm at the intruder.

Everything about the picture bespeaks the courtesan—even the name Olympia, which may have had as one of several possible sources the brazen courtesan of the play of Dumas fils, *La Dame aux Camélias.* In his painting Manet has succeeded in completely modernizing Titian's classic theme and in making it his own. Consciously or unconsciously he had avoided the pitfalls to which Baudelaire had called attention in his *Peintre de la vie moderne:*

> If a painstaking, scrupulous, but unimaginative artist has to paint a courtesan of today and takes his *inspiration* (to use an accepted expression) from a courtesan by Titian or Raphael, it is more than likely that he will produce a work

which is false, ambiguous, and obscure. The study of a masterpiece of that time and type will tell him nothing about the bearing, the glance, the forced smile, or the real life appearance of one of those creatures whom the dictionary of fashion has successively classified under the coarse or facetious titles of *fallen* or *kept women,* women of *easy virtue* and *tarts.* [OC, II:696]

The glance, the mien, the bearing of Olympia are indeed of her own time. Despite his compositional borrowings, Manet had remained profoundly original. Like Baudelaire he had come to realize that "almost all our originality comes from the stamp that *time* imprints upon our feelings" (*OC,* II:696). In fact, if the composition of the picture is borrowed from Titian, the tone or flavor may well have been inspired by Baudelaire himself. Wearing only a bracelet, earrings, a black ribbon around her throat, a flower in her hair and slippers on her feet, Olympia brings to mind the woman of Baudelaire's celebrated poem, "Les Bijoux."

Diderot wrote in his Salon of 1767: "A nude woman is not indecent; it is an undressed one who is."[69] In what follows, it almost seems as if he had had some prescient knowledge of Manet's picture:

> Imagine the Medici Venus before you and tell me if her nudity bothers you. But put little embroidered slippers on her feet. Fasten her tightly fitting white stocking with a rose-colored garter on her knee. Arrange a bit of ribbon in her hair, and you will strongly feel the difference between the decent and the indecent.

The ornaments worn by Olympia and, in particular, the ribbon tied around her throat, help to create an impression of being undressed rather than nude, and it was in part for this very reason that she shocked and horrified the public, much as her counterpart in "Les Bijoux" had done eight years before. Not only the ornaments worn by Olympia remind us of Baudelaire's poem, but certain phrases he had used ("the triumphant air," "her eyes fixed on me, like a tamed tigress") seem as true of Manet's courtesan as of Baudelaire's.

One could even say that the slender figure of the girl reflected Baudelaire's taste for the slender or thin woman, echoed in such poems as "Une Martyre," "Danse macabre," or "Le Vin du solitaire." Moreover, in his discussions with Manet he must have expressed his ideas about the nude figure. "The thin woman is a well of mysterious pleasures," he had written in 1846 in "Choix de maximes consolantes sur l'amour," and in his miscellaneous notes he had noted paradoxically: "There is in thinness an indecency which makes it charming" (OC, II:548, 595).

Equally Baudelairean in character are the black woman holding the bouquet of flowers and the cat so reminiscent of the cats that prowl through many of Baudelaire's works. Curiously enough, it was the cat that aroused the greatest furor on the part of the spectators. Given an almost diabolic significance, it provoked either laughter or scorn and inspired the public to rename the picture *La Vénus au chat*.

Yet *Olympia* should not be considered a mere transcription of "Les Bijoux" or even its principal source, although it can hardly be denied that Manet must have been encouraged by Baudelaire to turn to scenes of contemporary life and that his reading of *Les Fleurs du Mal* must have stimulated his imagination. One must not forget, however, that Titian's *Venus of Urbino* also wore a bracelet and that the slight but elegant figure of the young girl represented, as Sandblad points out, the contemporary ideal of attractive womanhood. Nor can one shut out insistent echoes of Goya's *Maja desnuda*. Manet's eyes, like those of Baudelaire, were open to the beauty of the past and to that of the present, to absolute beauty and to relative beauty. Inevitably his art reflected the full range of his vision, and the evocative words of his intimate friend and mentor were an important part of that vision.

Bewildered and dismayed by the hostile attitude of the public and critics, Manet wrote to Baudelaire in Brussels, telling how much he longed to talk with him and to learn his opinion about the finished work. Though Baudelaire must have seen the *Olympia* while his friend was working on it in 1863 (the date usually given for its composition), he evidently was not aware of some of the changes or additions, for in his reply he asked if there were really a cat in the painting. His reply to Manet was blunt and severe, evidently calculated to jolt the artist into a fighting spirit. While emphasizing the "irresistible charm" of his work, he reminded him that Chateaubriand and Wagner had also been scorned and mocked and that, while they were models, each in his own genre, Manet was "*only the first in the decrepitude of [his] art*" (*Corr.*, II:497).

Baudelaire was disturbed by Manet's discouragement and confided his worries to two of their common friends. To Champfleury he wrote: "Manet has great talent, a *talent which will stand the test of time* [my italics]. But he has a weak character. He seems to me crushed and stunned by the shock" (*Corr.*, II:502). And to the kind and charming Madame Meurice he wrote, urging her to bolster Manet's courage: "Manet has such light and brilliant faculties that it would be unfortunate if he became discouraged. He will never overcome the lacunae in his temperament. But he has a *temperament*, that is the main thing" (*Corr.*, II:501).

Baudelaire was not using an empty phrase, for he believed temperament to be a prime requisite of every great artist. As early as 1846 he had written, "An artist without temperament is not worthy of painting pictures, and, as we are wearied of imitators, and, above all, of eclectics—he would do better to enter the service of a painter of temperament, as a humble workman" (*OC,* II:419). Baudelaire's severe but encouraging letter must have served the purpose, for his friendship with Manet continued as warm as before. Years later the artist was to show to his good friend Mallarmé the "bonne et terrible lettre," which he had kept all those years.

To reproach Baudelaire, as do most critics, for not having written an article in defense of Manet at this juncture is completely unrealistic. The poet was far too ill to do more than try to encourage his friend—too ill even to do his own work. In his letter to the artist he admitted: "As for finishing *Pauvre Belgique,* I am unable to do so; I have lost my strength, I am dead. I have a considerable number of *prose poems* to publish in

two or three magazines. But I can't do any more" (Corr.,
II:497).

Moreover, at this point it was next to impossible for him to
find a publisher willing to accept his work. Even had he done so,
his praise might have done more harm than good. As George
Heard Hamilton reminds us, "To a later generation, the support
and encouragement of Charles Baudelaire would seem invaluable, but, in the early 1860s, praise from the author of Les Fleurs
du Mal was suspect in the extreme."[70] The poet-critic's support
of Manet was well known both in art circles and by the general
public. The critic Charles Monselet had called Manet "a pupil of
Goya and of Charles Baudelaire," and as late as June 15, 1864,
the newspaper Charivari presented a crude caricature of the poet
and painter.

Even more implausible is the criticizing of Baudelaire for not
having made Manet the subject of Le Peintre de la vie moderne.
Although, for want of a publisher, the now-famous essay appeared as late as 1863, it had been written almost four years
earlier, between November 15, 1859, and February 4, 1860.
And in 1859 Manet's work was still far removed from
Baudelaire's ideas of modernity.

It is true that, as a student, Manet—under the influence of
Courbet, Champfleury, and certainly Baudelaire himself—had
rebelled against the artificial and the unnatural and had advocated painting models clothed in the manner of the day. But it is
also true that his work between 1850 and 1859 mainly consisted
of copies of old masters in the Louvre, painted under the supervi-
sion of Couture. Baudelaire's cryptic comment about the Buveur
d'absinthe ("one must be oneself") clearly indicated his feeling
about the derivative character of Manet's painting at that time.
Today Manet scholars agree that the artist's originality did not
reveal itself until a number of years later. And even in his own
day, three of Manet's close friends and staunch admirers—Zola,
Mallarmé, and Duret—acknowledged the dependence of his early
style on the past.

Though Baudelaire had good reason for not centering Le
Peintre de la vie moderne on Manet and for not defending him

when the *Olympia* was under attack, one wonders why he did not write an article between 1861 and 1864, before leaving for Brussels. Unfortunately, Baudelaire knew only a small proportion of Manet's work. If Zola in 1867 had seen only thirty or forty canvases, as he claimed, Baudelaire must have seen even fewer before he left for Belgium. Though many of them were still far too derivative, one or two were certainly worthy of his critical attention.

However, to have written an article in defense of Manet would not have been as simple as it might appear to us today. While 1861 was a year of triumph for the artist (his *Guitarrero* won honorable mention in the Salon of that year and he was beginning to gain the attention of the public and of his fellow artists), for Baudelaire it was disastrous. He did succeed in publishing the second edition of *Les Fleurs du Mal* in 1861 and in finishing his articles on contemporary writers as well as his essay on Wagner. But his wretched health, the failure of his candidacy for the French Academy, and his final break with Jeanne Duval left him humiliated and broken. Moreover, had he written in support of Manet, it is highly probable that he would not have found a publisher. The two periodicals on which he had depended, the *Revue fantaisiste* and the *Revue européenne,* had ceased publication, and he had quarreled with the editors of the *Revue des Deux Mondes* and the *Revue contemporaine.* "I am without a journal," he wrote his mother on Christmas Day in 1861, and once again his thoughts turned to suicide.

In 1862 Baudelaire published his first and only formal defense of Manet in the form of a short review that appeared in *Le Boulevard,* a small newspaper circulating mainly in cafés frequented by artists. Manet had contributed an etching, *Les Gitanos,* to a portfolio of etchings published by the Société des Aquafortistes, of which Baudelaire was one of the sponsors. In his review, Baudelaire singled out Manet and Legros, briefly praising their taste for "modern reality" and for their "active and ample imagination."

In 1863 Baudelaire again failed to defend Manet publicly when the artist came under attack after exhibiting his two paintings *La Musique aux Tuileries* and *Le Déjeuner sur l'herbe*. His silence has been interpreted as a sign of his disapproval, yet, as we have seen, *La Musique* had been done in the company of Baudelaire and perhaps even at his instigation. Even had he tried, Baudelaire could have done little to help his friend, for the notoriety he had won with *Les Fleurs du Mal* would only have reflected on Manet. Moreover he was unable to find a publisher for his own collected art and literary criticism; he was obsessed with the idea of his literary impotence; and in January 1862 he had experienced what he believed to be a sign of oncoming mental illness. In his *Journaux intimes* he had noted: "Now I suffer constantly from dizziness, and today, January 23, 1862, I have experienced a strange warning. I have felt pass over me the wind of the wing of madness" (*OC*, I:668).

But though Baudelaire failed to support Manet publicly in 1863 and 1864, he did everything possible to influence those who could be of any help. He wrote Chennevières, the director of fine arts, asking him to give special attention to the hanging of Manet's paintings in the Salon of 1864 and, in a long letter, tried to convince Théophile Thoré that Manet's paintings were not pastiches of Spanish artists.

Despite his liking for Manet, however, Baudelaire had reservations about his art. His letter to Madame Meurice mentioning certain lacunae in the artist's temperament and his letter to Manet himself telling him frankly that he was only the first in the decrepitude of his art speak for themselves. Yet both comments are understandable in the light of Baudelaire's aesthetics.

Manet could not help knowing that the poet-critic believed that France was in a period of artistic decline, that the great tradition had been lost, and that a new tradition had not yet been established. In the *Salon de 1846* and often thereafter Baudelaire had emphasized the fact that the art of his day had become decadent and anarchic. Artists had failed to find the element of relative beauty that belonged to their age and had settled either for philosophic (didactic) art or for technique for the sake of technique. In still other cases they had simply gone on imitating a past which had lost its validity for them and, in so doing, had become what Baudelaire called "artistic monkeys."

Surely Manet discussed these ideas with Baudelaire and understood that the poet's harsh statement was only another way of saying that he, Manet, was the best in a period of artistic decadence in France. The fact that the artist harbored no grudge and that years later he showed the "bonne et terrible lettre" to Mallarmé, as has been mentioned, seems evidence that he did not entirely disagree.

As for the lacunae to which the poet referred in his letter to Madame Meurice, it is not hard to guess his meaning. Baudelaire must have been disturbed by the lack of movement in Manet's work, for he considered movement, together with color and atmosphere, essential to all great art. The tight draftsmanship and the almost photographic stillness of Manet's figures were the antithesis of the writhing fluency and the dynamic flow that he prized in the work of Delacroix: "Delacroix is the only artist today whose originality has not been invaded by the tyrannical system of straight lines; his figures are always restless and his draperies fluttering. From Delacroix's point of view line does not exist . . ." (OC, II:434).

Likewise, Baudelaire would have been bothered by the lack of emotion and the strange impassivity of Manet's figures: the nude woman in *Déjeuner sur l'herbe,* oblivious of the gesture of one of her companions and looking away from him over her shoulder as if a photographer had called her to look in that direction; the cold, almost arrogant impassivity of Olympia, who, ignoring the maid and proffered bouquet, stares straight ahead as if awaiting the click of a camera; the artist's parents, completely unrelated physically or psychologically, looking off into space.

It has been said that this curious lack of emotion—of melancholy in particular—prevented Baudelaire from appreciating Manet just as its presence in Delacroix explained much of his admiration for the Romantic painter. As we have already noted, the poet showed a strong predilection for melancholy and maintained that melancholy made Delacroix "the true painter of the nineteenth century." But there is no reason to believe that absence of melancholy prejudiced him against Manet any more than absence of modern subjects lessened his appreciation of the painter of *La Mort de Sardanapale.*

Baudelaire may also have been thinking of what John Rewald calls a "curious lack of imagination," which led him to borrow subjects and compositional elements from the old masters and prompted Degas to remark that Manet "never did a brushstroke without the masters in mind."[71] It is true that, in his review of 1862, Baudelaire had praised Manet's taste for reality and his ample imagination. But Baudelaire was alluding to works such as the *Ballet espagnole, Les Gitanos,* and *Lola de Valence,* in which the exotic aspects of contemporary life are portrayed with little reference to the old masters.

Moreover, Manet was certainly not lacking in originality or imagination in his *style* of painting, especially in that of his later works. In this respect he was much like Baudelaire himself, who, despite his borrowings from others, almost always remained profoundly original in style and treatment.

Far more serious in Baudelaire's eyes must have been Manets inability to work from imagination and memory. "All good and true draftsmen draw from the image fixed in their minds, and not from nature," he had written in *Le Peintre de la vie moderne,* for only by relying on memory and imagination could an artist, he believed, escape the hoard of trivial details besieging his attention and thus establish a proper hierarchy within his painting (*OC,* II:698). The ability to paint from memory was one of the things he most admired in Daumier and Guys and one of the things that Manet lacked most conspicuously. To his friend Proust, Manet once confided: " 'When I start something, I tremble at the thought that the model may fail to appear, that I will not see him as often as I would like. They come, pose, then leave, saying: "He will finish all right by himself!" No indeed, one cannot finish anything by oneself.' "[72] And as late as 1881, when he refused, because of ill health, to illustrate Mallarmé's translation of Poe, he added significantly: "I don't have a model, and above all I don't have any imagination."[73]

Yet he obviously agreed with Baudelaire as to the importance of the imagination and memory, for he once admonished a young painter in words that recall those of the poet: "Knowledge is all well and good, but for us, you see, imagination is more important."[74] And a year before his death, his advice to Jeanniot was again reminiscent of Baudelaire: "And then cultivate your memory, for nature will never give you anything more than suggestions."[75]

It is unfortunate that Baudelaire did not live to see Manet's work after 1865. But the friendship between the two was to continue until the poet's death in 1867. In his conversations with Duret and Mallarmé, the artist sometimes recalled the events of their association, and Baudelaire himself, on that autumn day in 1866 when Manet failed to appear, seems to have expressed in his cry of "Manet, Manet" the deep affection he felt for one with whom he had shared some of the happier moments of his life.

ARTHUR STEVENS

In Belgium, where he hoped to escape his creditors and find a publisher for his complete works, Baudelaire continued to take a deep interest in the plastic arts. The distinguished Belgian dealer Arthur Stevens, well known both in France and Belgium, had encouraged the poet to undertake the visit, and he and his two brothers Alfred (who had settled in France) and Joseph, both artists, were among those whose company Baudelaire enjoyed. Despite his friendship for Arthur, Baudelaire was well aware of his rather pompous self-importance and, in a letter to Nadar (August 30, 1864), wryly remarked that Arthur "passes in France for the King of the Belgians and in Belgium for the Emperor of the French and naturally boasts of having his wishes carried out in both countries" (OC, II:401).

In his unfinished *Pauvre Belgique,* Baudelaire shows himself acutely aware of the emptiness and the excessive materialism of Stevens's fashionable society paintings: "The great misfortune of this scrupulously careful painter, is the fact that the letter, the bouquet, the chair, the ring, the point-lace, etc. . . . become, turn by turn, the important object, the object that stares us in the face.—In short, he is a *completely* Flemish painter inasmuch as there is perfection in *nothingness,* or in the *imitation of nature,* which is one and the same thing" (*OC,* II:932).

Baudelaire was especially fond of Joseph Stevens, the animal painter, whose pleasant conversation and good sense of humor appealed to the embittered poet. Known especially for the wit and vigor with which he painted dogs, Joseph is today considered among the finest representatives of Realism as a result of his strong technique, the acuity of his observation, and the naturalness with which he handled his subjects. To Joseph, Baudelaire dedicated his prose poem "Les Bons Chiens" after an amusing incident that took place in the Tavern Horton. The artist had been wearing a waistcoat whose color and design Baudelaire had praised extravagantly on several occasions. When, one evening, the artist entered the tavern wearing the waistcoat in question, Baudelaire once again exclaimed about its beauty, whereupon Joseph, in the presence of their mutual friends, suddenly took it off and gave it to the delighted poet. Baudelaire later expressed his gratitude by writing the prose poem, in which he included a description of a painting by Stevens that he had seen in the home of the Belgian senator Prosper Crabbe.

FÉLICIEN ROPS

Baudelaire was especially fond of the painter and printmaker Félicien Rops, who, he wrote Manet, was the only real artist he had found in Belgium. In contrast to the stolid, unimaginative Flemish whom he despised, Rops was handsome and high-strung—at one moment full of laughter and fire, at another filled with despair; a cultivated dandy and libertine, he had both charm and a lively, irreverent wit.

Baudelaire was naturally attracted to Rop's art, for his realism was neither materialistic nor imitative. Instead, as the distinguished art historian Paul Haesaerts maintains, his realism was "psychological (à la Lautrec) or caricatural and satanic (à la Barbey d'Aurevilly)."[76] His entire work, Haesaerts continues, "is an unfolding of macabre or erotic scenes alive with all the human passions, where, in a sort of pleasure mingled with despair, the idea of death is joined to the instincts of lust and lucre."

Rops designed and etched the frontispiece of *Les Epaves* (1866) in accord with an idea which Baudelaire had suggested six years earlier to the artist Bracquemond, who was to have done the frontispiece for the second edition of *Les Fleurs du Mal.* Baudelaire had been so dissatisfied with Bracquemond's version that, despite the changes made by the artist, he finally gave up the idea of using it at all.

In his *Propos sur Baudelaire,* Jacques Crépet finds Rops's etching quite unsatisfactory and suspects that Baudelaire must have found it equally disappointing from the artistic standpoint.[77] It is true that in a letter to Rops the poet terms the frontispiece "excellent" and full of "ingenium" (he uses the Latin word), but he has no other words of praise (*OC*, II:617). Moreover, while apologizing for his temerity in criticizing matters of technique, he admits his regret that the light seen in the preparatory drawing was absent from the finished work. The frontispiece is cluttered and essentially mediocre and, to me at least, Baudelaire's marked reserve and lack of enthusiasm indicate the disappointment which he tried to conceal from his friend. After all, the poet owed to Rops some of the happiest moments of his self-imposed exile, as he acknowledged in the inscription on the photograph which he gave to the artist.

NADAR

Baudelaire's interest in the arts extended even to photography, which he discussed at some length in the *Salon de 1859.* Associating it with the Realistic movement, he denounced the modern tendency to equate photography with art and maintained that it was time for the former to return to "its real purpose, which is that of being the servant to the sciences and arts." Photography, he continued, must not be allowed to encroach upon "the domain of the impalpable and the imaginary, on all that whose value lies only in what man's soul has added" (*OC*,

II:618, 619). Yet Baudelaire obviously felt that photography could have a certain artistic value, for in a letter to his mother (December 23, 1865) he asked her for a photograph—one that would be "an exact portrait but with all the softness of a drawing" (*Corr.*, II:554).

Though he maintained in 1859 that photography was the refuge of would-be painters or painters too ill-endowed to succeed, Baudelaire was the friend and admirer of three outstanding photographers of his day: Nadar, whose portrait-photographs of almost all the celebrities of his day are still well known and highly regarded; Carjat, whose haunting photograph of Baudelaire was cherished by the poet himself ("I have seldom seen anything as good"); and the Belgian Neyt, who was with Baudelaire the night he suffered the final attack of apoplexy that left him speechless and partly paralyzed (*OC,* II:322).

Of the three, Nadar was closest to the poet, being one of his oldest and most intimate friends. Their acquaintance dated from their Bohemian days (1844), when Nadar drew the design for the cover of the *Mystères galans des Théâtres de Paris,* and lasted until Baudelaire's death in 1867. Nadar was one of the faithful who often came to the nursing home of Doctor Duval, where the poet had been brought after his return to Paris, to encourage and cheer the poet in every way possible. In order to offer him a little diversion, he arranged to take Baudelaire out for lunch once a week with a small group of friends, all former companions who had grown accustomed to his sign language. At first Baudelaire was delighted at the opportunity of meeting with his old friends and was always ready and eager for Nadar's arrival and for their carriage ride to the restaurant. Soon, however, he refused to accompany Nadar on the excursions, indicating that the meetings were so fatiguing that they counteracted the benefits of the treatment he was receiving. After Baudelaire's death, Nadar, fearing that the poet would be dealt with unjustly in the newspapers, asked permission to write an obituary notice for *Le Figaro.* The article, published on September 10, proved to be one of the most intelligent and perceptive written about the poet.

Nadar, whose real name was Félix Tournachon, was greatly admired by Baudelaire for his generosity, his versatility, and his enormous vitality. "Nadar is the most amazing manifestation of vitality," he wrote in his *Journaux intimes*. "Adrien told me that his brother Félix had all his vital organs in duplicate. I have felt envious at seeing him succeed so well in all that is not abstract" (*OC,* I:695).

Nadar began his career by contributing sketches and articles to humor magazines, founded *La Revue comique,* and then opened a photographic studio with his brother Adrien. In the 1850s the studio became a favorite meeting place for artists, musicians, men of letters, and famous people of all kinds. An experimenter, he was among the first to photograph by electric light and the first to photograph the city of Paris from a balloon (1856). His exploit has been immortalized by his friend Daumier, who in one of his most delightful lithographs portrays a fiercely intent Nadar standing eagerly bent over the edge of the balloon's gondola, his top hat flying in the air and his camera focused on the city below. The lithograph is appropriately entitled *Nadar Elevating Photography to the Level of Art.*

Nadar became so interested in aeronautics that he built *The Giant,* the largest balloon in the world at that time. On its second ascension it was carried to Germany, where on descending near Hanover it went out of control and dragged its hapless passengers through the countryside over some twenty-five miles of bumpy ground. Baudelaire had evidently been invited by Nadar to be one of the passengers on the ascent which he was to make from Brussels during the festival celebrating the thirty-fourth anniversary of the Belgian revolution in 1830. On August 30, 1864, the poet wrote his friend in Paris, alleging—strangely and unconvincingly—that he would be visiting the provinces from September 8 to 20 and suggesting that a Mr. O'Connell, who wanted desperately to make the trip, be allowed to take his place. Furthermore, on September 2, the poet wrote Ancelle that if by chance he were in Brussels on the 25th—"which I doubt"—he would accept Nadar's kind invitation. "To escape these dreadful people in a balloon, to land in Austria, in Turkey perhaps, every wild adventure appeals to me, provided it is amusing" (*Corr.,* II:404–05).

According to Maurice Kunel, who recounts information furnished by Georges Barral, Nadar's assistant, Baudelaire was present on September 26, the day of the flight, and actually boarded the balloon. When it was discovered, however, that the balloon was overloaded, the poet, as one of the last registrants, was obliged to withdraw.[78] The trip proved to be successful, save for an unexpected descent at Ypres.

Many years after the death of the poet, Jacques Crépet persuaded Nadar to publish his memories of his longtime friend. The result was *Charles Baudelaire intime,* subtitled *Le Poète vierge* (1911), in which the author maintains somewhat surprisingly that Baudelaire never lost his virginity. The fact that Nadar could offer no real proof to substantiate his case and that Baudelaire contracted syphilis as a young man would seem sufficient reason to discredit his theory.

Baudelaire was not exaggerating in his claim that the cult of images was "ma primitive, mon unique passion." Had he written his own epitaph, he could have added that art remained an absorbing passion until the very end of his life. It was while revisiting the church of Saint-Loup in Namur (March 18, 1866) that he suffered the initial attack of the illness that two days later was to leave him partially paralyzed and still later speechless.

On previous visits to Namur, Baudelaire had admired the baroque, or what he called the Jesuit, style of its churches. The church of Saint-Loup had especially excited his interest, and his description of its beauty ("a sinister and elegant wonder" resembling "the interior of a catafalque embroidered in *black,* in *rose* and in *silver*") seems today strangely premonitory. Accompanied by his friends Rops and Poulet-Malassis, the poet was extolling the carving of the confessionals, which he had previously characterized as "varied, exquisite, delicate, baroque, a *new antiquity*" (*OC,* II:951–52). Suddenly, he stumbled and fell. On regaining his feet with the aid of his companions, he maintained that he had slipped and fallen, but he remained unusually quiet and preoccupied. He returned to Brussels only to experience more devastating attacks from which he was never to recover. After a stay of two and a half months in his hotel room and in a Catholic nursing home, where he scandalized the good sisters by shouting in impotent rage, "Crénom" (damn it), the only word he could pronounce, Arthur Stevens and his mother brought him back to Paris. There he spent his last days in the nursing home of Doctor Duval.

For Baudelaire the lovely church of Saint-Loup had indeed proved to be a catafalque—a catafalque whose beauty seemed peculiarly fitting for one who had found in art one of the greatest joys of his life.

2 *Baudelaire and Music*

I

N THE WORLD OF MUSIC also Baudelaire was very much a man of his time. Although he had made no formal study of music (his whole musical education, he wrote Wagner, was restricted to having heard some beautiful works of Weber and Beethoven), his essay *Richard Wagner et Tannhäuser à Paris* is one of his finest works and one of the most fascinating nontechnical analyses ever made of the music of the great German composer.

Baudelaire may have known little or nothing about music, as he maintained, but it is nonetheless clear that he was instinctively and keenly sensitive to its beauty and that he reacted to this beauty much as he did to that of the plastic arts. In both instances, the shock of pleasure he felt in confronting a magnificent work of art—what he called "volupté"—was intense and profound. But in the case of music the nature of Baudelaire's "volupté" seems always to have a special character and to be more or less the same, whether evoked in his poetry or in his descriptions of his reaction to the music of Wagner.

To read the poem "La Musique" is to understand better his passionate, almost erotic response, both physical and psychological, to the beauty of music. "Music engulfs (possesses) me like the sea," he wrote in the opening line. Like the huge, rolling waves of the ocean, it lifts him into the vast heights toward his "pale star." At other times it becomes, like a sea that is becalmed, the "mirror of [his] despair."

RICHARD WAGNER

The music of Wagner produced in Baudelaire a similar sensation.
"I had a feeling," he wrote Wagner after attending the three
concerts Wagner gave in Paris in 1860, "of pride and joy in
understanding, in being possessed, in being overwhelmed, a truly
sensual pleasure like that of rising in the air or being tossed on
the sea." "Throughout," he continued, "there is something
exalted and exalting, something aspiring to mount higher, something excessive and superlative" (*Corr.*, I:673). And in the essay
itself he describes at greater length the exhilarating sense of being
freed from the bonds of gravity, and the ecstasy, composed of
sensuous delight and knowledge, of soaring above and beyond
the natural world in a luminous region whose horizon was filled
with a vast diffused light.

At times his description seems almost a pure paraphrase of
his magnificent poem "Elévation" with its joyous rhapsodic
emotion, its soaring movement, its spiritual and physical ecstasy.
Were it not for the fact that it had been written many years before, one would certainly believe that it had been inspired by the
music of Wagner, as was once believed by a number of critics.

There is good reason, however, to suppose that the poem,
with its imagery so much like that used by Baudelaire in describing his reaction to Wagner's music, was inspired by another musical experience. In his remarkable book *L'Univers poétique de
Baudelaire,* Lloyd James Austin argues convincingly that "Elévation" may well have been a translation of the musical experience
to which the poet alludes in a letter written to Poulet-Malassis on
February 16, 1860.[1] Austin reminds us that the poet, in attempting to explain his enthusiasm for the Wagnerian concerts, wrote
to his friend and publisher: "That music has been one of the joys
of my life; I haven't felt so carried away for fully fifteen years"
(*Corr.*, I:671).

To what music Baudelaire was referring one can only guess,
but it may well have been that of either Beethoven or Weber, for
the names of both composers are mentioned admiringly in his

writing, and it is clear that their music moved him deeply. It is widely believed that Baudelaire had thought of giving to his poem "La Musique" the title "Beethoven"—Beethoven, who, he wrote in his essay on Banville, "began to stir the world of melancholy and incurable despair piled up like clouds in man's inner sky" (*OC,* II:168).

And the poet's fondness for Weber's music is especially apparent in his comparisons of Delacroix's painting to the music of the great composer: to "a stifled sigh from Weber" in the poem "Les Phares" and to "a plaintive and profound melody from Weber" in his *Salon de 1846.* Curiously enough, Weber, who was idolized by both Wagner and Liszt, used the leitmotif and conceived the idea of the *Gesamtkunstwerk*—total art work— long before Wagner. Baudelaire could well have had in mind the powerful and doom-filled strains of the Wolf's Glen scene from *Der Freischütz* or the *Oberon* or *Euryanthe* overtures that at times anticipate the music of the great German composer.

Baudelaire's response to music as seen in the Wagner essay and in his poem "La Musique"—his feeling of soaring into space, of an ascent into the luminous confines of the starry spheres—was not unusual in the literature of the Romanticists. But in no other writer is it more frequently used to translate a musical experience than in the work of E. T. A. Hoffmann. Both Jean Pommier and Antoine Adam have noted passages in Hoffmann that are reminiscent of "Elévation." Adam remarks on the kinship between certain lines of "Elévation" and Hoffmann's statement, "Invisible wings beat the air around me, I float in a perfumed atmosphere." Pommier goes so far as to surmise that Hoffmann's pages on Beethoven, Mozart, and Haydn (*Kreisleriana*) may have prepared Baudelaire for the visual and spiritual translation he later gave to Wagner. And in pointing out relationships between the two writers he even notes in passing that "*Elévation* describes an effect similar to that produced on Kreisler by a certain thought: an unknown rapture raises him with its powerful wings above the mocking world below."[2]

But the similarities are not limited to one or two cases. The fact is that Hoffmann's *Kreisleriana,* so much admired by Baudelaire and even quoted by him on a number of occasions, abounds in passages that suggest both the theme and imagery of Baudelaire's poem. "Music opens up to man a kingdom, a world which has nothing in common with the world of the senses which surrounds him," Hoffmann wrote in his chapter on Beethoven, and it soon becomes evident that this world, like that of "Elévation," is always one of infinite space in which the soul takes flight on wings of song.[3]

So frequent are the allusions in *Kreisleriana* to an ascent into space, to a soul which soars above "the earthly mire," to wings that climb and plunge and float in "the misty ether" that Baudelaire, given his enthusiasm for "the divine Hoffmann," as he calls him in *Du vin et du hachisch,* could hardly have escaped the contagious influence of the imagery.[4] Antecedents may be found in the *Kreisleriana* even for the famous lines with which Baudelaire concludes his poem. This is not to deny, however, that similar antecedents may be found in other writers. Yet "the language of flowers and of mute things" found in "Elévation" is nonetheless strikingly reminiscent of Kreisler's remark that "Only by music can man understand the sublime song of. . . . trees, flowers, animals, stones, and waters."[5]

Strangely enough, the prose poem "Le Thyrse," dedicated to Franz Liszt, begins with the very rhythm of "Elévation": "Dear Liszt, through the mists, beyond the rivers, above the cities . . . I hail you in immortality." The mere remembrance of a particular type of music seems capable of recreating for Baudelaire the ecstatic vision of his great poem.

A few notations in the *Journaux intimes* likewise attest to the intense interest of the poet in music as well as his belief that music has the power of producing "those happy impressions that almost all imaginative men have known in dreams while they were asleep" (*OC,* II:784). "Music hollows out the sky," he wrote at one point (*OC,* I:653); at another, "Music gives the idea of space" (*OC,* I:702); and at still another he notes: ". . . cult of multiplied sensation expressing itself through music. Refer to Liszt" (*OC,* I:701). The simple word "Music" appearing in a note in the *Journaux intimes* together with a list of other topics such as slavery, magistrates, bureaucrats, society women, prostitutes, etc. suggests Baudelaire's intention of using music as a subject for an article (*OC*, I:695).

Baudelaire's interest in music must have been stimulated and strengthened by his close literary friends Champfleury, Charles Barbara, and Gérard de Nerval, all connoisseurs and lovers of music and all Wagner enthusiasts. Champfleury testifies to Baudelaire's love of music in the first version of his *Aventures de Mademoiselle Mariette,* which appeared in the *Corsaire* in 1847. Before having the poet (whom he actually names, though only in the 1847 version) recite his sonnet "Les Chats," he says of him by way of introduction: "19 March 1840.—We spent a pleasant evening with a friend who shares my weakness for pantomime, painting, religion, and music" (*OC,* II:950).

Charles Barbara (1822–66), to whom Champfleury dedicated his 1860 article on Wagner, was equally fond of music. A musician and writer of rather mediocre talent, Barbara belonged to a group centering on Henri Murger whose members were so poor that they called themselves "Water drinkers" ("Buveurs d'eau"). In Murger's well-known novel *Scènes de la vie bohème* he appears under the name of Carolus Barbemuche. Among his works, Barbara published the novel *L'Assassin du Pont-Rouge,* in which a poet, who remains anonymous, recites Baudelaire's sonnet beginning "Que diras-tu ce soir?"

Baudelaire seems to have felt sincere affection and compassion for the unfortunate Barbara, whose unhappy life finally led him to suicide. In his essay on *Madame Bovary,* the poet-critic devoted a paragraph of warm praise to his music-loving friend—"a rigorous and logical thinker, eager for intellectual honors. . . . If I do not express here all the admiration inspired in me by the author of *Héloise* and *L'Assassin du Pont-Rouge,*" he concluded, "it is because he fits into my theme only incidentally as a part of the historical record" (*OC,* II:79).

Baudelaire's kindness to Barbara is attested by Asselineau, who wrote in his biography of the poet: "How many days he wasted—wasted as far as his own work was concerned—in disposing of the manuscript of a friend, in introducing him to a publisher or to a director of a theater! Poor Barbara knew it; Barbara, whom he adopted because of his restive, obstinate temperament and his excessive shyness, and whom he loved for his perseverance and for his honest hard work."[6]

In his manuscript notes, Asselineau suggests that Baudelaire's feeling for Barbara was perhaps also based on gratitude. Asselineau assumed—quite incorrectly—that it was Barbara, one of the editors of the provincial newspaper *Le Journal du Loiret,* who first introduced Baudelaire to Poe by transmitting to him the stories that had appeared in translation in their newspaper. "It could be," he added, "that the devoted friendship which was constantly shown by Baudelaire to Barbara had no other cause than gratitude for that transmission."[7]

Asselineau was mistaken in his facts, for Baudelaire had first encountered Poe in the socialist newspaper *La Démocratie pacifique* in 1847, as W. T. Bandy has pointed out in his edition of Baudelaire's *Edgar Allan Poe: Sa vie et ses ouvrages.* "It may be," Bandy explains, "that Asselineau decided to omit the reference to *Le Journal du Loiret* in the final text of his biography of Baudelaire, because he was not certain of its accuracy."[8] What Asselineau's incorrect assumption does prove, however, is that Baudelaire and Barbara had much in common and that to their love of music and literature in general was added their interest in the American writer made famous in France and in all Europe by the author of *Les Fleurs du Mal.*

Just when Baudelaire gained his knowledge of Wagner remains something of a mystery. Though he did not meet the German composer until 1860, he knew him by reputation as early as 1849 and perhaps even earlier. In a letter addressed to an unknown correspondent—evidently a publisher who "share[d his] admiration" for Wagner—he recommended a study of *Tannhäuser* and a series of articles on the evolution of music done by a Mr. Schoman, who had had to leave Dresden because of the revolution. "In complying with his request," he concluded, "you will serve the cause of one [Wagner] whom the future will enshrine as the most illustrious of masters" (*Corr.,* I:157).

To write so glowingly of one whom he did not know and whose music he had not yet heard—as far as we know—indicates that Baudelaire must already have read or heard about the German composer and that his knowledge was based on that of persons in whom he had complete trust. He could hardly have failed to read the article that had appeared in the *Journal des Débats* two months earlier (May 18, 1849) written by Franz Liszt, the friend and loyal defender of Wagner. The study, introduced by Hector Berlioz, who was then favorable to Wagner, was a discussion of the opera *Tannhäuser,* which Baudelaire was not to hear until 1861.

The following year (1850) Nerval, who was a close friend of Liszt, published several articles on the fetes honoring Goethe and Herder in Weimar, where a performance of *Lohengrin* was conducted for the first time by the brilliant Hungarian composer. Nerval, who did not arrive in time for the performance, was aided by Liszt, who suggested and even dictated the favorable study of Wagner's music that appeared (September 18 and 19) in the form of two articles in *La Presse.*[9] The first was later reproduced in his *Lorely* (1853). The studies retrace the poetic and musical evolution of Wagner, hail the "alliance intime" of poetry and music advocated by the composer, and urge French writers and composers to follow his example.[10] Still other articles were published by Nerval in the *Revue et Gazette Musicale de Paris* (September 22) and in *L'Artiste* (October 1, 1850).

Baudelaire would surely have read Nerval's articles and been impressed by Wagner's emphasis on the interdependence of the arts and on the fusion of poetry and music. He himself, from his early years, had been concerned with the relationship between the different art forms and with the underlying principles which bind them together. At the same time, he was well aware of the dangers that could result from the spurious encroachment of one art upon the other.

Even before the Weimar festival Baudelaire and Nerval may have discussed the problem together, for in the year 1850 they were evidently quite close. The two short notes (addressed, the one to "Mon cher Gérard" and the other to "Mon cher ami") in which Baudelaire requested tickets for the play *Le Chariot d'enfant* suggest that they were on fairly intimate terms (*Corr.*, I:164, 165). In fact, Baudelaire's letter of 1849, in which he predicts the future greatness of Wagner, may well have been inspired by Nerval's enthusiasm as well as by the judgments of Champfleury and Barbara.

Wagner continued to be a "cause célèbre" among French intellectuals and aesthetes. In October 1850 Liszt himself wrote an account of the fetes at Weimar and attempted to give a brief sketch of the Wagnerian system—a new system "which will perhaps be a revolution," as he wrote. Rejected by the *Revue des Deux Mondes*, it was finally published through the efforts of Nerval in the *Journal des Débats* on October 22, 1850.

On November 24, 1850, Parisians were given an opportunity to hear Wagner's music for themselves when the Belgian director Seghers conducted the overture to *Tannhäuser*. According to Léon Guichard, Seghers wrote to Francis Wey, a man of letters and a friend of the artist Gustave Courbet, asking him to bring Nerval to the concert.[11] And interestingly enough, Gautier devoted a half-column review to the music in his drama criticism of December 2.

The review is said to have been ghostwritten by the musician Ernest Reyer, one of Gautier's good friends and cronies, though there is little or nothing that the critic could not have said on his own. What was important for the Wagnerites was his recognition of the composer as "one of the great music celebrities of modern Germany . . . a sort of Berlioz extravagantly admired by some and challenged by others."[12] From the tone of the review and from his request that the Symphonic Society make known the "masters of the day," it is clear that Gautier saw himself as a sort of standard-bearer and that he was anxious to do for music what he had done for Romantic drama in the days of Hugo's *Hernani*.

There was to be no letup in Wagnerian criticism, and Baudelaire had ample opportunity to note the arguments both for and against the German composer. In 1851, Liszt published a book on Wagner to which Baudelaire was to refer in his 1861 essay. The following year the well-known Belgian music critic François-Joseph Fétis wrote a series of articles for the *Gazette musicale de Paris* (June 6 to August 8, 1852) in which he violently attacked Wagner's ideas and accused him of being, among other things, a Realist.

His harsh criticism angered both Baudelaire and Champfleury. In his essay of 1861, Baudelaire was to term the pamphlet "indigestible and abominable," and a number of years earlier, in 1855, Champfleury had expressed his long-festering indignation in connection with his defense of the artist Gustave Courbet. In his open letter to George Sand, written at the time of the artist's private exhibition of his paintings, Champfleury compared the public's treatment of Courbet with that afforded Wagner. Both were being accused of Realism—a term of opprobrium at that time—simply because they were introducing innovative ideas into the arts. "A hyper-romantic German musician, M. Wagner, whose works are unknown in Paris," Champfleury wrote, "has received extraordinary maltreatment in the musical journals by M. Fétis, who accuses the new composer of being tainted with *Realism*. All those who put forward new aspirations are called Realists."[13]

In 1857 Gautier once again entered the arena. Invited to Wiesbaden to attend a performance of *Tannhäuser,* he afterward wrote a long review published on October 29 and 30 in *Le Moniteur* in which, "deeply moved by the presentation," as Baudelaire wrote in his 1861 study, ". . . he translated his impressions with the plastic sureness that gives an irresistible charm to all of his writings" (*OC,* II:780).

But this time Gautier's review was not without reservations. Though he found much to admire—especially the pilgrim's chorus and the music that opens the second act, both of which were "full of grandeur, of character and conviction, in short the music of a master"—he regretted the absence of melody and frankly questioned the belief that Wagner was destined "to dethrone the great masters of the art."[14] In Wagner he found nothing really Romantic, in the French sense of the word, nothing really revolutionary. Instead, he had found a return to the older forms. "His orchestra is full of fugues, of flowery counterpoints, of canons executed with great skill." He had gone expecting Berlioz; instead, he had found, in the better moments, only Rossini.[15]

Gautier had little technical knowledge of music, as his daughter Judith readily admitted, and it is generally agreed that Ernest Reyer, despite his denial, furnished him with at least the technical sections of the article.[16] Gautier's judgments may have reflected to a degree the opinions of Reyer, but his own taste and judgment (Judith insisted on his genuine love for music), his liking for what he called "the sensualities of melody and the delights of rhythm" could explain much of what he wrote.[17] Gautier concluded with the hope that *Tannhäuser* would soon be heard in France. Later he boasted that he was the first in Paris to write about the opera.

Eighteen fifty-seven was the year in which Baudelaire published his *Fleurs du Mal,* dedicated to Gautier, "the impeccable poet . . . my very dear and most venerated master and friend." Obviously the two friends must have seen each other often, and Gautier's visit to Wiesbaden must surely have been a lively topic of conversation. The strictures of "le bon Théo" undoubtedly rubbed off on Baudelaire. How else explain the change from the poet's enthusiastic praise in his letter of 1849 to the somewhat unfavorable attitude that he felt before hearing the concerts of 1860? In his famous letter to Wagner (February 17, 1860) he admitted, "The first time I went to the Théâtre des Italiens to hear your works I was not favorably disposed and, to tell the truth, I was even badly prejudiced: but I deserve to be excused; I have been duped so often; I have heard so much music by insufferably pretentious charlatans" (*OC,* II:1452).

To attract the attention of the public the three Wagnerian concerts were given (at the Salle Ventadour) on January 25 and February 1 and 8. It was not the first time that Wagner had come to Paris with the hope of presenting his works at the Opéra. His first visit, from September 1839 to April 1842, had been without success, and the German composer finally left Paris with only five francs in his pocket and with all his hopes of glory vanished in thin air. He made several shorter visits in the 1850s.

Finally, on September 15, 1859, believing that Parisians were prepared to give his music a more favorable reception, Wagner returned and settled down with his wife in a charming home on the Champs-Elysées, where every Wednesday evening he entertained a group of friends who came there more or less regularly. Among them were to be found Emile and Blandine Ollivier (Blandine was the daughter of Liszt and the Countess d'Agoult, and the sister of Cosima), Frédéric Villot, curator of the imperial museums, to whom Wagner addressed his *Lettre sur la musique,* Léon Leroy, Auguste de Gasperini, Champfleury, and, after 1860, Baudelaire—at least on occasion.

Champfleury seems to have been especially close to Wagner. In his *Journal* entry for March 14, 1861, the famous actor François Got tells how he had often met the German composer "in the company of Murger, Champfleury, Courbet, etc. . . . in a shabby restaurant on the rue Jacob."[18] Since Got does not specify the period in which he had seen the friends together, Guichard assumes rightly or wrongly that he was referring to an earlier visit when the penniless composer led a more or less Bohemian existence while he was struggling to establish a reputation for himself. That Baudelaire was not one of the group seems certain, judging by the tone of his letter and by Wagner's own testimony in his autobiography.

The three concerts given by Wagner in 1860 created a veritable sensation. The audience was on the whole favorable, but the press was generally hostile. Champfleury was the first to defend the German composer. In fact, his brochure *Richard Wagner,* dated January 27, 1860, was written after the first concert and attracted attention not only in France but also in Germany, where it was translated into German and widely published. His article was later published in 1861 by Poulet-Malassis in *Grandes figures d'hier et d'aujourd'hui,* where it was followed by a second article, somewhat shorter, entitled "Après la bataille" and by a short story, "Une Visite à Beethoven," written by Wagner himself.

Despite its title, Champfleury's brochure was not a study of Wagner's work and theories. Instead, it was an account of his impressions on hearing the music of a friend in whose genius he firmly believed. Wagner's music was for him, as it was for Baudelaire, "a revelation," and, like the author of *Les Fleurs du Mal,* he "understood" the thought of the master. Attacking the critics—among them Fétis père, who had likened Wagner to Courbet—he denied Berlioz's charge that the music lacked melody, and in words reminiscent of Baudelaire and of Wagner himself, compared it to the the great voices of nature—to that of the sea and of the forest.[19]

Wagner was highly pleased with Champfleury's article and later praised it warmly in his autobiography:

> In a series of light and airy aphorisms he displayed such a comprehension of my music, and even of my personality, that I never again met with such suggestive and masterly appreciation, and had only come across its equal once before in Liszt's lucubrations on *Lohengrin* and *Tannhäuser.*[20]

In the *Journal des Débats* for February 9, 1860, Berlioz himself published a review of the concerts. After praising the excerpts from *The Flying Dutchman, Lohengrin,* and *Tannhäuser,* he maintained that he understood nothing of the prelude to *Tristan and Isolde* and made a point of differentiating his own music from that of Wagner.

Perhaps Berlioz's review proved to be the last straw for Baudelaire, who in his 1861 article accused the composer of *Les Troyens* of showing "much less warmth than one might have expected from him" (*OC,* II:781). Whatever the case, on February 17, 1860, he sent a letter to Wagner which, he said, was prompted by the "outrageous, ridiculous articles in which every effort is being made to defame your genius" (*Corr.,* I:672). The letter may be considered a spontaneous, though greatly abbreviated first draft of the article he was to write a year later

after attending a performance of *Tannhäuser*. After expressing
his admiration in terms that recall the spiritual and aesthetic experiences evoked in the poems "La Musique," "Elévation," and
"Correspondances," he signed his name without adding an address "because you might think I have a favor to ask of you."

Wagner did not answer the letter personally but asked
Champfleury to thank Baudelaire for him and invite the poet to
his Wednesday evening receptions. Though Baudelaire was
touched by the invitation, he was too engrossed in pressing financial problems to be able to accept immediately. To
Champfleury he sent a note asking him to express his deep
gratitude to the composer and to assure him of the honor it
would be for him to shake the hand of so great a genius. In his
autobiography Wagner recounts his side of the story and tells
how he was struck by the author's "fantastic terms" and "auda-
cious self-assurance":

> My acquaintance with him [Baudelaire] began with a letter in
> which he told me his impressions of my music and the effect
> it had produced upon him, in spite of his having thought till
> then that he possessed an artistic sense for colouring, but
> none for sound. His opinions on the matter, which he ex-
> pressed in the most fantastic terms and with audacious self-
> assurance, proved him, to say the least, a man of extraordi-
> nary understanding, who with impetuous energy followed
> the impressions he received from my music to their ultimate
> consequences. He explained that he did not put an address to
> his letter in order that I might not be led to think that he
> wanted something from me. Needless to say, I knew how to
> find him, and had soon included him among the acquain-
> tances to whom I announced my intention of being at home
> every Wednesday evening.[21]

The Wednesday evening soirées gave Baudelaire an opportunity to meet and talk with some of the most distinguished men of
his day, among them the composers Gounod, Berlioz, Saint-
Saëns, and Liszt.

On March 12, 1860, the emperor, at the instigation of the

Princess Metternich, requested that a performance of *Tann-häuser* be given at the Opéra. After a long and arduous prepara-tion (164 rehearsals), the moment finally arrived. All Paris was agog. Friends and enemies alike were on hand to applaud or to shout their disapproval. There had been nothing like it since the reception given Victor Hugo's *Hernani* some thirty years earlier.

The first of the performances began on March 13, 1861, and proved to be a fiasco. Two more were equally disastrous. After the third, Wagner was forced to admit defeat and withdrew the opera. The anti-Wagnerians had won the day by resorting to every means of harassment, from whistling hunting tunes and playing flageolets to shouting insults and indulging in fisticuffs. At times Wagner had to suspend a performance as long as a quarter of an hour before the music could be heard over the noise and tumult. In the uproar that ensued, Baudelaire didn't hesitate to enter the fray when called upon to do so. Some time later Catulle Mendès, then a young man of nineteen and the founder of the *Revue fantaisiste,* wrote of his experiences: "In 1861, Charles Baudelaire and I exchanged blows with the hecklers; I remember having even received certain thwacks which I returned with interest."[22]

The reasons for the hostility to *Tannhäuser* were varied and many. The members of the aristocratic Jockey Club were in-censed at Wagner's refusal to introduce the traditional ballet in the second act. Others, who had viewed Wagner sympathetically as a revolutionary and as a victim of Saxon tyranny, were an-noyed that he was being befriended by the Princess Metternich and members of the German aristocracy. Music critics, like Gus-tave Héquet of the *Illustration* and Scudo of the *Revue des Deux Mondes,* were angered by Wagner's presumption in initiating a new system and by talk of the "music of the future." French musicians and composers resented the fact that the music of a German was being given preference by the emperor over their own: Gounod was waiting to present *La Reine de Saba;* Berlioz, who was said to be beaming with delight on leaving the perfor-mance, had yet found no opportunity to present his opera *Les Troyens.* Incidentally, Baudelaire was well aware of Berlioz's antipathy. In his article of 1861 he commented ironically, "M. Berlioz avoided giving his opinion; negative courage. Let us thank him for not having added to the universal insults" (*OC,* II:812). But more than anything else, the failure of *Tannhäuser* resulted from the fact that the general public, accustomed to traditional opera, was unprepared for what it heard.

It was the men of letters in France who, sympathetic both to Wagner's ideas and to his music, came to his support. And first and foremost among them was Charles Baudelaire. Infuriated by the outrageous behavior of the audience and by the animosity of the critics, he hastened to publish an article that he had begun some time before. In his letter of 1860 to Wagner, Baudelaire alludes to a study which he had begun to prepare but which he had evidently abandoned ("I had begun to write a few thoughts on the passages from *Tannhäuser* and *Lohengrin* which we had heard; but I realized the impossibility of saying everything") (*Corr.,* I:674). Evidently the enmity shown Wagner both by the general public and by so many of the critics acted as a stimulant, and he lost no time in finishing what he had begun thirteen months earlier.

The essay, dated March 18, appeared in the *Revue européenne* on April 1, about two weeks after the opening night (March 13, 1861). In a letter to his mother (April 3, 1861) Baudelaire claims to have improvised it in three days at the printers—an obvious exaggeration on his part. The major part of the essay had evidently been written in the time that elapsed between the concerts of 1860 and the first performance of *Tannhäuser,* as we know from a letter written to Poulet-Malassis on July 28, 1860, in which the poet complained of having to take time from working on his Wagner essay in order to settle more pressing business. What he composed or improvised at the last moment were mainly the final pages, entitled *Encore quelques mots,* added after the opera had been pronounced a failure. Another letter to Poulet-Malassis, dated March 23, 1861, explains how he had been detained at the printers for three days, from ten in the morning until ten in the evening, in order to finish the Wagner study which was to appear in the *Européenne.*

The article, together with a postscript dated April 8, 1861, was later published as a brochure by Dentu on May 4, 1861.

Baudelaire's study on Wagner and *Tannhäuser* proved to be one of his most brilliant and most satisfying works, despite his lack of any technical knowledge. It is all the more amazing considering that it was composed during a period of great emotional stress—a period when his unhappiness was so great that he seriously considered suicide for the second time in his life. The poems he wrote in the 1860s reveal his frustration and despair, his longing for understanding, and his dread of time and its inexorable laws. His discovery of Jeanne's infidelity in 1861 only made matters worse. In the midst of all his troubles, the music of Wagner became one of his chief consolations, and the essay he wrote reflected his passionate love of the music as well as all the major aesthetic preoccupations of this period of his life.

For some time he had been dreaming of an alliance between poetry and music, encouraged perhaps by his former talks with Nerval as well as other friends, and further stimulated by the knowledge he had acquired about the theories and aspirations of the German composer. In Wagner's music he found a magnificent example of this alliance. In his unfinished article *L'Art philosophique*, composed about 1859, he had warned against the danger of one art attempting to *replace* another: "Is it the inevitable result of decadence that today each art manifests a desire to encroach on its neighbor ... ?" (*OC*, II:598). But in Wagner, Baudelaire found an amalgamation of the arts that enriched the total effect without one art detracting from the other.

Baudelaire's criticism was intended not so much for connoisseurs of music as for "the poetic reader" to whom he had referred in the *Salon de 1846*. The technical information that he lacked he drew from Liszt, Berlioz, and Wagner himself, often using extensive quotations and paraphrases from their works. Obviously he had learned much from them and from his music-loving friends, but even without their guidance he was drawn to the music of the German composer almost instinctively. Baudelaire was not exaggerating when in his letter to Wagner of 1860 he wrote, "It seemed to me that the music was *mine,* and I recognized it as every man recognizes the things he is destined to love" (*Corr.*, I:673). Just as he had recognized certain aspects of himself in Poe a number of years earlier, so he saw reflected in the music of the Master the qualities he most admired and that are everywhere found in his own work.

What impressed him most, he wrote, was the sense of "grandeur . . . the solemnity of great sounds, of the great aspects of Nature, and the solemnity of the great passions of man." The reader is reminded of Baudelaire's own poetry in which, through the magic of his art, he endows the most ignoble subject with a grandeur and even sublimity of tone completely alien to a Champfleury or to other writers of his time. The "nervous tension" and "the violence of passion" which to him explained much of Wagner's genius are equally present in *Les Fleurs du Mal,* whether in the poems of despair or in those expressing a love-hate relationship. In literature and the plastic arts, he was fascinated by the fearful majesty of Lady Macbeth or by the overwhelming power of Michelangelo's *Night;* in nature, the vast expanse of sky and sea moved him deeply. In much the same way he was awed by Wagner's supreme gift for "painting space and depth, both material and spiritual" by means of his music.

Baudelaire recognized in Wagner's music not only the grandeur that he most sought in art and in life, but also a similarity in certain of their philosophic beliefs. To his delight he discovered that the very theme of *Tannhäuser* was based on the principle that dominates and explains almost all of his own work—the duality of man. "Every well-balanced mind bears within it two infinites, heaven and hell," he wrote in his discussion of the drama, "and in every image of one of these infinites he suddenly recognizes half of himself" (*OC,* II:795). In *Les Fleurs du Mal,* this duality serves as a sort of cohesive that binds together the whole and gives meaning and unity to the totality of the work. The same duality is at the heart of *Tannhäuser* and explains the character and role of its protagonist: "*Tannhäuser* represents the struggle of the two principles that have chosen the human heart as their chief battlefield—flesh against spirit, hell against

heaven, Satan against God" (*OC*, II:794). Moreover, Tannhäuser's aspiration to suffering and his "joy in damnation" are
completely Baudelairean in nature and must have strengthened
the poet's feeling of affinity with the composer.

Baudelaire was struck by Wagner's ability to suggest—
without the aid of the libretto—the psychic duality that constitutes the drama of *Tannhäuser* through melody that was either
"diabolically voluptuous,". expressing "the raging song of the
flesh" ("all the onomatopoetic dictionary of love"), or serene
and spiritual, reflecting "the beatitude of redemption" and "the
yearning of the spirit for an incommunicable God."

About 1859 or 1860, Baudelaire had defined pure art as "a
suggestive magic containing at one and the same time the object
and the subject, the world exterior to the artist and the artist
himself" (*OC*, II:598). In Wagner, he found one who was capable of creating this suggestive magic through music—"an artist
capable of translating the tumult of the human soul by a
thousand combinations of sound" (*OC*, II:781).

The imagination which enables the creative artist to suggest
and translate emotions or even ideas is also necessary to the listener, Baudelaire adds: "In music, as in painting and even in
literature, which is nevertheless the most concrete of the arts,
there is always a lacuna that is filled by the imagination of the
listener" (*OC*, II:781–82). It is hardly surprising that the Symbolists came to regard both Baudelaire and Wagner among their
most illustrious and important precursors. Baudelaire's observation, however, was not inspired by Wagner alone. His statement
was a logical development of his conviction, stated as early as
1846, that the poetry of a picture "lies in the soul of the spectator, and genius consists in awakening it" (*OC*, II:474).

In his essay on Wagner, Baudelaire revitalizes many of the
key ideas that he had already voiced in his criticism up to that
time. Of these, none is more effectively and poetically presented
than his theory of synaesthetic correspondences, which he had
first mentioned in the *Salon de 1846* and which he develops
more fully in his discussion of *Tannhäuser*. "True music suggests

analogous ideas to different minds," he maintains, and as proof he compares his own reveries suggested by the music with those of Liszt and Berlioz, from whose works he quotes at length.

But of even greater importance in Baudelaire's essay on Wagner was his discovery of what might be called his critical method. Although the poet-critic had long since renounced the idea of being guided by a "system," he had stressed from the beginning (*Le Salon de 1846*) the need for a critic to see a work of art through his own temperament in order to make a meaningful translation of his experience. "I was content to feel," he acknowledged in the *Exposition universelle* of 1855, after first admitting the futility of adhering to any critical system (*OC*, II:578). To sense the artist's experience and to recreate it for the reader was, he believed, the main purpose of the open-minded critic.

Evidently it was not until he composed his study on *Tannhäuser* that he seems to have realized the role that intelligence had been playing in his criticism. Intrigued by the repetition of certain melodic phrases which he had first noticed in the music from *Lohengrin*, he became obsessed by the desire to penetrate more deeply into the understanding of the composer's intention and method—"to discover the why and wherefore, and to transform pleasure into knowledge" (*OC*, II:786).

Consciously or unconsciously, he was articulating a precept that he had been observing for some time and that was actually an important element in his critical approach. But his confrontation with the music of his great contemporary finally forced him into this definition and made him realize that criticism was not only the recreation of the beauty contained within a work of art but also the search, through analysis and generalization, of the laws that govern artistic phenomena.

The essay itself is proof of the validity of the method that he describes, for it reveals not only the imagination of a creative artist recreating an aesthetic experience but also the curiosity and intelligence of an analytical mind seeking to discover the means by which an artist's genius finds expression.

Wagner seems to have been less enthusiastic about Baude-

laire's study than he had been about that of Champfleury. In his
autobiography, *My Life,* he contented himself with a rather
laconic remark: "Baudelaire distinguished himself by an ex-
ceedingly witty and aptly expressed pamphlet on this topic."[23]
But in a warm and gracious letter (April 15, 1861) he told the
poet how he had gone to his lodging several times to find and
thank him personally for "those beautiful pages which told me,
like the finest poem, the impressions which I can boast of having
produced on a constitution as superior as yours" (*PLB,* p. 400).

Baudelaire's enthusiasm was such that he had even thought
of going to Vienna with Champfleury to hear *Tristan and Isolde.*
When the presentation of the opera was postponed, Wagner
wrote his friend Gaspérini (September 18, 1861) asking him to
inform Baudelaire and Champfleury of the change in plans. Explaining that the two friends had expressed a wish to go to
Vienna for the occasion, he added: "I don't know if they were
too serious about this matter; at least, it showed good will on
their part" (*PLB,* p. 395).

FRANZ LISZT

It was through Wagner and his wife that Baudelaire first made
the acquaintance of the brilliant pianist and composer Franz
Liszt. In his 1861 article on Wagner, Baudelaire often refers to
the famous Hungarian composer, whom he describes as an "illustrious pianist, who is also an artist and philosopher" (*OC,*
II:783). Not only does he quote extensively from Liszt's book
Lohengrin and Tannhäuser, he also compares the composer's interpretation of the *Lohengrin* overture with his own and with
that of Berlioz. All three interpretations, he notes, are examples
of correspondences between sound and color and demonstrate
the fact that "true music evokes analogous ideas in different
minds."

Evidently Liszt had been given Baudelaire's brochure on
Wagner—no doubt a presentation from the poet-critic himself or
from one of his friends—and had expressed a desire to meet the
author. At any rate, there exists an undated letter addressed to

Liszt which Baudelaire seems to have written and left at the composer's residence on finding him absent:

> I met Madame Wagner today who informed me that you had received my brochure on Wagner and that you would be glad to see me. I wanted to forestall your visit, fearing that you wouldn't find me, since I am very busy. I know that you are leaving on the twentieth. I shall come back and see you. For many years I have been wanting to find the occasion to express to you all the admiration inspired in me by your character and your talent. [*Corr.*, II:162]

W. T. Bandy, who was the first to publish the letter, believes it was written sometime between the first and twentieth of May, since Baudelaire's pamphlet appeared around the first of May 1861, a few days before Liszt's arrival in Paris.[24]

Though little is known about their personal relationship, a comment made by Wagner in his autobiography suggests that the two were often together during the Hungarian composer's short stay in Paris. Wagner speaks of a lunch at Gounod's at which both Liszt and Baudelaire were present. The guests, he wrote,

> had a very dull time, which was only enlivened by poor Baudelaire, who indulged in the most outrageous witticisms. This man, *criblé de dettes,* as he told me, and daily compelled to adopt the most extravagant methods for a bare subsistence, had repeatedly approached me with adventurous schemes for the exploitation of my notorious fiasco [*Tannhäuser*]. I could not on any account consent to adopt any of these, and was glad to find this really capable man safe under the eagle-wing of Liszt's "ascendancy." Liszt took him everywhere where there was a possibility of a fortune being found. Whether this helped him into anything or not, I never knew. I only heard that he died a short time afterwards, certainly not from excess of good fortune.[25]

The nature of the "adventurous schemes" proposed by Baudelaire is not known. Crépet believes they may have been connected with the poet's desire to become a theater director. An equally plausible explanation may be found in Asselineau's comment that Baudelaire had a tendency to discuss theatrical or operatic projects as a pretext for talking with persons he liked or admired.[26]

Among other things, Baudelaire and Liszt shared a fascination for gypsy life, which served both poet and musician as inspiration for their genius. Baudelaire had celebrated gypsies in his poem "Les Bohémiens en voyage" as well as in the pages of *Du vin et du hachisch* in which he describes the wandering of Paginini and a Spanish guitarist throughout the countryside.[27] Liszt, on the other hand, not only composed music that was inspired by the passionate gypsy melodies of his native Hungary, but also published a book, *Des Bohémiens et de leur musique en Hongrie* (1859), of which he gave an inscribed copy to Baudelaire in return for an inscribed copy of *Les Paradis artificiels* offered him by the poet.

Undoubtedly Liszt's study of gypsy life and music must have further stimulated Baudelaire's interest. Robert Kopp suggests that the incident of the three wandering musicians found in the prose poem "Les Vocations" may have been inspired by Liszt, who in his book recounts in prose translation the story of the three gypsy musicians taken from the ballad of the poet Lenau.[28] Moreover, there is no doubt that the influence of the Hungarian composer explains the notation found in *Mon Coeur mis à nu:* "Exalt vagabondage and what may be called Bohemianism. Cult of multiple sensations expressed through music. Refer to Liszt" (*OC,* II:114).

Liszt, in turn, must have been impressed by Baudelaire's study on Wagner and *Tannhäuser,* for, not long after leaving Paris, he wrote to his daughter Blandine Ollivier (July 7 and again July 27) asking for two copies of the brochure.

Baudelaire's deep respect for Liszt was undoubtedly increased by the musician's charismatic personality and by what he considered his dandyism. Though Liszt remained in Paris only until June 7 or 8, Baudelaire forgot neither the man nor his genius. Two years later in his necrological article on Delacroix,

he mentions Liszt's "delightful study of Chopin" and, in a letter
to the editor of *Le Pays* (December 2, 1863), speaks of his intention to include the Hungarian composer (together with
Chateaubriand, de Custine, Paul de Molènes, Barbey d'Aurevilly) in a series of portraits of dandies that he was planning to
write.

In the prose poem "Le Thyrse," which he dedicated to
Liszt, Baudelaire best reveals the sincerity of his esteem for one
who, he believed, represented certain aspects of his own poetic
ideal. In his essay *De l'Essence du rire,* published some years
earlier, Baudelaire had written, "The artist is an artist only in-
sofar as he possesses a dual nature and is conscious of every
aspect of that duality" (*OC,* II:543). And in his prose poem it
becomes clear that this duality was one of the things that he most
admired in the musician: "The thyrsus represents your astonishing duality, mighty and venerated master, dear Bacchant of mysterious and passionate Beauty.... The staff represents your will,
straight, firm, and unshakable; the flowers, the wanderings of
your imagination" (*OC,* I:336).

But what strikes the reader most forcibly in the poem is the
warmth of personal feeling, the note of affection, that is seldom
found in the poet's praise of genius—not even in the homage that
he had paid to Delacroix, Poe, and Wagner. In a long dithyram-
bic sentence whose opening lines recall the rhythm of "Elévation"
and whose final line reiterates the sentiment he had expressed
to Madame Sabatier in his poem "Hymne," he concludes:

> Dear Liszt, through the mist, beyond the rivers, above the
> cities where pianos sing your glory, where the printing-press
> translates your wisdom, in whatever place you may be, in the
> splendors of the eternal city or in the haze of dreamy coun-
> tries consoled by Gambrinus, improvising songs of delecta-
> tion or of ineffable sorrow, or confiding to paper your ab-
> struse meditations, singer of eternal Pleasure and Anguish,
> philosopher, poet and artist, I salute you in immortality.

In Brussels, Baudelaire was not to forget his interest in Liszt's
music. In a letter written to the poet in May 1865, Manet ex-

plains that at long last he was sending him the "rapsodie de Lizt [*sic*]" which Baudelaire had requested a long time before. His wife, an accomplished musician, had lent it to a friend, he explained, and he had only just succeeded in getting it back (*PLB*, p. 234).

After his return to Paris, one of the few consolations in Baudelaire's bleak life was hearing extracts from the music he loved played for him by his friends Madame Manet or Madame Meurice, who came to visit him from time to time in the nursing home of Doctor Duval, where he spent his last days.

3

Baudelaire and Politics

BAUDELAIRE'S INTEREST IN the art and music of his day is not too surprising. But that for a few years he was also concerned with politics and social reform seems somewhat extraordinary. The poet even played a small part both in the revolution of 1848 and in the June insurrections, though his role mainly assumed the form of a protest against the existing order of things. It is now common knowledge that in 1848 Baudelaire took his place at the barricades on February 24, became a member of the *Société Républicaine centrale,* and founded the short-lived newspaper *Le Salut public* with Champfleury and Charles Toubin.[1]

Toubin, a friend and medical student, tells how on the evening of February 22, 1848, he and Baudelaire in the company of Courbet and the musician Promayet witnessed the killing of an escaping unarmed revolutionary by an officer of the military guard. Horrified by the incident, Courbet and Baudelaire reported the matter to *La Presse.* A few days later, Baudelaire, Champfleury, and Toubin published the first number of their own paper, *Le Salut public* (February 27), which the poet himself, dressed in a white smock, sold on the streets. The second issue (March 1 or 2), which also proved to be the last, was adorned with a vignette drawn by Courbet and allegedly based on Delacroix's *Liberty Leading the People.* The design was executed as a wood engraving by Rodolphe Bresdin, whose poverty and pathetic life inspired Champfleury to write his moving story *Chien-Caillou.*

In the meantime Jules Buisson, painter and engraver and

Baudelaire's friend of earlier years, tells how he saw the poet on February 24 carrying a gun and shouting, "We must go and kill General Aupick."[2] Whether or not the incident was completely true (Buisson often seems a little spiteful in his recollections), it is less revealing of the poet's attitude during this period than of the keen interest he took in socialist thought and in less sensational activities.

Baudelaire's service (during April–May 1848) on the editorial staff of *La Tribune nationale,* a supposedly moderate Republican newspaper, has often been mistaken as an indication of political vacillation on his part. However, Marcel Ruff has pointed out the fallacy of this belief and maintains that *La Tribune* expressed "opinions just as advanced as *Le Salut public* and that its increasingly violent opposition to the government [was] incontestably an opposition of the left."[3] Moreover, the poet's participation, however slight, in the June insurrection offers further proof that he remained true to his convictions.

It was only after the coup d'état of Louis Napoleon on December 2, 1851, that Baudelaire, disillusioned by the futility of the revolution of 1848 and by the ineffectual and contradictory theories of Utopian reformers, withdrew from political life and took refuge in the philosophical and metaphysical thought of Joseph de Maistre and of Edgar Allan Poe, both of whom strengthened his own belief in the natural perversity of man. To his legal guardian, Ancelle, he wrote in disgust on March 5, 1852: "You didn't see me at the polls; my mind is made up. *December 2nd has physically depoliticized me.* There are no more general ideas. It's quite obvious that *all Paris* is *Orleanist,* but that doesn't concern me. If I had voted, I could only have voted for myself. Perhaps the future belongs to classless men? (*Corr.,* I:188)

The sincerity of Baudelaire's revolutionary activities and of his concern for social and economic betterment has often been questioned. And yet, despite the poet's natural egocentricity, there is reason to believe that his involvement was far more than a result of his taste for adventure and excitement or of his wish to revenge himself on his stepfather, General Aupick. The compassion for the poor and downtrodden, to which Asselineau has testified eloquently in his biography of the poet, was seemingly present even in the heart of the child.

Memories of the suffering and poverty of the working classes that produced the outbursts of violence while he was a school-boy in Lyons as well as the firsthand accounts of the misery of those workers told him by his close friend Pierre Dupont, the humanitarian and socialist poet and songwriter, made a deep impression on him and inspired the moving passage contained in his essay on Dupont written in 1851.

> Whatever the party to which one belongs, whatever the prej-udices in which one has been nurtured, it is impossible not to be moved by the sight of that sickly throng breathing the dust of workshops, swallowing lint, becoming saturated with white lead, mercury, and all the poisons necessary to the creation of masterpieces, sleeping among vermin in the heart of districts where the humblest and greatest virtues live side by side with the most hardened vices and with the dregs from prisons—that sighing and languishing throng to which *the earth owes its marvels,* which *feels flowing in its veins an ardent red blood,* which looks long and sadly at the sunshine and shadows of the great parks and, for its only comfort and con-solation, bawls at the top of its voice its song of salvation; *Let us love one another.* [OC, II:31]

Moreover, the same compassion is found in his works both before and after his socialist period—in such poems as "Les Pe-tites Vieilles," "Le Crépuscule du soir," "Le Crépuscule du ma-tin," "La Mort des pauvres," and most notably in a great many of his prose poems.

Perhaps Baudelaire's explanation of Wagner's revolutionary opinions is the best clue to the poet's own motivation. In his 1861 essay on Wagner, he wrote what seems even more true of himself than of the German composer whom he was defending:

> I find the explanation of Wagner's revolutionary opinions in that capacity for suffering that is common to all artists and

that is all the greater as their instinct for the just and the beautiful is more pronounced. Embittered by so many disappointments, disillusioned by so many shattered dreams, impelled by an error that is understandable in such an excessively tense and sensitive mind, there came a time when he felt obliged to postulate a spiritual complicity between bad music and bad governments. Possessed by the supreme desire of seeing routine conquered once and for all by the ideal in art (it is essentially a human illusion), he brought himself to hope that political revolutions would promote the cause of revolution in art. [OC, II:787]

However, in the case of Baudelaire, his "instinct for the just and beautiful" was intensified not only by "disappointments and shattered dreams" but perhaps even more by the new contacts he made after his return from the voyage imposed on him by his family. His association and friendship with staunch Republicans like Daumier, Thoré, Nadar, and Dupont and with socialist thinkers and sympathizers like Courbet and Champfleury did much to increase his awareness of an oppressed proletariat. Gradually but surely he was becoming more and more aware of the discontent that was to erupt in the revolution of 1848.

During this period most writers—Hugo, George Sand, and Lamartine, to mention only a few—were involved with social reform, and in fact the whole Romantic movement was changing direction under the influence of the socialist thinkers. Even writers who are not usually considered *engagés* became involved in the movement for reform. For a short time Leconte de Lisle was a regular contributor to the Fourierist periodical *La Phalange,* while Sainte-Beuve was attracted successively by the Saint-Simonians, by Lamennais, and by Proudhon.

Everywhere in France the question of social injustice was being hotly debated. Lamennais, Leroux, Fourier, Louis Blanc, and Proudhon, among others, were all calling attention to the social evils of the day and suggesting various types of reform. Moreover, social problems were not being discussed as separate and distinct entities but rather in conjunction with aesthetic, religious, and metaphysical theories with which they were thought to be interrelated. For, as Léon Cellier observed, social and mystical considerations were inextricably mingled for the Romanticist.[4]

In his autobiographical notes Baudelaire cites among his "secondes liaisons littéraires" Sainte-Beuve, Hugo, Gautier, and Esquiros (OC, I:785). The name of Esquiros is of particular interest not only because, with Nadar and the abbé Constant, he collaborated with Baudelaire in the anonymous publication of the *Mystères galans des théâtres de Paris* (1844), but also because he undoubtedly did much to encourage the poet's interest in idealistic social republicanism.

Both Esquiros and the abbé Constant (later known as Eliphas Lévi) were engrossed in various forms of semimystical socialism and somewhat later in occultism. Baudelaire must surely have known the poem "Les Correspondances" of Constant and evidently took more seriously Esquiros's idea of correspondences than his knowledge of political and economic theory. In fact, in the electoral meetings of April 1848, where Esquiros spoke as a candidate, Baudelaire took delight in embarrassing him and Arsène Houssaye with questions on political economy about which the poet appeared to know more than either candidate.

Like so many others of his time, Baudelaire must have been swayed by Lamennais's passionate denunciation of social injustice. Though he offered no positive doctrine for economic reform other than the practical application of the teaching of Christ, the famous preacher and writer exerted a powerful influence on the people of his day and, together with Victor Hugo, did more than anyone else to arouse the public conscience and give a new direction to the Romantic movement. Claude Pichois sees in "Les Châtiments de Dieu," published in the second number of *Le Salut public* and apparently the handiwork of Baudelaire, the unmistakable imprint of the eloquence that marks the Abbé's *Paroles d'un croyant* (1834).[5]

Other social thinkers and reformers likewise aroused the poet's curiosity and attracted his attention, among them Charles Fourier, Pierre Leroux, and Pierre-Joseph Proudhon. That

Fourier had a strong influence on Baudelaire has been suggested by Jean Pommier in *La Mystique de Baudelaire* and reaffirmed by Pichois in his essay "Baudelaire en 1847."[6] As in the case of Esquiros, the poet seems to have been interested less in Fourier's ideas of social reform—among them the establishment of cooperative communities called phalanges—than in his discussion of universal analogy which the poet-critic, in his essay on Hugo, compared unfavorably to Swedenborg's presentation.

Echoes of Fourier, Pichois notes, are perceptible in the dedication of the *Salon de 1846* to the Bourgeois, in the choice of the second title, *Les Limbes,* for the future *Les Fleurs du Mal* (Fourier had called the beginnings of the socialist and industrialist period "les périodes lymbiques"), as well as in "the rich gamut of transpositions and symbols contained in universal *analogy.*"[7] Pichois also suggests that the dogmatic style affected by Baudelaire in his early writings as well as many of his ideas pertaining to political economy stemmed from a knowledge of Fourier's works.

Evidently Baudelaire was also drawn to the theories of Pierre Leroux and Pierre-Joseph Proudhon. According to Mouquet and Bandy, it was the poet who, on June 3, 1848, in proposing to the readers of *La Tribune nationale* a slate of candidates, including Proudhon and Pierre Leroux, urged the voters to choose candidates who were committed to social reform. With growing passion he wrote: "Do you want . . . to have noble and courageous defenders, men who are sincerely devoted to the sacred cause of the people? Choose men of the people, choose men who are one with the people, men who are ready to fight and die for them."[8]

Leroux, who was imbued with the democratic ideal, believed, like Blanqui and Louis Blanc, that all capital should be common property. But unlike George Sand, whose social novels were steeped in Leroux's philosophy, Baudelaire was more attracted to the aesthetics of the social reformer. In 1831, Leroux had published an article in the *Revue encyclopédique* in which he applied to aesthetics the centuries-old philosophy of universal analogy. Though the poet could hardly have failed to read the article, given his fascination with the subject, it is the passage from Hoffmann's *Kreisleriana* on the relationship between colors, sounds, and perfumes that he cites in the *Salon de 1846* and accepts as his own.

Proudhon went even further than Leroux and denounced property as theft ("la propriété, c'est le vol")—unfortunately a somewhat exaggerated statement of his real beliefs. Though Proudhon's significance has been strangely overlooked, it was he who came to play the most important role in Baudelaire's socialist period and whose social, political, economic, and even religious ideas won the approval of the poet, at least for a short time. Even after turning away from socialism and rejecting all else, Baudelaire continued to respect Proudhon as an economist and to defend him against his critics.

The diverse influences felt by the poet and the large quantity of material being published must have bewildered him with their conflicting views and theories. Many years later, in the opening paragraph of his prose poem "Assommons les pauvres," written about the time of the death of Proudhon in January 1865, Baudelaire refers to his early reading of the many socialist tracts:

> For two weeks I had stayed in my room, surrounded with books in vogue at that time (sixteen or seventeen years ago); I mean books that are concerned with the art of making people happy, wise and rich, in twenty-four hours. I had thus digested,—or rather swallowed—all the lucubrations of all those custodians of the public happiness—those who advise the poor to become slaves and those who convince them that they are dethroned kings.—It is not surprising that I was then in a state of mind bordering on bewilderment or stupidity. [*OC*, I:357]

Moreover it seems that even as his interest in the revolutionary movement grew, Baudelaire ironically was aware of his irresolution and ineffectual action. He was predicting his own course of action in 1848 when, at the conclusion of his story *La Fanfarlo* (published in 1847) he says of the protagonist, Samuel Cramer, who represents Baudelaire himself: "I recently learned that he was founding a socialist paper and that he wanted to go in for politics" (*OC*, I:580).

In later years Baudelaire's continuing puzzlement about his attitude and activities during the revolutionary period—despite his explanation or perhaps rationalization in his essay on Wagner—is evident from a notation found in his *Journaux intimes* (*OC,* I:679). Looking back on the past within the privacy of his journal, he saw in what he called "My intoxication in 1848" proof of the concept of original sin and the perversity of man which he had so enthusiastically noted in de Maistre and Poe. "Taste for vengeance. Natural pleasure in destruction," he remarks with the stern severity of a de Maistre, remembering no doubt the less commendable aspects that had marked his spirit of revolt.

A far more valid explanation of the poet's conduct is to be found in the comment that immediately follows: "Literary intoxication; memories of what I had read."

No doubt it was the "literary intoxication" of the voluminous reading to which Baudelaire refers in "Assommons les pauvres" that was largely responsible for his actions in 1848 and even for certain ideas which he continued to hold until the end of his life. It must have been in 1847—a year in which, except for the publication of *La Fanfarlo,* little is known about Baudelaire—that the poet found himself, as he admitted, "bewildered" by the diversity and contradictory nature of the socialist literature, by "the lucubrations of all those custodians of the public happiness." As Claude Pichois points out in his essay "Baudelaire en 1847," the poet was trying to find himself in 1847: "He was trying to find himself and risked losing his way—all the more so, since like Sainte-Beuve, he was a man curious about everything, tempted by everything."[9]

PIERRE-JOSEPH PROUDHON

Much has been written about the influence of Swedenborg and Fourier in particular on the impressionable mind of the young poet. Very little has been said about that of Pierre-Joseph Proudhon, who seems to have made a far greater impression on Baudelaire as a social reformer. "An individualist tinged with anarchism," as he is often described, Proudhon devoted his life to seeking legislation that would end the oppression and exploitation of the poor and establish equality, justice, and liberty for all. To achieve his goal, Proudhon sought the abolition of capitalistic profit not through violence but through economic reform—through the establishment of a "Banque du Peuple" which was to institute "free credit." To the young and still little known Karl Marx, who had written proposing an alliance, he answered with blunt candor: "I am a revolutionary, not a bully (bousculeur)" (*POC*, VII:9).

Though Proudhon was opposed to both the February revolution ("They have started a revolution without an idea") and to the June insurrection, he rose to the defense of the militants in spite of his disapproval. As a result of his stand, he was violently attacked on all sides and paradoxically came to represent, as Daniel Halévy has remarked, the very incarnation of the revolution—"the ridiculous fanatic who said that God was evil; property, a theft..." (*POC*, III:36).

Proudhon continued to express his ideas frankly and fearlessly throughout his life, even during the three years that he spent in prison (beginning June 5, 1849) as a result of two impassioned articles directed at the future Napoleon III. He never failed to champion the cause of the working class in the articles and books that he wrote constantly. On his death in 1865, it is said that between five and six thousand Parisian workingmen marched in the funeral cortège to the cemetery.

Baudelaire's friendship and admiration for Proudhon seem at first glance somewhat incongruous, given the differences in their tastes and personalities. Yet there is reason to believe that for a short period of time the author of *Les Fleurs du Mal* was not only intrigued by Proudhon's social and political doctrines but also more influenced by them than is usually believed.

The very questions that Baudelaire asked of Esquiros and Houssaye in the electoral meeting of 1848 were, according to T. J. Clark, author of *The Absolute Bourgeois*, those which Proudhon had treated in his *Système des contradictions économiques ou Philosophie de la misère*, published two years earlier.[10] Baudelaire's extensive acquaintance with the ponderous, all-embracing work is attested by the fact that he copied from it a passage pertaining to the problem of aesthetics and morality:

> Art, in other words the quest for beauty, the perfecting of truth, in his person, in his wife and children, in his ideas, his words, his actions, his products: such is the final evolution of the worker, the phase destined to bring to a glorious close the circle of nature. Esthetics, and above esthetics, Morality,—in them is to be found the keystone of the economic edifice.
> [*POC*, I: pt. 2, 375]

Moreover, the fact that Baudelaire, as we have seen, proposed the name of Proudhon as one of the candidates for the National Assembly is proof in itself of his esteem. Perhaps the liberal tendencies of *La Tribune nationale,* recently noted by Marcel Ruff, may be attributed to Proudhon's influence on the editorial staff of the newspaper and on Baudelaire in particular. According to Clark, *La Tribune* grew more favorable to Proudhon's ideas after the beginning of June. Its final number (pp. 301–02), he maintains, not only contained a long quotation from the newspaper published by Proudhon himself but also gave "cautious *backing* to the notorious proposal for a Bank of Exchange."[11]

What remains, however, as indisputable proof of the poet's sincere interest in the ideas of Proudhon is the discovery of two letters warning the social reformer of possible attempts against his life and urging him to take steps to protect himself. The first, dated August 21, reveals a youthful, almost naive exhilaration that seems quite uncharacteristic of the later Baudelaire.

> Citizen, An unknown but devoted friend insists upon seeing you, not only to learn from you and to take a few moments of your time, as perhaps would be his right, but also to inform you of things pertaining to your safety that you may not know. Even if the person writing you should reveal only what you already know, I don't think it would be absurd on his part, admiration and fellow-feeling justifying him sufficiently.

I wrestled for a long time with my indolence to write you a very long letter; but I preferred to dare to tackle you directly. Today policemen on all sides kept me from entering; for I was hoping to get this note to you through other agents with whom I am a little acquainted. If you don't find it odd that a wretched stranger should ask an immediate reply from a man as busy and pressed for time as you—I shall wait in that case *indefinitely* in the café-restaurant at the corner of the rue de Bourgogne.

Charles Baudelaire

Avenue de la République, 18, Neuilly

With my eternal and most sincere devotion and admiration. [*Corr.*, I:150]

In the second letter, which Pichois believes was written either the same day or the following day, Baudelaire's admonitions are even more explicit and insistent. The tone and style of the letter are plainly evidence of his haste and excitement.

This is what I had to tell you; and it seems to me useful; for, either you know it and it is my duty to tell you anyway, not knowing whether you really know it; or you do not know it, and it is a good thing that you find it out.

There are rumors of troubles. Who will create them? We don't know. But at the next demonstration, even one that is anti-working class, in other words, at the next pretext you may be assassinated.

It's a real conspiracy.

To begin with, deliberate, vague, and incipient, developing as far as you are concerned in the same way that a few years ago the desire to kill Henry V developed:—*Doubtless one must not wish for anyone's death, but it would be a fortunate event if an accident were to get rid of him.* The other possibility is more clear: *at the next opportunity, we know where he lives, and we will easily know how to find him elsewhere. Leave it to us.*—You are the great scape goat.—Be assured that there is no exaggeration in all this; I can't give you any proofs. If I had any, I would have sent them to the police without consulting you. But my conscience and my intelligence make me an excellent informer where my convictions are concerned. In other words, I am certain of what I am telling you, namely that the man who is especially precious to US is in danger. It has reached such a point that, remembering several conversations that I have overheard, should there be an attempt on your life, *I could give you names,* so foolhardy is ferocity.

I thought that today you would deign to honor me with a reply. Furthermore, I had no thought except to suggest some improvements in your paper that I think are important, for instance, for the weekly issue, suggestions about the reprinting of all the back issues, and in the second place, the opportunity there would be to publish an immense poster, signed by you, by other representatives, and by the editors of your paper, printed in enormous quantities and ORDERING the people to sit tight. Your name at present is better known and more influential than you realize. An uprising can start by being Legitimist and end by being Socialist; but the opposite can also happen.

He who writes you these lines has complete confidence in you, as do many of his friends who would march blindfolded behind you because of the assurances of knowledge that you have given them.

Thus, at the next sign of trouble, even the most insignificant, *stay away from home.* If you can, secure a secret guard or ask the police to protect you. On the other hand, the *government would perhaps be very glad to accept such a gift from* ferocious property holders; so it is perhaps better to protect yourself.

Charles Baudelaire
[Corr., I:151-52]

Some time later in 1848 Baudelaire had his first personal encounter with Proudhon in the office of the newspaper *Le Représentant du peuple,* where he had gone to meet Jules Viard. Viard was not in the office; instead Baudelaire found Proudhon, with whom he struck up a conversation. Years later (1865) Baudelaire described the meeting in a letter to Poulet-Malassis. "Citizen, it's dinner time; shall we dine together?" Proudhon asked the young poet. Baudelaire went on to add: "We went to a small restaurant recently established on the rue Neuve-Vivienne; Proudhon talked on and on, violently, profusely, initiating me, a stranger to him, into his plans and projects, and pouring out, unintentionally so to speak, a deluge of clever remarks" (*Corr.*, II:470).

That Baudelaire encountered Proudhon on a number of occasions after that date seems quite safe to assume. In fact, in a letter to Sainte-Beuve written many years later (1866) he writes: "I have read much of his work and knew him a little" (*Corr.*, II:563). During this period the poet was a close associate not only of Champfleury but also of the artist Gustave Courbet, who had done the vignette for the second and final edition of *Le Salut public*. Proudhon, who had settled in Paris in 1847, was an intimate friend of both Champfleury and Courbet; a few years later he was to become particularly close to Courbet, who, like him, had grown up in the Franche-Comté. Proudhon came to replace Champfleury as Courbet's aesthetic and philosophical mentor.

It was at the Brasserie Andler, two doors from Courbet's studio on the rue Hautefeuille, that Proudhon occasionally joined the friends and admirers of the artist, who came to talk, listen, argue, or be entertained. The more elite group, Gerstle Mack tells us, included such well-known persons as Corot, Daumier, Baudelaire, Champfleury, Proudhon, Gustave Planche, Desnoyers, Pierre Dupont, and many others.[12]

In his *Souvenirs,* Champfleury, as we have seen, nostalgically recalls the evenings spent in "le temple du réalisme" and describes the spirited conversation and the air of gaiety that prevailed. That both poet and reformer occasionally attended the dinners is suggested by Champfleury's lively account. Only Proudhon and Baudelaire, he reports, seemed to disapprove of the new school of poetry, which had abandoned rhyme, and failed to join in the singing of the rhymeless couplets.[13] Of Baudelaire, Champfleury adds: "The gaiety didn't succeed in cheering that poor troubled soul, and after long and frequent attendance in the temple, the poet was the only dissident who was conspicuous by his non-conformism."[14]

Whether through personal persuasion or through his publications, Proudhon managed to convert both Champfleury and Baudelaire to his way of thinking. Baudelaire was obviously referring to his friends Champfleury, Dupont, and Courbet when, in his second letter to Proudhon, he wrote that many of his friends "would walk behind you blindfolded in return for the assurances of knowledge that you have given them" (*Corr.*, I:152). And in his *Souvenirs,* Champfleury himself ruefully admitted his conversion to Proudhon's philosophy: "For a short time, under the Republic, I believed in Proudhon's ideas; I have long since made confession of my sins."[15]

Baudelaire's championing of Proudhon's ideas was evidently no secret. In his review of *La Presse de 1848,* Jean Wallon, the Bohemian philosopher—the model (with Marc Trapadoux) of the philosopher Colline in Murger's *Scènes de la vie de Bohème*—wrote with indignation and disgust about Baudelaire's *Les Limbes,* whose publication had been announced.

Today we see announced in *L'Echo des marchands de vin: Limbes,* to be published on 24 February at Paris and Leipzig. They are doubtless Socialist verses, and in consequence bad verses. Yet another new disciple of Proudhon, due to *too much* or *too little* ignorance.... For the last few months everybody seems to have lost his head, nobody believes in literature any longer, everyone has rushed into Socialism— without seeing that Socialism is the absolute negation of art.[16]

Proudhon's name must often have been on Baudelaire's tongue in 1849. As we have seen, the artist Eugène Delacroix noted in his *Journal* under the date of February 5: "M. Baudelaire came as I was resuming work on a small figure of a woman in the Oriental style.... He talked to me about the difficulties that Daumier has in finishing. He jumped to the subject of Proudhon whom he admires and whom he calls the idol of the people. His views seem to me extremely modern and quite progressive."[17]

Coming from Delacroix, the last remark was hardly intended as flattery.

Eighteen fifty-one and 1852 showed no lessening of Baudelaire's support of Proudhon. Laudatory comments appearing in two essays published in 1851 indicate a growing esteem for the social philosopher. "Proudhon is a writer whom Europe will always envy us," he wrote in *Les Drames et les romans honnêtes,* and in his essay on Pierre Dupont he repudiated for the first and only time in his life his admiration for René and Obermann and adopted the philosophy of action that was being preached by the socialist thinker: "Take flight then, deceptive shades of René, Obermann and Werther; vanish into the mists of nowhere, monstrous creations of idleness and solitude.... The spirit of *action* [my italics] leaves no more room for you among us" (*OC,* I:34). The word *action* was obviously the key to the poet's belief in Proudhon's ideas—action that was for him "the sister of the dream"—for unlike the Utopian philosophers of the day, who offered only beautiful but vague and impossible dreams, Proudhon preached action based on concrete proposals, such as free exchange and cooperation between small trader and worker.

That Baudelaire was thinking of Proudhon and that he was well acquainted with his work is proved by the paragraph that immediately follows his attack on the passivity of the Romantic hero:

> When I glance over the work of Dupont, I am always reminded, probably because of some secret affinity, of that sublime movement of Proudhon, full of tenderness and enthusiasm. He hears someone humming the Lyonese song:
>
> > Come, be of good cheer
> > Good workers!
> > Take courage in your work!
> > Let us be the first.
>
> and he cries: "Go to work with a song, predestined race, your refrain is more beautiful than that of Rouget de Lisle." [*OC,* I:34]

Baudelaire's surprising rejection of the School of Melancholy, accompanied as it is by his praise of Proudhon, leads one to believe that the poet's brief acceptance of utilitarian art ("art was henceforth inseparable from morality and utility" [*OC*, I:27]) may also have been inspired by the aesthetic ideas of the socialist reformer. Proudhon's influence likewise helps to explain the concluding paragraph of Baudelaire's essay *L'Ecole païenne:* "Literature must go and renew itself in a better atmosphere. The time is not distant when it will be understood that every literature that refuses to walk hand in hand with science and philosophy is a homicidal and suicidal literature" (*OC*, I:49). The passage on aesthetics and morality that the poet had copied from *Philosophie de la misère* would indicate that he had found the ideas of Proudhon of more than cursory interest.

Sainte-Beuve's great respect for Proudhon's intelligence and probity and the fact that after the revolution of 1848 the socialist philosopher actually came to replace Gautier in the "dilection" of the critic may have done much to encourage and confirm Baudelaire's opinion.[18] Sainte-Beuve never flagged in his support, for after the death of Proudhon in 1865 he published a series of four laudatory articles based on the life and correspondence of the social reformer between 1835 and 1848—articles which Baudelaire, in a letter to his guardian, Ancelle, on December 26, 1865, described as "miracles of intelligence and suppleness" (*Corr.,* II:557).

It was to these articles that Baudelaire referred in the letter written to Sainte-Beuve from Brussels on January 2, 1866: "I have read much of his work and knew him a little. Pen in hand, he wasn't a *bad sort;* but he wasn't and never would have been, even on paper, a *dandy*. That's what I shall never forgive him" (*Corr.,* II:563).

Baudelaire's reservations, based on Proudhon's utilitarian concept of art—a concept which he himself had adopted for a brief moment—were obviously well justified. Despite his claim to competence, the socialist philosopher viewed the arts only as an instrument for the improvement of society. As Gerstle Mack has observed, "Proudhon could never see anything in a picture except a sociological tract."[19] Baudelaire was not alone in deploring Proudhon's taste in literature and the arts. Champfleury, Théophile Thoré, and Sainte-Beuve himself were among those who recognized his aesthetic shortcomings.

Baudelaire's letter to Sainte-Beuve was written long after he had abandoned his concern for social and political reform and long after Poe and de Maistre had come to replace Proudhon in his hierarchy of values. Yet he was never to reject the soundness of Proudhon's thought in matters of political economy. A year before writing his letter to Sainte-Beuve, he dispatched a note to Ancelle (February 8, 1865) warmly defending a letter written by Proudhon to the editor of the *Journal de Liège:*

> Proudhon's letter didn't impress you enough, and you are too quick to call him a fool. I sent you that letter to prove to you that Proudhon, whatever one says, *had never changed.* At the end of his life, as at the beginning, the questions of production and finance were those that obsessed him especially. If it were a question of art, yes, you would be right in saying of Proudhon: *He is mad.*—But in economic matters he seems to me eminently respectable. [*Corr.,* II:453]

Baudelaire came to view Proudhon much as he did Victor Hugo, as another letter to Ancelle shows (February 21, 1865). Reporting to his guardian comments that Thoré had made to him criticizing the "the rustic affectation of Proudhon, an affectation of crudeness in everything, the coarse manners of a peasant," he concludes: "Thus one can be both *a wit* and *a boor,* as one can possess at one and the same time a *special genius* and yet be *a fool.* Victor Hugo has certainly proved that to us" (*Corr.,* II:459–60).

It would seem almost inevitable that the interest Baudelaire showed in Proudhon's thought between 1848 and 1852 be reflected in at least some of the verse composed during those years. Curiously enough, Baudelaire himself has written the words "socialisme mitigé" on a manuscript copy of "La Rançon," a poem composed before the beginning of April 1852. In their critical edition of *Les Fleurs du Mal,* Crépet and Blin, noting the comment that appears in parentheses after the text, suggest that the poem and the author's notation are to be explained "by the very surprising and ephemeral adherence of the poet to Proudhon's ideas about 1848 (Utilitarianism, Mutualism, etc.)."[20] René Galand in his recent book, *Baudelaire, Poétiques et Poésie,* as well as Clark in *The Absolute Bourgeois,* both specifically name Proudhon as the poem's principal source of inspiration.[21] Clark even suggests that the sentiments expressed in the poem parallel rather closely the passage in *Philosophie de la misère* (the book from which Baudelaire had copied some lines on aesthetics and morality) in which Proudhon had celebrated "man's dual idealization of work and love."

Like Proudhon, Baudelaire combines socialist sentiments with biblical allusions in "La Rançon." To pay for his ransom, man must cultivate the fields of Art and Love (Charity) with the plow-share of reason. At the Last Judgment he must be able to show not only a harvest of grain but also of flowers whose form and color will gain the approval of the Angels. The stilted moralism and uninspired treatment, so uncharacteristic of Baudelaire, help to explain why the author excluded the poem from the 1857 and 1861 editions of *Les Fleurs du Mal.* But even in later publications he suppressed the final quatrain, whose socialist sentiment could not even be qualified as "mitigé" since it suggests the revolutionary idea that the crops be held in common.

A far greater poem, "Le Reniement de Saint Pierre" likewise seems to reveal the influence of Proudhon but with no detriment to its intrinsic aesthetic value. Like "La Rançon," "Le Reniement" was written sometime before April 1852 and published as one of the *Douze Poèmes* in October of that year. Whereas some critics, placing it between 1844 and 1848, see in it merely an attempt to shock and scandalize a complacent public, others situate it closer to 1852 and stress its strong social and political overtones. Whatever the date of composition, "Le Reniement" is undoubtedly the product of the sociopolitical climate of the period and reflects, consciously or unconsciously, the religious and social thought of Proudhon.

In many ways the poem is not unlike a number of Romantic poems written during the first half of the nineteenth century. The idea of a cruel, wicked God governing the world was commonplace during the Romantic period, and the fact that Baudelaire adopted the theme is not extraordinary. It is one of his most powerful poems and reveals an undeniable note of conviction and sincerity.

Qu'est-ce que Dieu fait donc de ce flot d'anathèmes
Qui monte tous les jours vers ses chers Séraphins?
Comme un tyran gorgé de viande et de vins,
Il s'endort au doux bruit de nos affreux blasphèmes.

Les sanglots des martyrs et des suppliciés
Sont une symphonie enivrante sans doute,
Puisque, malgré le sang que leur volupté coûte,
Les cieux ne s'en sont point encore rassasiés!

—Ah! Jésus, souviens-toi du Jardin des Olives!
Dans ta simplicité tu priais à genoux
Celui qui dans son ciel riait au bruit des clous
Que d'ignobles bourreaux plantaient dans tes chairs vives.

Lorsque tu vis cracher sur ta divinité
La crapule du corps de garde et des cuisines,
Et lorsque tu sentis s'enfoncer les épines
Dans ton crâne où vivait l'immense Humanité;

Quand de ton corps brisé la pesanteur horrible
Allongeait tes deux bras distendus, que ton sang
Et ta sueur coulaient de ton front pâlissant,
Quand tu fus devant tous posé comme une cible,

Rêvais-tu de ces jours si brillants et si beaux
Où tu vins pour remplir l'éternelle promesse,
Où tu foulais, monté sur une douce ânesse,
Des chemins tout jonchés de fleurs et de rameaux,

Où, le cœur tout gonflé d'espoir et de vaillance,
Tu fouettais tous ces vils marchands à tour de bras

Où tu fus maître enfin? Le remords n'a-t-il pas
Pénétré dans ton flanc plus avant que la lance?

—Certes, je sortirai, quant à moi, satisfait
D'un monde où l'action n'est pas la sœur du rêve;
Puissé-je user du glaive et périr par le glaive!
Saint Pierre a renié Jésus ... il a bien fait!

Particularly reminiscent of the literature of the day are the opening stanzas, in which Baudelaire denounces God's sadistic pleasure and malevolence in the face of suffering humanity. Critics have rightly compared the poem to "Le Désespoir" of Lamartine, "Le Mont des Oliviers" of Vigny, to the "Ténèbres" of Gautier, and "Le Christ aux Oliviers" of Nerval, as well as to a number of others. Yet despite similarities, there is a marked difference between Baudelaire's poem and those of his fellow Romantics. Lamartine makes no mention of Christ but denounces a cruel God, who, spurning the world he has created, "from his imperfect work, turned his face / And kicking it disdainfully into space / Returned to his repose."

Vigny, like Baudelaire, is concerned with the role of both God and Christ. His God, like that of Lamartine and Baudelaire, is cruel and silent—indifferent even to the prayers of his own son. But Vigny's Christ, on the other hand, in contrast to that of Baudelaire, is unwilling to accept death and begs to live long enough to bring "hope" and "certitude" to a suffering Humanity. Nerval's Christ, vainly seeking a God in an empty universe, seems more concerned with his own personal fate than with that of Humanity: "The god is gone from the altar where I am the victim. . . . God does not exist! God no longer exists!" Gautier scornfully rejects both God and Christ, but his despair, unrelated to social and political problems, derives from his nihilism and from his personal obsession with death.

In all these cases the underlying tone is markedly different from that of "Le Reniement de Saint Pierre." It is not the metaphysical pessimism of the Romantics that Baudelaire is expressing, although verbal echoes, particularly of "Le Désespoir" and "Ténèbres," can be heard. On the contrary, as Antoine

Adam has pointed out, "In Baudelaire's poem there is much less metaphysics than certain commentators believe and a greater concern for the concrete reality in which he lived."[22]

That this preoccupation with the contemporary scene had been strengthened and determined by Proudhon seems almost undeniable. Proudhon was passionately, almost obsessively, concerned with the question of religion, and he spoke and wrote freely on the subject throughout his lifetime. Moreover, his religious thought was by no means restricted to his *Carnets* and to his *Bible annotée;* in most of his important works it often appears as an essential part of his argument. In Proudhon can be found the same mingling of political, social, and religious ideas that appears in "Le Reniement de Saint Pierre." As early as 1846 in his *Philosophie de la misère* Proudhon denounces God with the same frenzied virulence that marks "Le Reniement":

> Thy name, for so long the scholar's last word, the judge's sanction, the prince's strength, the poor man's hope, the repentant sinner's refuge, well, this ineffable name, henceforth doomed to scorn and anathema, will be jeered at among men! For God is stupidity and cowardice; God is hypocrisy and lies; God is tyranny and wretchedness; God is evil! [*Poc,* I: pt. 1, 383–84]

The ringing words were not soon to be forgotten. In 1848 when Proudhon was under attack for defending the June insurrection—in which Baudelaire, incidentally, and not Proudhon had taken part—the *Journal des Débats* repeated the celebrated formula, "Dieu, c'est le mal" [God is evil] and added to it an even more famous dictum of the social reformer: "La propriété, c'est le vol" [Property is theft]. The fact that, encouraged by his friends, Proudhon published an explanation of the notorious passage on May 6, 1849, in the newspaper *La Voix du Peuple*—a newspaper which he himself was to publish during his imprisonment—must have attracted even greater attention to his pronouncements.

In fact, Alison Fairlie has pointed out in her study *Leconte de Lisle's Poems on the Barbarian Races* that the famous statement "Dieu, c'est le mal" proved to be a "byword" throughout the mid-nineteenth century and that "letters of Leconte de Lisle to Ménard in 1849 show Proudhon's theories to have been a subject of frequent discussion among their group...." Moreover, in a penetrating analysis of Leconte de Lisle's poem "Qaïn," Fairlie demonstrates that of all the influences to which the author may have been subjected, "Proudhon was the more direct influence for the development of the thought."[23]

Much the same may be said of Baudelaire. Although there may be no direct relationship between his invective and that of Proudhon, it seems safe to assume that the poet was as much encouraged by the thought and the scornful diatribes of his political colleague as by those of his Romantic *confrères*.

But it is in the verses addressed to Christ that Baudelaire differs most from his fellow poets and, at the same time, seems more closely allied to Proudhon. Where Vigny had rejected God rather than Christ, Baudelaire rejects Christ himself and for the very reasons cited by Proudhon both in his *Carnets* and in his published work. Baudelaire's denial of Christ, like that of Proudhon, is based neither on hate nor fear. On the contrary, while admitting his "divinity," he speaks to him with almost a note of tenderness ("Ah! Jesus, remember the Garden of Olives! ... when you felt the thorns sink deep / Into your skull where dwelled infinite Humanity"). It is rather the mob ("vile executioners ... that lewd mob of bodyguards and scullions") on whom the poet vents his anger.

Yet despite his obvious sympathy and admiration even for the Christ, who had come with heart "swollen with hope and courage" to fulfill "the eternal promise," Baudelaire rejects him more in sorrow than in anger. "Did you dream of those days so splendid and so fair when ... you lashed with might and main those vile money changers, / In short, when you were *master*" [my italics], he asks. "Didn't remorse / Pierce deeper than the spear into your side?" he continues. And the questions reveal the very reasons for Baudelaire's denial. It is not so much Christ himself that the poet rejects as Christ's failure to fight evil in the world, his failure to continue seeking reform through positive action as he had done in driving the money changers from the temple. For if dreams are not accompanied by appropriate action (if "action is not the sister of the dream"), evil is allowed to prevail and good is inevitably overcome by wrong.

"Combatir es la vida del hombre sobre la tierra" [To fight is man's life on earth] Unamuno was to write many years later in his story of Juan Manso, who was made to atone for a life of inaction and complacency in the face of wrongdoing by being sent back from the very gates of Paradise to combat the evil of this world. Baudelaire, accepting Proudhon's doctrine of reform, is saying much the same thing. If suffering and evil, poverty and misery, injustice and corruption are to be destroyed, man must be encouraged to struggle ("take up the sword and perish by the sword"). The words could almost have served as a battle cry for social revolution or as a call for revolt against the infamous coup d'etat of Napoleon III. True, Baudelaire is distorting the meaning of the biblical account on which the poem is based, but no more so than Vigny had done in "Le Mont des Oliviers."

Baudelaire's theme was the very one that Proudhon had been stressing and that he continued to stress throughout his life. As early as 1843, in his book *De la Création de l'ordre dans l'humanité,* he had pointed out that Christ failed in his mission on earth when he declared that his kingdom was not of this world. Three years later (1846), in his *Philosophie de la misère,* it became even more evident that his hostility to religion was based primarily on the fact that it teaches acceptance and resignation and that it puts off to the next world the remedy for the injustices of this world. Christianity had lost its way, Proudhon believed, by extending its protective wing over social injustice. Hence he concluded: "Let the priest finally get it into his head that sin is poverty, and that true virtue, that which makes us worthy of eternal life, is to struggle against religion and against God" (*POC,* I: pt. 2, 412).

Repeatedly Proudhon returned to the theme of a Christ who had failed to combat the evils of his day and who, despite his saintliness, his intelligence, his indignation in the face of corruption, proved to be an "irresponsible reformer" (*POC,* II:307).

In his failure to see that the regeneration of humanity could only be brought about by revolutionary action, Christ himself was destroyed, while evil lived on after him with renewed vigor.

A note written in the *Carnets* and dated "6/7 novembre, 1847" explains in greater detail Proudhon's aversion to the philosophy of Christ:

> In vain, Christ, the Missionary of resignation, has told us: *Blessed are the poor, blessed are the persecuted, blessed are they who mourn, blessed are they who hunger for justice;* if he has not proved the necessity and the justice of wretchedness; . . . Ah! Christ, in your day you were perhaps a great politician speaking in this way to your flock; but you lacked logic, you contradicted your own words in justifying tears and poverty by persecution and injustice.[24]

Then, in words that bear a striking resemblance to those of "Le Reniement," he adds:

> *As for me, I deny you* [my italics] and I shall burn your Gospel, for neither you nor your Gospel represent humanity; neither you nor your Gospel are eternal. I rebel, in my thoughts, against your words; as I shall rebel against the society which you have made, as soon as I have enough strength.

The passage constitutes the very theme of "Le Reniement de Saint Pierre" and could even have been the subject of a conversation between Bandelaire and Proudhon, for, as the philosopher Théodore Ruyssen points out, "what Proudhon wrote for himself, reflections on the events of the day, work projects, lists of readings to undertake, etc., he would say or write for the use of the public as well" (*POC*, XV:8).

On April 1, 1850, while Proudhon was serving his prison term in the Conciergerie,[25] he returns to the subject of Christ's role as redeemer of mankind and asserts with somewhat more restraint: "Posterity will perhaps find that the Redeemer of the world, in shedding his blood for us on the cross, has done us more harm than good." In the eyes of Proudhon, who scorned all "utopistes" (and in this category he included not only Saint-Simon, Lamennais, Fourier, and Leroux, but Karl Marx as well), Christ was "the greatest of utopians, author of a social and religious utopia." In his judgment, only action that seeks to bring about positive social reform is worthy of man's endeavors.

And so in his *Carnets* of 1850 he summarized, as it were, the goal of all his efforts: "Since February especially I have been trying to push socialism into the path of reforms, or rather of practical and positive realities; I have not ceased to combat Utopia in all its forms, sentimental, political, economic, and theosophical."[26]

Baudelaire's poem was in a sense a comparable endeavor. It too was a condemnation of a "utopiste" who eschewed active, positive reform and who offered only a weak palliative as a remedy for suffering and injustice. Like Proudhon, Baudelaire could only scorn those for whom "action is not the sister of the dream." To interpret the French word *action* as "reality," as a number of critics have done, seems quite unnecessary, for Proudhon and Baudelaire at this point strongly believed that only when accompanied by action could the Utopian dreams of reformers be made reality.

"Le Reniement de Saint Pierre" is not the only poem of *Les Fleurs du Mal* which reveals the influence of Baudelaire's association with Proudhon. Though less powerful and gripping, "Abel et Caïn" and "Les Litanies de Satan," which with "Le Reniement" constitute the section entitled *Révolte,* are equally typical of Baudelaire's and Proudhon's religious and social ideas during the Second Republic.

In "Abel et Caïn," Baudelaire has changed the original roles of the two brothers, just as he has changed the usual order in which their names have appeared since biblical times. Abel represents the bourgeoisie—rich, comfortable, and self-satisfied; Cain, the proletariat—starving, homeless, and desperately struggling to exist. This transformation was far from new. In fact, Cain, like Prometheus and Satan, was being frequently used in English, French, and German Romantic literature to typify Man's rebellion against divine injustice.

About 1850, as scholars have pointed out, inspired by social thinkers and reformers—not the least of whom was Proudhon—the myth came to serve as an allegory of the struggle between classes and of the growing demand for social and economic justice. It is this sentiment that the poet expresses in "Abel et Caïn," and it may well be that his interest in Proudhon's social, religious, and economic ideas did much to encourage both his choice of subject and his treatment.

Jacques Crépet was the first to cite a significant passage, taken from an article by Louis Goodall that appeared in the *Figaro* in 1856, which characterized the evolution of the figures of Cain and Abel in the literature of his day.

> Abel, the earliest type of the good young man, . . . was the first representative of the School of Good Sense, as he was the first bourgeois.
>
> And Cain, the ferocious Cain,—Cain the rebel, Cain the fratricide,—at the same time that his brother was founding the school of wisdom, of moderation and of good sense, was creating that of moral insurrection, of wild fantasy, of rebellion carried to its bitter end, and of an out and out Romanticism.
>
> Yes indeed, Cain was the first romantic, and the precursor of Shakespearean tragedy, of Byronic drama, and of the Hugolian theater.[27]

In Baudelaire's poem, Cain is not so much the ferocious Romantic as he is an abject creature living like a cold and hungry animal (the reader is reminded of the poet's description of the factory workers in his essay on Dupont). In the concluding section Baudelaire, reminding Cain that his task is still incomplete and that the plowshare ("le fer") of the prospering Abel will be conquered by the pike of the long-suffering Cain, utters a sharp command that has all the force of a battle cry:

> Race of Cain, ascend to heaven
> And cast down God upon the earth!

Shocking though the charge may be, it is no more so than the poet's denial of Christ in "Le Reniement," and it is a logical conclusion to Proudhon's celebrated observation that "God is evil" ("Dieu, c'est le mal"). Antoine Adam and Claude Pichois agree that the poem belongs to the period 1848–52, but whereas Pichois sees a metaphysical element in the highly charged last lines (*OC,* I:1082), Adam insists that "it is a call to a revolt that is *not metaphysical in the slightest*" (my italics).[28] To me, at least, Adam's observation seems incontrovertible, for if Cain and Abel represent the opposing classes in the social and economic struggle of 1848, God obviously represents the monstrous tyranny imposed on the poor by a greedy, heartless society.

"Les Litanies de Satan," an early poem dating perhaps from the same period as "Le Reniement" and "Abel et Caïn," owes much to traditional Romanticism, though Proudhon's influence was more than likely responsible for its inspiration. The Satan of the poem is not the Satan of the two postulations or the Satan whom Baudelaire in his letter to Flaubert described as "that evil force exterior to man" which explains some of his sudden acts and thoughts (*Corr.,* II:53). And it is not the Satan to whom, around 1846, a group of young men paid worship each Sunday, reciting verses and composing invocations in his honor.[29] Baudelaire apparently was not a member of such a group, though he must certainly have been interested in their activities and may even have conceived the form of his poem as a result of his knowledge of their rituals—in this case the litany based on the liturgy of the "miserere."

This is rather the Satan of the Romanticists, who, according to Mario Praz, modeled their protagonist on the Lucifer of Milton—a Lucifer "majestic though in ruins," a fallen angel who remembered Paradise and whose sad and tragic beauty recalled his former grandeur.[30] It is the Satan admired alike by English, German, and French Romanticists—a Satan who was to become one of the most important ancestors of the Romantic hero.

Baudelaire possibly knew of Shelley's admiration for Milton's Satan presented in his *Defense of Poetry,* which—though written in 1821—remained unpublished until 1840. "Nothing can exceed the energy and magnificence of the character of Satan as expressed in *Paradise Lost,*" Shelley had written. "It is a mistake to suppose that he could ever have been intended for the

popular personification of evil." And the English poet even went
on to maintain the moral superiority of Satan over God.[31]

If, however, Baudelaire was unaware of Shelley's panegyric,
he could hardly have failed to note Chateaubriand's pro-
nouncement in *Le Génie du Christianisme* that Satan was "one
of the most sublime and pathetic conceptions ever to have been
conceived by the mind of a poet."[32] Baudelaire's own definition
of virile beauty shows to what extent he had accepted the Miltonic conception of Satan as affirmed by the author of *René* and
Atala. After citing the characteristics of what he called "mon
beau" in his *Journaux intimes*, he adds, "it would be hard not to
conclude that the most perfect type of virile beauty is *Satan*—in
the manner of Milton" (*OC*, I:658).

Baudelaire must also have been struck by the many Romantic
works, both by major and minor writers—particularly those of
George Sand—in which Satan, like Cain, assumes a Promethean
aspect or becomes a symbol of heroic energy—a symbol of the
revolt of a whole Romantic generation against divine or earthly
injustice. In this aspect "Les Litanies de Satan" conforms to the
revolutionary sentiment of both Proudhon and Baudelaire in
1848: God is evil; Christ has failed in his mission; Satan remains
as the one who, in Baudelaire's poem, having endured tragic defeat in proud silence, becomes for suffering humanity, "the
familiar healer of human anguish, . . . who to console frail
mankind in his torment," has offered him the means with which
to revolt against the oppressor ("has taught us to mix sulphur
and saltpeter").

There can be little doubt. "Les Litanies de Satan," like the
other two poems of *Révolte* in *Les Fleurs du Mal*, is an expression of that same revolutionary sentiment which incited him between 1848–51 and which in part he was to lose.

After the coup d'état of December 2, 1851, Baudelaire, as we
have seen, was left in a state of complete disillusionment—
"physically depoliticized," as he wrote Ancelle on March 5, 1852,
too disgusted even to bother to vote. Contrary to his own words,
however, he never fully succeeded in renouncing his interest in
politics. On May 16, 1859, he wrote to Nadar, "I have con-

vinced myself twenty times that I was no longer interested in politics, but for every serious question, I am again seized by curiosity and passion" (*Corr.*, I:578).

And as late as January 1862 he wrote to Sainte-Beuve commenting on the eminent critic's plan to reform the French Academy, "Your Utopia has given me new pride. I too had built a Utopia and sought reform—is it the *remains of the revolutionary spirit* [my italics] that prompted me, as it also did long ago, to make plans for a constitution?" (*Corr.*, II:220).

Baudelaire's letters from Brussels are filled with references that reveal his fascination with political events both in Belgium and elsewhere. Perhaps it was "the remains of [his] revolutionary spirit" that caused him to write Ancelle on July 14, 1864, in regard to "the extraordinary situation in which the Chamber and Ministry found themselves": "I was hoping for gunfire and barricades. But these people are too stupid to fight for ideas" (*Corr.*, II:388).

Nor did Baudelaire ever lose interest in Proudhon's ideas, despite his rejection of socialism in favor of the philosophies of Poe and de Maistre, who, he wrote in his *Journaux intimes,* "taught me to think" (*OC,* I:669). His feelings toward the social reformer were somewhat ambivalent, as we have seen, for, like Théophile Thoré, he found the peasant manners and appearance of Proudhon too crude to suit his aristocratic taste. Physically and spiritually, Proudhon was anything but the dandy that Baudelaire so much admired. Wearing his broad-brimmed hat made of white rabbit-skin that, according to Champfleury, "resembled a pale sun or a large Brie cheese," Proudhon sometimes cut a rather comic figure that must have been embarrassing at times to his fastidious friends.[33]

Moreover, Proudhon's utilitarian conception of art was equally distasteful to Baudelaire, as Sainte-Beuve well realized. In his reply to the poet, who had written from Brussels commenting on the articles that Sainte-Beuve had devoted to the reformer, the critic admitted almost apologetically,

Proudhon . . . must have been the most antipathetic of men to you. All these socialists and political philosophers want nothing from literature except an institution or a tool with which to teach people morality. It is the viewpoint the most opposed to ours, born as we were in a period of happy and brilliant fantasy, of free imagination, more and more nourished in the gardens of Alcinous. [*PLB*, p. 346]

Sainte-Beuve was quite right. Baudelaire detested Proudhon's literary and aesthetic tastes. Yet, despite this aversion, he did not alter his opinion of the reformer's intelligence, particularly in matters pertaining to political economy. And so, even as late as 1865, he defended Proudhon's ideas of economics as "eminently respectable," was highly amused at the thought of Proudhon's marginal notes made on a copy of Hugo's *Les Misérables* ("logic correcting the absence of logic"), and was incensed by the "disgusting riot" that forced Proudhon to leave Belgium as a result of a public too obtuse to understand the irony of his comment about the annexation of Belgium by Napoleon III.

Though Baudelaire refers on several occasions to Proudhon in his *Pauvre Belgique,* his notes are too terse and too vague to do more than alert the reader to his continuing interest in the socialist philosopher. However, Baudelaire was obviously inspired by him to write his puzzling prose poem "Assommons les pauvres," for at the conclusion of the manuscript copy appear the words, "What do you think about it, citizen Proudhon?"

Baudelaire begins the prose poem, as we have noted, with a reference to the period sixteen or seventeen years earlier when, after immersing himself in the socialist literature of the day, he found himself stupefied by all the conflicting theories that he had read. Leaving his room and going out in search of fresh air and refreshments, he encountered at the door of a cabaret a beggar, who with an unforgettably piteous expression in his eyes held out his hat begging for alms. Suddenly, at that same moment, Baudelaire heard in his ear the voice of his "good Demon" whispering, "He alone is the equal of another who proves it, and he alone is worthy of liberty who knows how to conquer it" (*OC*, I:358).

Immediately, Baudelaire fell upon the beggar, beating him unmercifully until the poor wretch, transformed by anger and by the injustice of his treatment, turned upon his persecutor and beat him in even worse fashion. "By my energetic medication," Baudelaire adds, "I had restored in him pride and life."

Thereupon, rising to his feet, he announced to the beggar, "Monsieur, *you are my equal!* do me the honor of sharing my purse with me; and remember, if you are really philanthropic, you must apply to all your confrères, when they ask you for alms, the theory that I have had the *pain* of trying on your back. He [the beggar] swore that he had understood my theory and that he would follow my advice" (*OC,* I:359).

Needless to say, the prose poem was rejected for publication and ever since has been subjected to various interpretations. Although some critics have seen in the apostrophe "What do you think of it, Proudhon?" a repudiation of Proudhon's theories, it should be noted that Baudelaire, like the reformer, is rejecting pity and Christian charity as ineffectual and demanding. Moreover, the description of the "*good* Demon" as "un grand affirmateur," "a Demon of *action,* a Demon of combat" recalls the "positive action" preached by Proudhon as well as the poet's wish expressed in "Le Reniement de Saint Pierre" that "action" be "the sister of the dream." Certainly Proudhon, believing as he did in the dignity of the individual, would have approved Baudelaire's view, "He alone is the equal of another who proves it, and he alone is worthy of liberty who knows how to conquer it."

To me, the prose poem is obviously intended as irony directed at the naiveté of the same Utopian humanitarians, described by Baudelaire, who preach "the art of making people happy, wise, and rich in twenty-four hours . . . those who advise the poor to become slaves or convince them they are all dethroned kings." Neither passivity nor willingness to accept alms is the cure for the poor and humble, but rather *action*—the need to stand up for one's rights, to fight, if necessary, as the Demon of action and combat had suggested. Then only will the oppressed become the equal of the oppressor and regain the dignity that has been taken from him. The victim's conviction of the validity of the theory and his promise to carry it out on others under similar circumstances supports the belief that the poem is not so much an attack on Proudhon as a way of lending approval to the theories of the social reformer by going even further than he.

To say, as some do, that the germ of the poem is found in the following passage that appears in *Le Peintre de la vie moderne* is to confuse the issue: "It is philosophy (I mean sound philosophy), it is religion which commands us to care for our parents when they are poor and infirm. Nature (which is nothing more than the voice of our self-interest) orders us to beat them" (*OC*, II:715). Here Baudelaire is speaking about original sin, about the evil in *natural* man which leads him to commit crimes and to destroy those whom religion teaches him to love. A few lines later the poet specifies that he is talking about "Nature as a bad counselor in moral matters, and about Reason as true redeemer and reformer...."

Even more invalid is the claim that the poem's idea lies in a letter to Nadar in which Baudelaire shamefacedly confesses that he had beaten a Belgian and "what was even more monstrous" that he was "completely in the wrong" in so doing. Moreover, in the same letter the poet explains that, the spirit of justice *regaining* the upper hand [my italics], he hurried after the man to make his excuses, but was unable to find him (*Corr.*, II:401).

Quite the opposite is true in "Assommons les pauvres." Prompted by the *Reason* of his "*good* Demon," Baudelaire beats his victim not through any evil impulse or through natural perversity but out of his intention to restore the man's dignity and self-pride. In other words, he acts as the beggar's benefactor rather than as his persecutor, and what is more, his victim understands and agrees to adopt the theory.

If a germ for the story must be found, it seems rather to lie in a notation that appears in the *Journaux intimes*.

When a man gets into the habit of laziness, of day-dreaming, of complete idleness to the extent of constantly postponing something important until the next day, if another man should wake him in the morning with a whip and beat him mercilessly until, not being able to work with pleasure, the latter worked out of fear, wouldn't that man with the whip be his *true friend,* his *benefactor* [my italics]? . . .

Likewise in *politics,* the real saint is he who whips and kills the people for the *good of the people* [my italics]. [*OC,* I:655]

Baudelaire's tendency to use extravagant language to astonish or even scandalize the reader is as noticeable here as in the prose poem, but it must be admitted that the shock value in both cases commands attention, whether or not one accepts the author's viewpoint.

Baudelaire must have decided to abandon the first title he had chosen for his prose poem. Originally, he had intended to call it "Le Paradoxe de l'aumône," but his love for the hyperbolic and for the "titre pétard" led him to substitute the title "Assommons les pauvres." The irony of both title and narration was too strong for the public taste, however, for the poem was rejected for publication and the apostrophe to Proudhon was later omitted either by Baudelaire himself or by his editors.

Had he read the prose poem, Proudhon would probably have understood it, if not approved of it. Like Baudelaire, Proudhon was fond—too fond—of the exaggerated but striking statement ("God is evil"; "property is theft") and much of the misunderstanding of his work came, as in the case of the poet, from this very fact.

Proudhon would surely have agreed that forceful action was required to restore liberty and equality to all. But where Proudhon would have blamed the existing system for the inequities, Baudelaire, under the influence of de Maistre and Poe, puts the blame on the individual himself. He almost seems to be saying, like Shakespeare's Cassius, "The fault . . . is not in our stars, But in ourselves, that we are underlings." That this belief applied not only to the moral progress of the individual but to the destiny of a nation seems to be suggested in a notation in his *Journaux intimes.*

The great glory of Napoleon III will have been to prove that the first one who comes along can govern a great nation by taking over the telegraph and the national press.

Those who believe that such things can be accomplished *without the permission of the people* and those who believe that glory can only be based on virtue are *idiots*.

Dictators are the *servants of the people*—nothing more—a damnably stupid role besides—and glory is the result of conformity of a mind with national *stupidity* [my italics]. [*OC,* I:692]

Unfortunately Baudelaire's remedy for social injustice seems as impractical and futile as was the February revolution of 1848, which Proudhon complained had been "started without an idea." But Baudelaire made no pretense of being consistent in his thinking, especially in politics. Perhaps that is why he wrote in his *Journaux intimes* under the heading *POLITICS,* "I don't have any convictions, as people of my century understand them, because I don't have any ambition. I haven't any basis for convictions. . . . However, I do have some convictions, in a more elevated sense which can not be understood by the people of my time" (*OC,* I:680).

4

Baudelaire and the Literary World

AS MIGHT BE EXPECTED, Baudelaire was nowhere more involved than he was in the literary world of his age. In mingling with poets, critics, journalists, and novelists of various schools and in experimenting with many divergent philosophies, he finally evolved and perfected, after a certain amount of groping and experimentation, the aesthetic ideas which had first appeared for the most part in embryonic form in his *Salon de 1846:* the importance of the imagination, modernity, correspondences, and supernaturalism. During the course of his career he came to know almost every important writer of his day and to find in his discussions with them, as well as in his omnivorous reading, the stimulus which helped to energize and sharpen his own thinking.

Before being sent on the long sea voyage by his family, Baudelaire's closest associates were his fellow students at the Pension Bailly. At the pension he became a member of the so-called Norman School formed by his good friend Le Vavasseur and made up of a few amateur poets (Prarond, Buisson, Chennevières, Dozon), all of whom were strongly influenced by the Romantic School and by Gautier and Sainte-Beuve in particular.

With the members of the Norman School Baudelaire planned to collaborate on a book of verse, but quietly decided at the last moment to withdraw his contribution rather than submit it to the critical suggestions of his colleagues. He also collaborated with Prarond on a verse drama, *Idéolus,* whose manuscript, left unfinished, was preserved by his friend and collaborator. Even after his return in 1844 to Abbeville, where he devoted his life to the publication of historical and archeological works, Prarond remained on friendly terms with Baudelaire. One of the last letters dictated by the ill poet, before he lost his power of speech, thanked his former companion for sending him a copy of his then unpublished *Airs de flûte sur des motifs graves,* which contained a poem dedicated to the author of *Les Fleurs du Mal.*

LOUIS MÉNARD AND THÉODORE DE BANVILLE

After his return to Paris from his sea voyage in 1842, Baudelaire saw less of his old school friends and formed a closer relationship with Louis Ménard and Théodore de Banville. In 1844 Ménard, "l'Helléniste du Parnasse" as he was later called, published a verse play called *Prométhée délivré* under the pen name of Louis de Senneville. Baudelaire's devastating and amusing review of the play in *Le Corsaire-Satan* on February 3, 1846, quickly put an end to their friendship. Eleven years later Ménard evened the score by writing a malicious review of *Les Fleurs du Mal* in which he described its author as an awkward boy, suffering from arrested development and trying to pass himself off as a devil with forked feet.

Banville, two years younger than Baudelaire, had established his reputation as a virtuoso poet at the age of nineteen with the publication of *Les Cariatides* in 1842. Four years later he published *Les Stalactites,* which, being more truly poetic than *Les Cariatides,* anticipated the poetry of the Parnasse. Throughout his life he remained a warm friend and admirer of Baudelaire except for a brief estrangement around 1859 caused by the latter's jealousy over the actress Marie Daubrun.

Though Banville was obviously one of those at whom Baudelaire scoffed in his essay *L'Ecole païenne,* elsewhere, especially in his essay on the poet, he spoke of him with only the highest praise. Generally speaking, Baudelaire and Banville were miles apart both in the mood and treatment of their poetry. The poet-critic was well aware that his brilliant young friend revealed none of that "essentially demonic tendency" which, he maintained, characterized "modern art" and that, unlike Maturin, Byron, Poe, and himself, he had no interest in delineating the "satanic side of man"... "the latent Lucifer hidden in every human heart" (OC, II:168).

Yet Baudelaire recognized certain traits in Banville which he not only prized but which he himself shared to a degree—and may even have envied. That his admiration was sincere is undeniable for Banville was one of those whom he continued to praise to the end of his life both in his correspondence and in his literary criticism. "Banville's poetry," he wrote in his essay, first published in 1861, "represents the beautiful hours of life, those hours when one feels happy to think and to be alive" (OC, II:163). Though Baudelaire's own personal idea of beauty ("mon beau"), as stated in his Journaux intimes, was closely associated with melancholy and sorrow, he did not deny in that same definition that beauty could also have "Joy" as one of its ornaments—an ornament that he considered somewhat commonplace, however (OC, II:657). He even praised his idol Delacroix for painting "the soul in its beautiful hours" (OC, II:637).

One of the qualities that Baudelaire most respected in Banville was what he called his "spiritual vitality" (my italics). A comment in his Journaux intimes seems both to explain and confirm what he meant by "spiritual," a quality which, it should be added, was one of the most important elements of his aesthetics: "Théodore de Banville is not exactly materialistic; he is luminous. His poetry represents the happy hours" (OC, II:656). Perhaps no better description could be made of Baudelaire's own exultant "Elévation."

But what Baudelaire and Banville had most in common was their tendency to seek in the past or even in dreams the happiness that had once been theirs. "Every lyric poet, by virtue of his nature, inevitably effects a return to the lost Eden," Baudelaire wrote in his essay (OC, II:165). Such poems as "Moesta et errabunda," "Le Balcon," "La Chevelure," "Un Fantôme," among many others, show how well the definition applies to his own work.

Baudelaire returns in a somewhat different way to this same theme in the final paragraph of his essay: "His [Banville's] poetry is not only regret and nostalgia for the Paradisiac state, but even a very deliberate return to it. From this point of view we can then consider him an original writer of the bravest type" (*OC,* II:168). The observation applies as much to himself as to Banville—perhaps even more so—for much of Baudelaire's verse as well as his whole life was an attempt to refind that paradisiac state which continued to haunt him awake or in dreams. In both Banville and Baudelaire that quest accounts for some of their most beautiful poems.

After Baudelaire's death in 1867, it was Banville and Asselineau who pronounced the moving funeral orations, and later the two friends collaborated in preparing the posthumous edition of the poet's works that appeared between 1868 and 1870.

THÉOPHILE GAUTIER

In the office of *L'Artiste,* a journal which had been taken over by Arsène Houssaye in 1844, Baudelaire renewed his acquaintance with other writers whom he had first met and known somewhat casually in earlier years: among them Gautier, Nerval, and Esquiros. Of the three, he occasionally saw Gautier at Madame Sabatier's famous Sunday dinners, where the latter was known for his earthy humor and the license of his conversation. Gautier's bawdy and often obscene letters to "la Présidente," as he called her, contrast sharply with the deferential, almost timid letters that Baudelaire wrote to his charming hostess during that same period.

Baudelaire was always to admire the perfection of form that marked the work of Gautier, and it was to him, "au poëte impeccable, au parfait magicien ès lettres françaises," that he was to dedicate *Les Fleurs du Mal.* In his essay of 1859 on Gautier he showed himself still dazzled by the "evocative magic" of the writer's masterful handling of words. It is true that on several occasions he referred somewhat critically to the author of *Emaux et Camées.* His letter to Hugo (September 1859) asking for a preface to his brochure on Gautier has often been cited as proof of his insincerity. Though he admitted "confidentielle-ment" that he was aware of the "lacunae of that astonishing mind," which he claimed he had deliberately overlooked in his essay ("I didn't lie, I hedged, I dissimulated"), he still uses the adjective "astonishing" in speaking of Gautier's intelligence (*Corr.*, I:597). His comment may have been prompted in part by his desire to win Hugo's favor and to obtain a letter-preface for his brochure. Yet there seems no more reason to doubt the hon-esty of his praise for Gautier, despite certain reservations he may have had, than to doubt his praise of Banville, whom he had mocked in his essay *L'Ecole païenne* and with whom he often disagreed.

Moreover, Gautier is described as "the most detached as well as the greatest of contemporary poets" in the preface to As-selineau's *La Double vie*, which had been inspired and corrected by Baudelaire and which Jacques Crépet maintains is a veritable Baudelairean manifesto (*OC*, II:1124). And throughout his cor-respondence, Baudelaire speaks of Gautier in the most flattering terms. Two of his letters in particular show the extent of his esteem. Writing to his mother in 1857, he expresses the certainty that his own poetry would some day take its place beside the best poems of Hugo, Gautier, and Byron (*Corr.*, I:411), and in his well-known letter of 1866 to Ancelle (*Corr.*, II:611) he included the name of Gautier among those whom he considered the truly great among his contemporaries. It is also significant that Baudelaire chose Gautier as the subject of one of the five lectures that he delivered in Brussels.

Undoubtedly Baudelaire was aware of certain limitations in Gautier's poetry, in particular the absence of a spiritual element, which was assuming more and more importance in his own aesthetics. We have only to contrast Baudelaire's definition of poetry found in his "Puisque Réalisme il y a" ("Poetry is what is most real, what is completely true only in *another* world" (*OC*, II:59) with Gautier's well-known comment, made to the Gon-courts: "I am a man for whom the visible world exists."[1]

Baudelaire must also have missed in Gautier's poetry the

more profound emotions, which appear only sporadically in his work. Ernest Raynaud has commented that, whereas Gautier remained a spectator, Baudelaire was a seer who sought the meaning and the "raison d'être" that lie beneath the surface of things.[2]

Yet despite these important differences, the two poets shared many ideas. Both were hostile to the idea of progress, both were pessimistic in their attitude toward life. "Art is what consoles us most for living," Gautier wrote in his preface to *Albertus* (1832), and Baudelaire could not have expressed it more succinctly. Both dedicated their lives to the creation of literature and made of it the sole purpose of life as well as its only real value.

Moreover, Gautier and Baudelaire alike disdained those artists and poets who were guided by nature alone, who were imitators rather than creators. When in his *Salon de 1846* Baudelaire affirmed that art must be "the sincere expression of [the artist's] temperament" (*OC*, II:419) or when in 1859 he maintained that "the true artist, the true poet, should only paint in accord with what he sees and feels" (*OC*, II:620), he was saying more or less what Gautier had written in his Salons of 1839 and 1841 in regard to the artist's "inner vision." Artists and poets who, for him as for Baudelaire, were alike in all but their choice of medium, carried within themselves, he wrote, their own little world from which they drew the thought and form of their work ("When M. Delacroix paints a picture, he looks within himself rather than looking out the window").[3]

The idea was, of course, not unique; others had expressed more or less the same belief, including Gautier's and Nerval's close friend Heinrich Heine (Salon of 1831), whom Baudelaire quotes in his *Salon de 1846:* "'In artistic matters I am a supernaturalist. I believe that the artist can not find all his forms in nature, but that the most remarkable are revealed to him in his soul...'" (*OC*, II:432).

It is somewhat surprising that Baudelaire saw in Gautier a decipherer and translator of divine hieroglyphics possessing an "immense, innate understanding of universal correspondences and symbols, that repertory of metaphor" (*OC*, II:117). Yet

Gautier was not entirely lacking in mystical qualities, as is evident in his statement that "spirit is everything, matter exists only in appearance; the universe is perhaps only God's dream or an irradiation of the Word in the vastness of the cosmos."[4] Moreover, as Joanna Richardson has pointed out in her biography of the poet, Gautier was one of the first to use correspondences freely, particularly the correspondences between color and music. "They are most often found," she claims, "when, his emotions stirred, his technical knowledge least strong, Gautier writes about music."[5]

The similarity of many of these ideas with those of Baudelaire and other men of his time is far from surprising, for, as has been already mentioned, literary and artistic problems were constantly being discussed—in cénacles, in cafés, in almost any place where artists and men of letters gathered. No doubt Baudelaire's and Gautier's agreement on many of these problems did much to strengthen the younger poet's beliefs and to increase his veneration of his elder.

Gautier, like his disciple, believed that poetry could be inspired by the simplest things in life: "Poetry isn't here any more than it is there, it is in us ... daughter of heaven as she is, she is not disdainful of the most human things. ... Poetry is everywhere."[6] Baudelaire was to go further and insist that poetry was to be found even in ugliness and evil, and to maintain that in *Les Fleurs du Mal* he had turned "mud" into gold.

But what seems to have most impressed Baudelaire, outside of the technical perfection of the elder poet's verse, was Gautier's obsession with death. As Georges Poulet has suggested, Gautier was haunted by the thought of death. Death was for him "a personal anguish," not the artificial theme that the Romantic poets held so dear to their hearts. Gautier's visual power, according to Poulet, only increased for him the horror of death, for in everything he saw and enjoyed he was conscious not only of its present beauty but of its inevitable ruination and of the decay that time would inexorably bring in its wake.[7]

Baudelaire liked *La Comédie de la mort* (in particular the "prodigious symphony" called "Ténèbres," so much like "a symphony of Beethoven"), *Albertus,* and certain poems in *España.* In his essay he notes how Gautier's melancholy, "more positive and more sensual" than that of Chateaubriand, "bordering at times on the sadness of the ancients," often revealed "the giddy sensation and the horror of nothingness" (*OC,* II:125–26). Baudelaire himself was often aware of this sensation of nothingness, but, unlike Gautier, his despair was at times so great that death and nothingness lost for him their horror and became a welcome escape from the even greater horror of life itself. In fact, his poem "Le Goût du néant" expresses this very desire for annihilation—for nothingness.

Scholars have pointed out echoes of Gautier's imagery in the poetry of Baudelaire—a matter of minor significance, it would seem, in the oeuvres of any poet or, for that matter, of any artist. Of far greater importance is the fact that Baudelaire was inspired poetically and aesthetically by his association with Gautier and that he was able to transform whatever inspiration he gained from him into something both more profound and infinitely more moving.

After Baudelaire's death, Gautier, who according to Asselineau felt for his confrere an affection "magistrale et quasi paternelle," wrote the necrological article that appeared in *Le Moniteur universel.*[8] He was also to write the long influential study which, after its publication in *L'Univers illustré* in 1868, served as the introduction to the third edition of *Les Fleurs du Mal,* published that same year by Michel Lévy frères under the editorship of Asselineau and Banville.

GÉRARD DE NERVAL

Less is known about Baudelaire's relationship to Gautier's close friend Gérard de Nerval, though it is evident from the few facts available that the author of *Les Fleurs du Mal* held him in high esteem, especially after 1855. Only two of Baudelaire's letters to Gérard exist—both of them short notes requesting tickets for Nerval's play *Chariot d'enfant,* which had been done in collaboration with Méry and opened at the Odéon on May 13, 1850.

Baudelaire seems to have followed Gérard's literary production with much interest. In his second note to Nerval in 1850, requesting tickets for his friend and future publisher Poulet-Malassis, he also asked for a copy of an extract from the *Nuits de Ramazan,* which had been appearing daily in *Le National* (March 7 to May 9, 1850). His own poem "Un Voyage à Cythère" was inspired in part by the author of "Les Chiméres." An autograph copy of the poem bears a dedication to Nerval with a note explaining that the "point de départ" had been found in some lines written by the eccentric poet. Baudelaire was referring to an article that Nerval had published in *L'Artiste* in 1844 in which he told of seeing the shores of "l'antique Cythère" during a Mediterranean voyage. As the boat approached the island, the poet thought he saw a small monument resembling the statute of some "protective deity." But as the boat drew closer to shore, he discovered that what he had presumed to be a statue was really a three-branched gibbet from which was hanging a rotting corpse. Around these lines Baudelaire built a sort of moral allegory in which, with its gruesome description of the decaying cadaver, he surpasses Villon in evoking the horror of death.

When "Un Voyage à Cythère" was published in 1855, there was no mention of Nerval, perhaps because the gentle pagan poet objected to the Jansenist interpretation that Baudelaire had given the spectacle of the hanged man, who, in the poem, is supposed to have died in "expiation for the infamous cult (infâmes cultes) and for the sins which had denied him a grave."

Nerval rejected Baudelaire's inference that these "infâmes cultes" were responsible for transforming the once beautiful island into a barren, rocky desert. That much is clear from a letter sent by Baudelaire to Gautier in 1852: "The *incorrigible* Gérard claims, on the contrary, that it was for having abandoned 'le bon culte' that Cythera was reduced to that state" (*Corr.,* I:180). It may be that Nerval was so disturbed at Baudelaire's contempt for Venus and for his beloved pagan civilizations that the author of *Les Fleurs du Mal* thought it best to omit the dedication as well as his explanation of the source of his inspiration.

Nerval's knowledge of music, as we have seen, as well as of German literature may have done much to broaden Baudelaire's aesthetic horizons. His translation of Goethe's *Faust* (1826–27), his enthusiasm for *Les Contes fantastiques* of Hoffmann, and his translation of Heine's poems (1848) further stimulated Baudelaire's admiration for the German writers. Moreover, Nerval's friendship with Liszt and his affinity for Wagner, based on their common belief in the alliance of music and poetry, surely communicated themselves to the author of *Les Fleurs du Mal*, as has been noted in a previous chapter. He may even have confessed to Baudelaire, as he did to Doctor Blanche in 1854, that his theories, "which I don't often expound, are related to those of Richard Wagner."⁹

After Nerval's tragic death on January 26, 1855, Baudelaire seems to have viewed him with a profound sympathy bordering on his feeling for Poe. In 1856, a year after it was discovered that the gentle, despairing writer had hanged himself one freezing January morning on a dark and desolate street known as the rue de la Vieille-Lanterne, Baudelaire defended his suicide in his essay on Poe and described him as "a writer, admirably honest, highly intelligent, who was always lucid" (*OC,* II:306). A few years later in his essay on Hégésippe Moreau, in which he compared and contrasted Nerval with Poe, he referred to him as "endowed with a brilliant, active, luminous mind, quick to learn" (*OC,* II:156).

It is rather disconcerting to note that Baudelaire thought of Nerval as only a writer of prose. "Gérard wrote many books, travel books or short stories, all marked by good taste," he wrote in his essay on Moreau—one of the very few references he makes to the writer's work. "Both Poe and Gérard," he adds, "were, in spite of their faults, excellent men of letters in the broadest and most delicate meaning of the word, bowing humbly to the inevitable law, working, it is true, when they chose and as they pleased, in accordance with a more or less mysterious method, but active, industrious, making use of their dreams or their meditations; in short, pursuing their professions with zest" (*OC,* II:157).

Baudelaire's failure to mention the poems of Nerval is strange, since their density, mystery, musicality, and especially their suggestive power were all qualities which he valued. Moreover, Nerval's poetry exemplified—perhaps too much so for Baudelaire's taste—some of his most important aesthetic ideas. In his essay on Wagner (1861), Baudelaire insists on the creative role of the reader: "In music, as in painting and even in literature, which is nevertheless the most concrete of the arts, there is always a lacuna that is filled by the imagination of the listener" (OC, II:781–82). And in his essay on Victor Hugo (1861) he praises the "*indispensable obscurity*" with which the exiled poet expressed "that which is obscure and vaguely revealed" (OC, II:132).

Both comments apply strikingly to the poetry of Nerval as well as to a few of Baudelaire's own poems, for example, "Harmonie du soir" or "Spleen" ("Quand le ciel bas et lourd . . ."). In both, images are no longer peripheral but become the poem itself and suggest rather than describe the author's "état d'âme." As a result, the reader is forced to enter the creative process and determine for himself the author's meaning or intention.

Perhaps Baudelaire found the obscurity of Nerval's verse too dense and the "lacunae" too great to allow for the reader's participation. In his own poetry, imagery is always rooted in solid reality and, though the element of obscurity is present, it is seldom, if ever, impenetrable. Nerval's symbols, on the contrary, dissociated and unexplained, are drawn from history, legend, myth, personal memories, and past experiences, actual and imaginary, and their heterogeneity and absence of transitions make the poems in question hermetic, except to the informed reader who knows something of the author's real and vicarious experiences.

Whatever the case, Baudelaire seems not to have realized the relationship that exists between his own poems that anticipate Symbolism and those of Nerval which carry to the furthest limits some of the very ideas that the Symbolists were to borrow from Baudelaire.

That Baudelaire in his last years came to associate his own

mental and physical condition with that of the deranged poet is clear in a letter he wrote to Malassis in 1861: "I felt afflicted with an illness like that of Gérard, that is with the fear of no longer being able to think or to write a line" (*Corr.*, II:135–36). And a year later, he may well have been thinking of Nerval when he wrote in his *Journaux intimes:* "Today, January 23, 1862 I have experienced a strange warning. I have felt pass over me the *wind of the wing of madness*" (*OC,* I:668).

LECONTE DE LISLE

According to Baudelaire, Leconte de Lisle was the only poet who could be compared to Gautier. In his essay on the Creole writer (1862), considered one of his finest, the critic was astute enough to realize that the originality of the Parnassian leader lay in his portrayal of the "powerful, crushing forces of nature" and in the "majesty of animals in movement and repose" and at the same time to note that through his interest in the pagan past he was seeking escape from the values of an age that he despised as much as Baudelaire himself.

Baudelaire never changed his mind about Leconte de Lisle's superiority as a poet. In one of his last letters to Ancelle, written from Brussels on February 18, 1866, in which he bitterly characterized the writers of his day as "la racaille moderne" ("modern riffraff"), Leconte de Lisle was one of the nine excluded from his denunciation. In the same letter he reminded Ancelle of the "profound saying of Leconte de Lisle": "All elegists are boors" (*Corr.*, II:611). In his turn, Leconte de Lisle published a favorable review of the 1861 edition of *Les Fleurs du Mal* on December 1, 1861, in the *Revue européenne.*

The two poets, however, were never close. According to Maurice Barrès, the Creole poet did not think very highly of Baudelaire as a person and found the latter's "wish to make an impression" quite "intolerable."[10] His judgment of Baudelaire's talent, on the other hand, was less severe. In her *Leconte de Lisle intime,* Jean Dornis (pseudonym for Mme G. Beer) cites a cryptic note in which the Creole poet summed up his opinion of his admirer: "*Baudelaire:* Very intelligent and original, but with a limited imagination and lacking in inspiration. An art too often clumsy."[11]

In spite of his reservations, however, both about Baudelaire's art and his eccentric behavior, Leconte de Lisle joined in the efforts of his friends to obtain financial aid from the government for the ill and dying poet.

CHAMPFLEURY

As we have seen, Baudelaire and Champfleury first met in the office of a small journal, *Le Corsaire-Satan,* in the 1840s and remained intimate friends until the poet's death in 1867. Champfleury was not long in introducing the young poet to his circle of friends, among them the painters Courbet and Bonvin, and the novelist Murger and his friends, many of whom served as prototypes for the latter's *Scènes de la vie bohème.*

In the 1840s and even in the early years of the Second Empire—despite the aristocratic and spiritual influence of de Maistre and Poe—Baudelaire, as well as Champfleury, remained on good terms with the members of La Bohème, a group of struggling writers and artists who differed greatly from the gay and lighthearted *bousingos* of ten years before. Most of them came from working-class homes (Murger was the son of a concierge, Pierre Dupont the son of a blacksmith in Lyons, and Courbet of a peasant), and many of them were to know only poverty, hunger, and cold. It was Champfleury who in 1846 persuaded Murger to write *La Vie de Bohème,* which was intended to be a realistic novel based on personal experience and observation. Champfleury gave his own, less sentimental picture of Bohemian life in *Les Aventures de Mademoiselle Mariette,* in the first version of which (1847) Baudelaire, as one of the characters, recites his famous sonnet "Les Chats."

Champfleury, Baudelaire, and Manet, like a number of others of their day, had a strong affinity for cats and saw in them the embodiment of their own spiritual and aesthetic natures. Baudelaire with his three poems on cats in *Les Fleurs du Mal* was especially noted for his predilection—a fact that was often ridiculed by a critical and hostile public.

Manet's interest in cats has been attributed in part to Baudelaire's influence. In fact, Bradford Collins sees the inclusion of the cat in Manet's *Luncheon in the Studio* (1868) as one of a number of iconographic symbols which seem to indicate the painting was intended as a homage to the poet, who had died the year before.[12]

In his charming book *Les Chats* (1869), a sort of feline *étude des moeurs,* Champfleury discusses the cat from the standpoint of history, types, and temperament. In a chapter devoted to cat-lovers, he recounts several anecdotes involving Baudelaire's fondness for cats and even includes Morin's etched portrait of Baudelaire seated with arms resting on a table, a cat perched on his shoulder, its body curved so as to follow the outline of the poet's head.

The endpiece of the book is a portrait of Champfleury himself, his hair on either side depicted so as to form cat's ears (a way of identifying himself with the animal), while behind him, crouched on a row of books, a real cat looks sleepily over his shoulder. For the second edition of *Les Chats* (1870), Manet did an etching and aquatint, *Le Chat et les fleurs,* as well as a striking lithograph, *Le Rendez-vous des chats,* that served as a poster to advertise the book.

The friendship between Baudelaire and Champfleury was strengthened by the interest they shared in pantomime, painting, religion, and music. We have seen how the two fought together to gain support for Wagner in France and how, for a short time, Champfleury shared—much to his chagrin a little later—Baudelaire's esteem for Proudhon. Where the two failed to agree was on the question of Realism, though for a while Baudelaire, through the influence of Champfleury, Courbet, and Pierre Dupont, came to be more receptive to the movement. In 1847, the poet wrote a favorable but uninspired review of the three volumes of Champfleury's stories—obviously the result of an attempt to be sympathetic yet objective toward works that he found mediocre. The flat, photographic realism of Champfleury, devoid of imagination, poetry, and beauty, was alien to the poet's temperament.

Champfleury's defense of Realism in his book *Le Réalisme,* one of the first studies of the movement, was more than Baudelaire could bear. In 1855 he began working on "Puisque Réalisme il y a," intended, as we have seen, to show his disapproval of the new movement and of the ideas of Champfleury and Courbet, who in his judgment had succeeded in capturing only external reality. Evidently, it was also to be an affirmation of the transcendental implications of poetry, for it is here that he defines poetry as "what is most real, what is completely true only in *another* world" (*OC*, II:59).

Though Baudelaire had rejected Realism around 1852, his friendship with Champfleury continued. Undoubtedly the latter's fondness for music (he had even thought of adopting it as a career around 1845) as well as his involvement in pantomime and the plastic arts did much to hold them together. Moreover, Champfleury, like Baudelaire and Nerval, was an ardent supporter of E. T. A. Hoffmann. For twenty years, beginning in 1853, he undertook the task of making Hoffmann known in France both as a writer and as a musician. He translated his tales and in his book *Les Excentriques* (1852) invented a musician, Dubois, who, like his prototype Kreisler, served as a spokesman for the author.

Champfleury remained a loyal friend of Baudelaire throughout the life of the poet and helped obtain a government pension for him during his final illness. While in Brussels Baudelaire composed the short poem honoring Daumier which Champfleury had requested for his book *Histoire de la caricature moderne.*

PIERRE DUPONT

During the time that he was associating with the members of Bohemia, Baudelaire, influenced by his young friends and by the social thinkers of the day, turned against the Neo-Classic movement and the School of Art for Art's Sake, for which he had felt a certain sympathy early in his career. Imbued with the social and democratic ideals that inspired the revolution of 1848 and fired by enthusiasm for the ideas of Proudhon, he denounced Neo-Classic art as a sterile and naive pastiche that had divorced itself from contemporary life and had rejected the relative or transitory beauty that for him was an essential ingredient of all great art. In his essay on Pierre Dupont he even went so far as to defend utilitarian art and to approve the social and humanitarian mission of the poet. In fact, as we know, it was Dupont, the patriotic Republican poet and songwriter, exiled in 1851 for his revolutionary songs, who, together with Proudhon, did most to stimulate Baudelaire's interest in utilitarian art and arouse his sympathy for the poor and downtrodden.

Dupont's friendship with Baudelaire dated back to at least 1840, and the two were most closely associated from 1846 to 1851, the period when the author of *Les Fleurs du Mal* was involved in the Socialist movement. Dupont was the son of a workingman in Lyons and had known poverty from early childhood. From him, Baudelaire learned much about the life of the working class and came to realize more fully their misery and suffering. In the notice which he wrote as a preface for the *Chants et Chansons* (1851) of Dupont, the poet-critic recalled the emotion that he had felt on hearing for the first time *Le Chant des ouvriers* (1846)—"that admirable cry of pain and melancholy" (*OC,* II:31).

Baudelaire's second essay on Dupont in 1861 was less fervent, for he had long since rejected the idea of utilitarian art. Yet he did not repudiate his belief that Dupont was a writer of moving songs who had made popular poetry acceptable and who possessed "that natural aristocracy of minds which owe infinitely more to nature than to art" (*OC,* II:175). One of Baudelaire's most musical poems, "Jet d'eau," is so similar in its ideas and rhythm to Dupont's "La promenade sur l'eau" that it is thought the two young men may have deliberately set out to treat the same theme in a friendly competition or that they may even have collaborated in its composition.

JULES BARBEY d'AUREVILLY

Though Realism may have helped Baudelaire see the weaknesses of Art for Art's Sake, it could never long appeal to one for whom imagination was the "queen of faculties" and for whom the spiritual qualities of art superseded the material. It was primarily his knowledge of the works of Joseph de Maistre and of Edgar Allan Poe, however, that caused him to cease his groping and return to certain basic ideas that he had propounded as early as 1845 and 1846. In Poe, whom he made famous in France and all of Europe through the translation of his tales and through three long critical essays, he discovered a spiritual brother and a sort of alter ego, and in both Poe and de Maistre he found confirmation of his own aristocratic conception of art.[13] The German writer E. T. A. Hoffmann also contributed to Baudelaire's conception of art; in his works, especially the *Kreisleriana,* the French poet appreciated not only the fantasy but even more the author's sense of universal unity and harmony.

A writer who shared Baudelaire's opinion of de Maistre and whose work revealed a similar sense of a world given over to evil was the novelist-critic-journalist Jules Barbey d'Aurevilly, whose dandyism, keen mind, flamboyant temperament, and militantly Catholic and Royalist views made him one of the more colorful figures of the nineteenth century. "Except for d'Aurevilly, Flaubert, Sainte-Beuve, I can't hit it off with anyone," the poet wrote to his mother on August 10, 1862 (*Corr.,* II:254). As Jacques Petit has pointed out, the statement takes on added significance when one realizes that of the three mentioned Barbey was the only one whom Baudelaire saw frequently.[14]

Though they had known each other since 1852 or 1853, their friendship really began late in 1854 when Baudelaire, seeking a pretext to meet Barbey, wrote asking to borrow some of his books, which he had promised to lend to Madame Sabatier. The two writers found they were alike in temperament and in their literary tastes. (Barbey concluded his letter of December 1854: "Friend of two days that seem worth ten years!" [*PLB,* p. 32]) Both had what Armand Chartier calls "a Jansenistic substratum" and were concerned with problems of sin and evil and eternal damnation.[15] In both could be found the same desperate quest for the infinite, the same pessimism and bitterness, the same liking for satanic literature, the same disgust for the ugliness and vacuity of their century.

Baudelaire was especially attracted by Barbey's *Du dandysme et de Georges Brummell,* which conceived the dandy not as a social fop in love with himself and engrossed only in mundane pleasure, but rather as a philosophic type in revolt against the vulgarity and crass materialism of contemporary bourgois society. Baudelaire developed the conception in *Le Peintre de la vie moderne,* in which he saw dandyism as "the last spark of heroism amid decadence" (*OC,* II:711). Ellen Moers describes Baudelaire's viewpoint as a "poetic distillation" of Barbey's work, though she freely admits that Baudelaire brought new power and depth to the tradition.[16] For the author of *Les Fleurs du Mal,* dandyism was "a kind of religion," and its members represented "a new aristocracy," characterized by a "quintessence of character and a subtle understanding of the whole moral mechanism of this world" (*OC,* II:711, 691).

Barbey's concept of dandyism evolved with the years and in time became more moral, more ascetic, and more human. For both writers, dandyism was characterized by an ethic related to stoicism, a psychological discipline marked by individualism and independence, and finally, to quote Chartier on Barbey, by "an aristocracy of the soul."[17] The term *dandy* was the highest compliment Baudelaire could pay, and, like Barbey, he came to apply it to artists and writers whom he admired and in whom he found ideas and sentiments compatible with his own.

The two writers' tastes in literature were much alike. De Maistre, Balzac, and Vigny were among those whom they thought the best; Hugo, with some exceptions, notably *La Légende des siècles,* was one of the chief targets of their animosity.

In their amicable debates, which treated everything from the idea of progress to the dogma of the Immaculate Conception, they liked to shock each other and were disappointed and somewhat irritated when they failed to do so. Their letters are full of wry pleasantries and of amusing and ironic modes of address. Baudelaire, who frequently encountered Barbey in the salon of the Lejosnes, often referred to him as "Vieux-Mauvais-Sujet" ("old reprobate"), a soubriquet affectionately bestowed on the novelist by the members of the salon. His real feeling for Barbey is concealed under a guise of irony in a letter to Asselineau written from Honfleur, February 20, 1859: "And what has become of that perfect monster, the *old reprobate,* that depraved creature who knows how to win one's affection?" (*Corr.,* I:552).

Barbey's terms for Baudelaire were equally outrageous: "Dear horror of my life," "monster," "my dear forgetful one." And he concludes his letter of August 13, 1860—one guesses half seriously—"Farewell last of my vices. When will you become a virtue?" (*PLB,* p. 59). For Barbey would have liked nothing better than to convert Baudelaire, as he himself had been converted.

Barbey's frank opinion of the poet was expressed in a letter to his friend Trébutien (editor of the works of Eugénie and Maurice de Guérin) asking that a copy of Eugénie's *Reliquiae* be sent to the author of *Les Fleurs du Mal.* His comments indicate that he was fully aware of the differences between them, and that their compatibility was based as much on their dislikes as on their affinities.

> He is a writer whose *power has been learned* and a thinker who does not lack depth, although.... Oh! there are many *althoughs!* He is on the wrong track. He is blasphemous. In short, he is everything that I've been! why shouldn't he become what I've become?... He doesn't share our faith or respect the things we do—but he does share our hatreds and contempts. Then too, in these beastly times when everything is out of gear, he is one of those whose heart is greater than his fortune. [*PLB,* pp. 39–40]

One of the things that the two friends obviously held in contempt was the ideology of Victor Hugo. Like Baudelaire, Barbey could not tolerate *Les Misérables.* His review of the novel criticized the political aims of Hugo so ferociously that friends and sympathizers of the novelist scribbled here and there on the walls of Paris, "Barbey d'Aurevilly idiot." In 1865 Barbey wrote a review of Hugo's *Chansons des rues et des bois* which, scathing as it was, did not satisfy Baudelaire. "Quel petit-lait!" ("How wishy-washy") he wrote scornfully to Lejosne on November 16, 1865 (*Corr.*, II:546).

At the time of the publication of *Les Fleurs du Mal* and the scandal that it provoked, Barbey did much to support its author. He spoke highly of the book to people of importance, like the Marquis de Custine; he even attempted to intervene with Pinard, the public prosecutor. In addition, he wrote a very fine review in which he characterized the book as a condemnation of the evil it evokes and noted (the first to do so) the "secret architecture" of the volume of verse. He concluded with the now well-known statement: "After *Les Fleurs du Mal*, the poet who brought them to blossom, has only two courses open to him: either blow out his brains ... or become a Christian."[18] Barbey was less enthusiastic about *Les Paradis artificiels*. Unlike Flaubert, who found the book a little too Catholic for his taste, he considered it "non-Christian."[19]

On his side, Baudelaire admired Barbey both as a man and a writer. He called Barbey's unpopular novel *L'Ensorcelée* a masterpiece and praised his *Du dandysme et de Georges Brummell*. In 1860 he wrote to Houssaye, editor of *L'Artiste*, that he wanted to do an article on Barbey as well as on Hugo, Wagner, and Paul de Molènes—"sincere praise, but in a very free and almost familiar tone" (*Corr.*, II:102). Unfortunately, his study of Barbey, like so many of his other projects, never materialized. He likewise intended to include Barbey, together with Chateaubriand and the Marquis de Custine, in a work to be entitled *Famille des Dandies* announced in 1860 but never completed. And in 1863—even though their friendship had cooled as a result of the break between Barbey and Sainte-Beuve—Baudelaire dedicated, perhaps ironically, his poem "L'Imprévu," "A mon ami, Jules Barbey d'Aurevilly."

In the light of his friendship with the poet and his open hostility to Victor Hugo, it comes as a surprise to learn that Barbey should write in the *Nain jaune* of November 7, 1867—scarcely two months after Bandelaire's death—"Let's be fair. Without M. Hugo the Father of us all, without M. Gautier..., without Edgar Poe... and even without M. Sainte-Beuve and his terrible saw-bones Joseph Delorme, what would [Baudelaire] be?"[20] This was not the first time that Barbey had denigrated Baudelaire's genius, for on May 6, 1866, even before the poet's death, Asselineau wrote Poulet-Malassis: "B. d'A. has never said and will never say anything but utter stupidities about B."[21]

HIPPOLYTE BABOU

One of the first to recognize publicly Bandelaire's great talent was Hippolyte Babou, who came to be on intimate terms with the poet around 1853–54. Babou was responsible for suggesting to Baudelaire the title *Les Fleurs du Mal* as the result of a long discussion on the subject that took place one evening among a group of friends at the Café Lemblin. In his article on Babou and Baudelaire, James S. Patty has pointed out that Hippolyte was also the first to praise with enthusiasm and perspicacity the eighteen poems of *Les Fleurs du Mal* that had appeared in the *Revue des Deux Mondes* on June 1, 1855.[22] From 1856 on he was one of a group including among others Baudelaire, Asselineau, Banville, and Monselet who were in close association with Poulet-Malassis, their editor.

The friendship between Baudelaire and Babou, who were both slightly hotheaded, was punctuated by several quarrels. Most notable was one provoked by an article, "De l'amitié littéraire," published by Babou in *La Revue française* on February 20, 1859. In it Babou attacked the cowardice of Sainte-Beuve—without mentioning his name—for having failed to lend Baudelaire any critical support: "To take foolish risks by acting in accordance with the demands of virtue and conscience would be in his opinion foolhardy and quixotic. That fine gentleman can praise *Fanny* [Ernest Feydeau] and remain silent about *Les Fleurs du Mal*."[23]

Though in his heart Baudelaire must have known that Babou

was right, he was angered and deeply upset by his friend's indiscretion. He wrote in haste to Sainte-Beuve (February 21, 1859) in an effort to explain his innocence in the matter and, three days later, poured out his distress to Asselineau and Poulet-Malassis. "Babou knows very well that I am a great friend of Uncle Beuve, that I value highly his friendship, and that *I* take pains to hide my opinion when it is contrary to his" (*Corr.,* I:555). Sainte-Beuve accepted Baudelaire's explanation and blamed only Babou for the incident.

After Baudelaire's death, Babou remained faithful to the memory of the poet. Convinced of the real greatness of his verse, he rose to the defense of his friend and, in an article entitled "Nos Alsaciens," vehemently attacked the critic Edmond Schérer, one of Baudelaire's most violent detractors, who, lacking Babou's intelligence and insight, had excoriated the author of *Les Fleurs du Mal.*

CHARLES AUGUSTIN SAINTE-BEUVE

In his brief autobiographical notes Baudelaire lists the name of Sainte-Beuve as one of the writers whom he met after his return to Paris in 1842. It was probably not until after 1844, however, that the poet came to be better acquainted with the eminent French critic, who, like Gautier, strongly influenced his literary inclinations, even as an adolescent. In a letter which he wrote that very year, he enclosed an early, somewhat mediocre poem in which he acknowledged his debt in the most flattering terms. Here the author of *Les Fleurs du Mal* first reveals the extent to which he had been swayed by the unhealthy romanticism of Sainte-Beuve's only novel, *Volupté,* and his *Poésies de Joseph Delorme.* He had absorbed everything, he wrote, "the miasmas, the perfumes, the soft whispering of dead memories" (*Corr.,* I:118).

Years later, in another letter sent from Brussels to the famous critic (March 15, 1865), the ailing poet again graciously acknowledged his debt: "You were absolutely right: *Joseph Delorme* is yesterday's *Fleurs du Mal.* The comparison is a glorious one for me. You will be kind enough not to find it offensive on your part" (*Corr.*, II:474). The critic, addressing Baudelaire as "Mon cher ami, mon cher Enfant," answered: "What you say is true: mine was not unlike yours; I had tasted of the same bitter fruit which turned out to be ashes. Hence your kind and loyal friendship for me—I have the same feeling for you, dear friend" (*PLB*, p. 343).

We do not know specifically what each writer valued or questioned in the other. Evidently Baudelaire had thought of writing an article to be called "Sainte-Beuve ou *Joseph Delorme* jugé par l'auteur des *Fleurs du Mal,*" for the title is listed among his prose works in 1866. As so often happened, the study was never done; at least it has never been discovered. However, critics have often noted thematic and stylistic similarities between the two writers: the intimate, often deliberately prosaic tone which Baudelaire seems to have adopted from the elder poet, the concern of both with the spiritual anguish of the period, their preoccupation with the various aspects of Parisian life. In fact, as Norman Barlow reminds us, "The available evidence of literary history accords to Sainte-Beuve the important distinction of having foreshadowed the 'Tableaux parisiens.'"[24]

All things considered, it seems strange that the famous critic did nothing to support the poet in his moments of need. He could not fail to have known how much a favorable article on his part would have meant to Baudelaire, for on several occasions the latter even suggested—with the greatest diffidence—that he write a notice of one of his works. Though "l'oncle Beuve" promised several times to write a review, he never did so and left unsaid the few words that might have done much to change the destiny of his admirer.

When Baudelaire announced his candidacy for the French Academy in December 1861, Sainte-Beuve in his official capacity was obliged to make some mention of him as well as of other candidates submitting themselves for election. The critic's characterization of Baudelaire's position in literature was marked by circumspection (Baudelaire had built for himself a "kiosk . . . at the farthest point of the Kamchatka of the Romantics") and also the most damning priase. After giving a distorted picture of the contents of Baudelaire's poetry, he concluded:

> The author is satisfied to have done something impossible in a field where it was believed no one could go. Does this mean, now, and when everything has been explained to respectable and somewhat astonished colleagues, that all these peculiarities, this spicy stew and these over-refinements seem sufficient qualifications for the Academy, and has the author seriously been able to convince himself of it?[25]

The poet, however, seemed oblivious to Sainte-Beuve's more disparaging observations and was made pathetically happy by the critic's comments on his refined appearance and manner. His letter of appreciation to Sainte-Beuve reveals how sensitive he was to the unfavorable opinion of him that was held by the general public:

> I have been very hurt (but I didn't say anything) to hear myself called for some years a boor, a surly and impossible man. Once, in a malicious newspaper, I read some lines about my repulsive ugliness, well calculated to alienate any approval (that was hard for a man who has so much loved the perfume of women). One day a woman said to me: "That's strange, you are very well-mannered; I thought you were always drunk and that you smelled bad." She had been taken in by the legend. [*Corr.*, II:219]

Ever since Babou's indictment of Sainte-Beuve, defenders of Baudelaire have censured the eminent *lundiste* for his failure to recognize publicly the poetic genius of his loyal and deserving friend. In a provocative article, "Sainte-Beuve, juge de Stendhal et de Baudelaire," Gérald Antoine and Claude Pichois seek the causes for this neglect. They maintain that to a great extent the traits that mildly alienated Sainte-Beuve from Baudelaire the man were the same that alienated him from Baudelaire the artist: "Excessive libertinism, but also misuse of intellectual faculties." "Sainte-Beuve remained constantly attached to his method, which was to think of the man, of his behavior. . . . His sin was not, as is often believed, infidelity, but perhaps on the contrary an excessive fidelity toward his fellow-creature—to the fatal detriment of the sacred cause of Art."[26]

That the critic's temperament, taste, and mentality were often at odds with those of the poet is clear from his own remarks and from those made by his faithful secretary, Jules Troubat. On one occasion Sainte-Beuve had noted: "I have seen my liberal-minded friend (B.D.) who said the strangest things about literature and poetry, but [who is] intelligent and enlightens me about the coming generations."[27] And in the *Lundis* he speaks of the "poisonous juice," that Baudelaire had extracted from every subject and from every flower. Then he adds, "He was moreover, a man of intelligence, quite likeable on occasion and very capable of affection."[28] Troubat likewise admitted that, though Sainte-Beuve appreciated Baudelaire's affection, his work did not permit him to "ramble and indulge in vagaries" and that the poet's conversation "took him away from his weekly tasks."[29]

The arguments of Antoine and Pichois are sound, but it also seems clear that Sainte-Beuve felt ill at ease in evaluating the younger generation of writers, perhaps fearing to be mistaken either through excessive praise or disdain. Had he not admitted that Baudelaire "enlightens me about the coming generations"? Moreover he naturally would have wanted to avoid government censure for condoning what was considered the immorality of *Les Fleurs du Mal*.

Despite everything, however, the letters exchanged between the two—especially the later ones—leave little doubt of their mutual liking and respect. The impatience that a man of Sainte-Beuve's temperament and regular work habits must have felt at Baudelaire's tendency to "flâner et de vagabonder, même en esprit" did not prevent him from speaking the truth when he wrote to Madame Aupick during her son's final illness: "There isn't a single man in the literary world who has shown me more friendship and for whom I in turn feel as much" (*PLB*, p. 326). One wonders what judgment he would have passed on the dead poet in the "médaillon" which he promised Madame Aupick he would compose and which, like his projected reviews, remained unwritten.

ALFRED DE VIGNY

Of the first generation of Romantic poets, whom he had read and adored as a child, Baudelaire continued to enjoy the works of Alfred de Vigny and Victor Hugo. For Lamartine's poetry he had little patience, finding it, like that of Musset, too sentimental, too personal, and too undisciplined in form. Furthermore, he had almost no personal contact with either Lamartine or Musset. Of Vigny, Baudelaire thought highly both as a man and a poet. The two writers had much in common, as Henri Peyre has observed, from their ideas on progress and modern society to their deification of the imagination.[30] Vigny was the only important poet of his day who fully appreciated the genius and originality of *Les Fleurs du Mal*. The warm letter he wrote from his sick bed in 1862 inviting Baudelaire to pay him a visit expresses true respect for the younger poet's "real and rare talent" and for "the real beauty of your poetry, still too little appreciated and too lightly judged" (*PLB*, pp. 382–83).

VICTOR HUGO

Though Baudelaire had little opportunity to discuss personally with Victor Hugo the latter's ideas on aesthetics, politics, and social problems, he was very much aware of all that the exiled poet wrote and said, and tended to react to it quite strongly, either negatively or positively. Baudelaire's acquaintance with Hugo's work dated from his schooldays in Lyons and in Paris. Both at the Collège Royal and at the Collège Louis-le-Grand he was known for his enthusiasm for Romantic poetry, especially that of Hugo, Lamartine, and Gautier. On December 5, 1837, he wrote his mother asking for a copy of Hugo's *Le Dernier Jour d'un condamné*, and a year later (August 3) he wrote telling her of his disgust for all modern literature save that of Hugo and Sainte-Beuve. The novels of Eugène Sue bored him to death, he confided. "I am disgusted with all that: it is only the dramas, the poetry of Victor Hugo and a book of Sainte-Beuve [*Volupté*] which have entertained me," he wrote with surprising good judgment for a boy of seventeen (*Corr.,* I:67).

In 1840 (February 25), the young Baudelaire wrote Hugo a highly flattering letter, prompted by his enjoyment on seeing a performance of Hugo's *Marion de Lorme.* That same year, Prarond tells us, he arranged to have himself introduced to Hugo—perhaps as a result of the letter—and the elder poet suggested "a stay in the country, work in solitude, a sort of retreat."[31] Distasteful as the advice must have been, Baudelaire gave no indication of his true feelings, though a quiet, secluded life was the last thing he would have wanted or accepted. Perhaps the meeting helped to dampen his fervor, for according to Prarond it was evidently around this time that Baudelaire, who had come to detest the work of Lamartine, spoke of Hugo with "deferential restraint, but without enthusiastic ardor. He, who recited a lot of poetry, seldom recited the poems of Hugo."[32]

According to his own admission, Baudelaire from this period on, saw little of the author of *Les Misérables,* in part because Hugo was furious at the coup d'etat of Louis Napoleon and remained in self-exile until the fall of the Empire in 1870. In a letter (September 1859) to the exiled poet asking for a preface to his essay on Théophile Gautier Baudelaire himself mentions that he had seen Hugo only twice some twenty years earlier.

In the meantime, Baudelaire had become much more critical of the elder poet. His comments in private varied from highly laudatory to most disparaging. In his correspondence and *Journaux intimes* he often gave vent to his animosity. He referred to Hugo in his *Journaux* as so "lacking in elegiac and ethereal qualities that he would horrify even a notary" and described him as priestlike, with his head always bent—"too bent to see anything except his naval" (*OC,* II:665). As late as 1865 he could write to Ancelle from Brussels: "One can be both a *wit* and a *boor*— just as one can possess a *special genius* and be a *fool* at the same time. Victor Hugo has indeed proved that to us" (*Corr.,* II:459–60).

Moreover, he could chide Madame Aupick for failing to appreciate in *La Légende des siècles* "the dazzling faculties that Hugo alone possesses" (*Corr.*, II:609). And in July 1857 he wrote to her at the time of the publication of *Les Fleurs du Mal,* "I know that the book with its faults and merits will take its place in the memory of the literary public beside the best poems of V. Hugo, of Th. Gautier and even of Byron" (*Corr.*, I:411).

Baudelaire's use of the word *best* explains his ambivalent attitude toward the elder poet. Much in Hugo he recognized in his more dispassionate moments as being truly great, and to compare his own poetry to the "best" in Hugo was the highest compliment he could pay.

In his published remarks, except in his early criticism, Baudelaire was usually fairly restrained. The *Salon de 1846* had been surprisingly outspoken in its expression of his critical views. In praising Delacroix he had contrasted the artist with the poet and had maintained that Delacroix rather than Hugo was the real head of the Romantic School. He had disparaged the poet for his artificiality and pedantic use of symmetry and antithesis—faults that are more damning in Hugo's earlier work, where they are less often redeemed by his more solid virtues— but had nevertheless admitted his amazing technique as well as his "nobility" and "majesty" (*OC*, II:430–31).

The praise that Baudelaire accorded Hugo beginning in 1859 may have been to some degree inspired by selfish reasons. The preface that he wanted Hugo to write for his article on Gautier would have increased its commercial value and importance, and Baudelaire was quite aware of that fact. But self-interest aside, his esteem for the poet's later work is unmistakable. His positive comments to his mother about *La Légende des siècles* testify to the sincerity of his appreciation and are too convincing to be questioned. Moreover the three poems that he dedicated to the exiled poet ("Le Cygne," "Les Sept Vieillards," and "Les Petites Vieilles") are proof in themselves of his admiration. "Les Petites Vieilles," he wrote Hugo (September 27, 1859), was actually an attempt to imitate the exiled poet—a fact that he confirmed in a letter (October 15, 1859) to Poulet-Malassis. It was, incidentally, in thanking Baudelaire for the dedication that Hugo shrewdly observed that the author in his three poems had created "un frisson nouveau" ("a new shiver") (*PLB*, p. 188).

Even more significant is the success with which Baudelaire revealed the true greatness of Hugo's poetic genius in his essay (1861) written for Eugène Crépet's anthology, *Les Poètes fran-çais*.[33] Despite a certain amount of vague, conventional praise and a tendency to gloss over that part of the work which ran counter to his own aesthetic beliefs, the essay remains one of the best studies of Hugo as a poet. In it, Baudelaire anticipated present-day revaluation of Hugo by recognizing the cosmic power, the epic strength, and the sense of mystery that charac-terize his later verse. Hugo, he maintained, was a "translator" and "decipherer" who was able to draw "from the inexhaustible storehouse of *universal analogy*" and who indulged in "all the reveries suggested by the infinite spectacle of life on earth and in the heavens" (*OC*, II:133–39).

It seems clear that Baudelaire's dislike for Victor Hugo was inspired mainly by the poet's personality and by his aesthetic and political beliefs. Hugo's conception of himself as "savior of the human race," a second Christ who could presume to give advice even to God himself (*Conseils à Dieu*) appeared to him both ridiculous and repugnant. Moreover, to a disciple of de Maistre and Edgar Allan Poe, the idea of progress and a belief in utilitar-ian literature were outright anathema, particularly in moments of anger and frustration—and there were many of them, espe-cially during the last years of his life. Finally, there is no doubt that the younger poet's irritation was exacerbated by his own lack of success and by his knowledge that an unjust fate had brought fame and fortune to Hugo and only poverty and obscur-ity to him.

Baudelaire's differentiation between the beauty of Hugo's verse and what he considered the utter stupidity of his beliefs is often revealed in his comments. In a letter to the critic Armand Fraisse (February 18, 1860), who had written an article on the exiled poet, he accused the critic of failing to make this distinc-tion:[34]

You haven't sufficiently distinguished between the *amount of eternal beauty* in Hugo and the comic superstitions introduced in his work by events, in other words modern stupidity or *wisdom,* the belief in progress, the salvation of the human race by balloons, etc. Such as it is, your article is the best I have read.—Generally the friends of Hugo are as stupid as his enemies; the result is that the truth will never be told. [*Corr.,* I:675][35]

Even the most indulgent commentators, however, feel that in his review of *Les Misérables* Baudelaire overstepped the boundaries of honest criticism. On April 3, 1862, Hugo had published the first part of *Les Misérables,* a powerful, uneven, and often ponderous novel in which the author preaches "la fraternité humaine et le progrès social." On April 20, Baudelaire published a review of the book in the newspaper *Le Boulevard.* It is this essay in particular which has provoked the reproaches of critics and won him the reputation of being hypocritical. Crépet and Blin have characterized the article as "reserved, even treacherous," while Margaret Gilman deplores its "sadly evasive conclusion" and its many "half-truths."[36]

At first glance the review strikes the reader as being inconsistent with Baudelaire's conception of art, but a closer examination indicates that, despite his flattery, Baudelaire is saying nothing which either belies his own convictions or contradicts his most cherished beliefs. On the contrary, he even succeeds in suggesting certain aesthetic and metaphysical ideas which are in opposition to those of Hugo. It is rather for certain things that he failed to say that the poet-critic can be faulted.[37]

That Baudelaire heartily disliked the novel cannot be denied, for he ridiculed it to his close friends as well as in letters to his mother. To make matters worse, after reviewing the book, he admitted to Madame Aupick: "This book is vile and idiotic. I have shown in this connection that I know how to lie. He wrote an absolutely ridiculous letter to thank me. This proves that a great man can be a fool" (*Corr.,* II:254).

When one knows Baudelaire's real opinion of *Les Misérables,* one wonders why he decided to write the review. The answer may be guessed from reading his correspondence. At this point Baudelaire's career was at low ebb. Many magazine editors showed no interest in his work; those who did could not help him because of the complaints of their subscribers. As usual, he was badly in need of money—so much so that he had had to beg his mother and Ancelle for assistance in paying for his lodging. His health was wretched and he had come to know the torturing fear of losing his mind. All his pent-up bitterness and resentment are reflected in a letter, written to Madame Aupick on December 11, 1862, in which he lashed out in an angry rage against all humanity: "*I abhor life*. Once more I say:—I am going to flee the sight of the human face, and especially that of the French" (*Corr.*, II:254).

Hugo, on the other hand, was at the height of his glory. Rich, powerful, admired by all, he had obtained everything that had been denied the author of *Les Fleurs du Mal*. In a letter to his mother, written a month before the publication of his review, Baudelaire admitted the sense of envy that he felt in contrasting his lack of success with the popularity and fame of Victor Hugo: "Hugo is going to publish his *Misérables*, a novel in 10 vols. Another reason why my poor volumes, *Eureka, Poëmes en prose* and *Réflexions sur mes contemporains* may not be seen" (*Corr.*, II:238).

Baudelaire's envy of Hugo's vigor and vitality, of his amazing virtuosity, and of his superb imagination and epic power was both inevitable and perfectly natural. Yet he had recognized and sincerely, though perhaps reluctantly, praised those very qualities in *Les Contemplations* and *La Légende des siècles*.

In his review of *Les Misérables*, however, Baudelaire's disordered state of mind and health left him in no mood to tolerate what he had called in his article on Gautier "la philosophaillerie moderne" resulting from "the notorious doctrine, the indissolubility of the Beautiful, the True, the Good" (*OC*, II:111). Hugo's belief in progress, in the natural goodness of man, in explicit morality, and in utilitarian literature—all of which were odious to the author of *Les Fleurs du Mal*—exacerbated his nervous and physical irritability and blinded him to the epic power and puissant imagination that he might otherwise have found in

Les Misérables. He who so passionately believed in the integrity of an art that exists in its own right could only be enraged by a book that, as Hugo himself wrote to Lamartine, had "fraternity as its basis and progress as its highest goal."[38]

Baudelaire was not alone in condemning the ideology of the novel, a fact which lends further credence to the belief that his antipathy was based on something other than mere envy or personal dislike. In a series of articles published in *Le Pays,* Barbey d'Aurevilly described the morality of *Les Misérables* as "inane evangelism," and labeled the novel as "*Le Compère Mathieu* du socialisme" and "the most dangerous book of this time."[39] Even Lamartine, who was affable enough to ask Hugo's permission to attack "le socialisme égalitaire" of the novel, called it "très dangereux" and commented in Baudelairean fashion: "This book accusing society would be more aptly entitled *The Epic of the Rabble;* now society is not made for the rabble, but against it. . . ."[40]

Moreover, Proudhon, with his immense distaste for utopian dreamers, also took time—much to Baudelaire's amusement—to analyze with his customary pedantic seriousness the weakness of Hugo's social and political ideas by carefully annotating the first two volumes. He couldn't bear to read more than the first two, according to Poulet-Malassis, Baudelaire's longtime friend and publisher.[41]

Asselineau, who knew and understood Baudelaire better than any of his other friends, correctly analyzed the poet-critic's private denunciation of the novel: "Basically, the book with its moral outrageousness, its leaden paradoxes, irritated him immensely. He abhorred false sentimentality, virtuous criminals, and angelic prostitutes. He said so often enough. When he came upon that kind of reasoning, he demolished it with a savage crudity."[42]

Under the circumstances, there is no denying that it would have been more honorable had Baudelaire not written his essay on *Les Misérables.* Yet a review of the novel assured him the opportunity of publishing an article, and Baudelaire badly needed such an opportunity.[43] His determined effort to gain recognition and to remind the literary public of his previous accomplishments as a critic is revealed in the notice that appeared in *Le Boulevard* on April 13—a notice which he may well have drafted himself:

> We have the pleasure of announcing to our readers that *Le Boulevard* will publish, in its next number, a critical article on *Les Misérables* by Charles Baudelaire. The author of *Les Fleurs du Mal* and of *Les Paradis artificiels* is, among the few writers continuing the great romantic school, one of the best suited to honor the master. He who has succeeded so well in explaining Victor Hugo the poet will explain Victor Hugo the novelist. [*OC*, II:1182]

Baudelaire could not express his opinion openly in the review since it was appearing in a paper that favored Victor Hugo. What is more, he had not forgotten that only the year before Eugène Crépet had refused to publish his essay on Hégésippe Moreau and had rejected his article on Auguste Barbier on the ground that it was overly severe in its judgment of the poet's didactic tendencies. Baudelaire's appraisals have since been confirmed by posterity, but Crépet, known for his democratic sympathies, disapproved his censure of Barbier, despite the high praise with which his strictures had been tempered.

Perhaps to avoid a similar rejection, Baudelaire chose an amusing though somewhat devious way to get around the problem of having to find something worthy of praise in a book that he disliked. At the beginning of his review, he could have stated categorically that *Les Misérables* was a utilitarian novel and that as such it was contrary to his idea of great art. He does say just that, but understandably his approach is less direct. He begins the essay with a long quotation taken from his 1861 article on Hugo, in which he had praised *Les Contemplations* and *La Légende des siècles* for the absence of "that sermonizing morality which, with its pedantic manner and its didactic tone, can spoil the most beautiful piece of poetry.... Morality does not enter into this art as its *express purpose;* it is intermingled with it and lost sight of, as in life itself. The poet is unintentionally a moralist *through the abundance and plentitude of nature*" (*OC,* II:218).

The quotation, far from being mere padding, is evidently a reminder to the reader of Baudelaire's aesthetic ideas and of his objection to the teaching of a moral lesson in particular. Its purpose becomes even more apparent when, without further comment, Baudelaire adds in the most unequivocal manner: "There is only a single line that must be changed here; for in *Les Misérables* MORALITY DOES ENTER AS ITS EXPRESS PURPOSE." As undeniable proof he proceeds to cite the very words of Hugo himself, taken from the preface of the novel: "So long as ignorance and poverty exist on earth, books such as this cannot be useless" (*OC,* II:218).

Baudelaire cannot refrain from adding: "So long as . . . ! Alas, you might as well say ALWAYS!" And with this dry comment he obviously hoped to remind the reader that his own views on progress were quite incompatible with those of the author of *Les Misérables.* Once again, without further comment, Baudelaire continues:

> But this is not the place to analyze such questions. We merely wish to do justice to the extraordinary talent with which the poet has seized public attention and bent it, like the recalcitrant head of a lazy schoolboy, toward the bottomless chasms of social ills. [*OC,* II:218]

To accuse Baudelaire of duplicity at this point is not to notice that his praise is directed at Hugo's ability as a *propagandist* rather than as an artist, that Baudelaire is praising his power to attract public attention to the social evils of the day. At the same time it should not be forgotten that he had just reminded the reader that the teaching of a moral lesson is incompatible with great art.

Throughout the rest of the essay Baudelaire continues in much the same vein. He subtly suggests that the novel was a thesis novel—a book of charity, "written to arouse and stimulate the spirit of charity." Although he commends warmly—and no doubt sincerely—Hugo's characterization of Fantine and his extraordinary ability to portray childhood, he suggests that most of the characters are living abstractions, representing ideas necessary to the thesis.

The mental conflict undergone by Jean Valjean is singled out for praise that seems too extravagant, but, ironically, what Baudelaire most appreciated was the evidence of original sin which Hugo had revealed in the heart of man: "One would have to search hard and a long time, a very long time, to find elsewhere pages equal to those which expose in so tragic a manner all the appalling Casuistry inscribed from the Beginning in the heart of Universal Man" (OC, II:222).

Baudelaire resorts to innuendo to make his final point. He repeats that Les Misérables was a book of charity, a call to order of a society too enamored of itself and too little concerned with the immortal laws of brotherhood. But even while agreeing with Hugo that "books of this kind are never useless"—a fact with which no one could disagree—he discredits the validity of the novel as a social document by a passing reference to the "intentional deception or unconscious bias in the manner in which . . . the terms of the problem are stated" (OC, II:224). The reader is left with the impression that, if Hugo had succeeded in proving his thesis, it was only by building a case to fit, by employing false or specious arguments.

And finally, Baudelaire could not resist ending the article with an affirmation of his own belief in original sin and a sly dig at the novelist's belief in progress. But first he clearly points out Hugo's inconsistency in accepting a philosophy that maintains the goodness of man, yet fails to hold God accountable for allowing the innocent to suffer: "He believes that Man is born good, and yet, even in the face of the constant disasters that befall him, he does not accuse God of cruelty and malice" (OC, II:224).

Far from accepting Hugo's ideas on the natural goodness of man, Baudelaire unequivocally declares his belief in original sin and closes the essay with a statement which must surely have proved irritating to the author of Les Misérables: "Alas, even after all the progress that we have been promised for so long, there will always remain sufficient indications of Original Sin to establish its everlasting reality!" (*OC*, II:224).

To Baudelaire's credit, not once did he call the novel a great work of art or praise it for anything more than its characterization or its effective propaganda. It is true he praised the *usefulness* of the novel, but for those who already knew Baudelaire's ideas or who read the self-quotation with which he began the essay, it is quite clear that in his judgment utility and didacticism were faults rather than merits in matters of art. And even the blindest of readers cannot fail to notice that Baudelaire and Hugo were in complete disagreement about such questions as progress and original sin.

Despite Baudelaire's claim to his mother that he had known how to lie—a claim obviously made in a moment of bravado—it would seem that Baudelaire was not as guilty of duplicity as has been believed. Casuistry perhaps, but not the lies of which he had boasted to his mother. What he evidently attempted to do was to write an article favorable enough to be published in *Le Boulevard,* yet consistent with his own aesthetic and philosophic ideas—a sort of tour de force, as it were.[44]

Victor Hugo appears to have been delighted with the review and, in a letter to Baudelaire written only four days later (April 24), expressed his appreciation and his belief in the affinities between his poetry and that of his critic. "We are devoting ourselves, you and I, to progress through truth," he concluded, after suggesting that Baudelaire "continue [his] fine work on this book" (*PLB*, p. 194). The suggestion was patently an invitation to review the volumes that were soon to appear: the second and third parts on May 24, the fourth and fifth on July 5. But Baudelaire could stomach no more. Hugo's assertion that the author of *Les Fleurs du Mal* was, like him, dedicated to "progress through truth" must have proved to be the last straw. Not only had Hugo failed to extract the full meaning of the review itself but, even worse, he was too blind to recognize that his conception of truth was diametrically opposed to that of his critic. For a disciple of Poe and de Maistre, *Les Misérables* could represent only the prostitution of art and the embodiment of false logic.

Given the circumstances, Baudelaire's final judgment was much less hypocritical than is often believed.[45] Despite his exasperation at what he regarded as the utter stupidity and irrationality of Hugo's thinking, he was able to see in the poet, if not in the novelist, those redeeming qualities which made him appear, even to the jaundiced eyes of the poet-critic, "un grand homme."

As Baudelaire grew more and more bitter with the deterioration of his health and mental faculties, he became less careful to hide his animosity for Victor Hugo. Before leaving for Brussels he write a letter to *Le Figaro* in which he suggested that the approaching celebration of Shakespeare's birthday was being used as a pretext to advertise Hugo's forthcoming book on the English drama.

In Brussels, Baudelaire first tried to avoid the Hugos, but finally, in May 1865, as he wrote his mother and Madame Meurice, he was obliged to dine with Madame Hugo and her sons. Though Victor Hugo was in Guernsey at the time, Baudelaire later dined with him and the rest of the family on several occasions when the elder poet was present in Brussels.[46] At first, Baudelaire remained firm in his dislike of the entire family. The pontifical Hugo bored and tired him, Madame Hugo seemed silly and her two sons complete blockheads. Soon, however, Baudelaire came to alter his judgment of Madame Hugo and became very fond of the frail old woman. When, shortly before his stroke, she insisted that her doctor go to see the ailing poet, he wrote his mother (February 16, 1866) that Madame Hugo, "who seemed only ridiculous to me at first, is decidedly a good woman" (*Corr.*, II:599). On one occasion, when illness prevented Baudelaire from dining at her home, she wrote him a friendly note assuring him of her family's devotion and reminding him that a place was always laid for him at their table.

Evidently Baudelaire was even planning to write a review of Hugo's latest novel, *Les Travailleurs de la mer,* but unfortunately the notes he had jotted down are so few and so terse that they do not reveal his attitude. On the whole, however, it would seem, as Léon Cellier suggests, that his reaction was not unfavorable. Cellier's interpretation of the final comment, "The ending is distressing—favorable criticism" ("Le Dénouement fait de la peine—critique flatteuse"), which has been called enigmatic by many Hugo critics, seems both logical and reasonable: "On one hand, Baudelaire recognizes that he was moved by Gilliatt's suicide; on the other, he considers that to recognize this emotive power is to praise the novel."[47]

On March 22, 1866, Madame Hugo, who had learned to like and pity Baudelaire, wrote her husband that her friend was doing a review, "but he doesn't have a newspaper at his disposal."[48] A few days later, she wrote her husband again, this time to inform him of Baudelaire's serious illness: "They have given him up and they are afraid that he may survive the loss of his intelligence. It is very sad, for Baudelaire had an exceptional mind."[49] When the poet lay helpless from his stroke, both Victor Hugo and his wife tried to obtain for him the best medical help available.

Hugo himself was always suspicious of Baudelaire's true sentiments. Though his own letters to the younger poet were as effusive and flattering as those of his correspondent, he was far more restrained in writing to Asselineau, who had sent him a copy of his biography of the author of Les Fleurs du Mal: "I met Baudelaire rather than knew him. He often offended me and I must have often annoyed him. I would like to talk about it with you. I agree with all your praise, but with some reservations...."[50]

One puzzling question will perhaps never be solved. In Baudelaire's famous letter to Ancelle (February 18, 1866), in which he named the writers whom he exempted from "all the modern riffraff" (Chateaubriand, Balzac, Stendhal, Mérimée, de Vigny, Flaubert, Banville, Gautier, Leconte de Lisle), the name of Hugo is absent. And so is the name of Sainte-Beuve. Perhaps the omission of their names was a mere oversight on his part, for the letter, written in a moment of rage and frenzy, reveals a state of mind bordering on hysteria. Or perhaps, knowing that all hope of publishing his collected works was gone forever, he deliberately and in anger omitted the names of the two writers: Sainte-Beuve, who could have helped him but failed to do so; Hugo, whose enormous success seemed so unjust compared to the failure of his own efforts and dreams.

GUSTAVE FLAUBERT

Among the novelists of his time whom Baudelaire greatly admired and also knew personally was Gustave Flaubert. The two writers, who occasionally met at Madame Sabatier's dinners, had much in common. Both believed that the chief goal of art was beauty and sought in that beauty a means of escaping the monotony and ugliness of reality. Moreover, beauty, in their judgment, was not restricted to the treatment of certain subjects. Quite the contrary. All subjects were equal, Flaubert maintained ("Yvetot is worth as much as Constantinople."),[51] and Baudelaire agreed. In his review of *Madame Bovary* (October 18, 1857), the poet-critic departed from prevailing criticism by stressing "the BEAUTY with which it was clothed" (*OC,* II:77). By softening what was "repugnant and grotesque" ... with the "opaline nightlight" of poetry, the author had proved, he affirmed, that "all subjects are equally good or bad, according to the manner in which they are treated, and that the most commonplace can become the best" (*OC,* II:84, 81). Baudelaire had, of course, done the same things in *Les Fleurs du Mal.*

Both writers detested Realism for the very reason that it lacked the beauty which they considered essential to all great art. Neither believed himself to be a Realist. In fact, in his review of the novel, Baudelaire defined Realism as "a repulsive insult flung in the face of every analyst, a vague and elastic word which for the ordinary man signifies not a new means of creation, but a minute description of minor details" (*OC,* II:80). Flaubert evidently felt much the same way. "I would like to write all I see, but transfigured," he wrote to Louise Colet in 1853.[52] And years later he admitted to George Sand: "I despise what is usually called Realism, and yet I have been made one of its high priests."[53] Yet neither writer rejected reality. Instead, they used it as a springboard (Flaubert actually called it such) from which they made the leap from the reality they knew and despised to the *vision* of reality which they created through their imagination and the magic of their art.

The two writers were likewise opposed to didactic art, though they did not hesitate to admit that true art is inevitably moral. Angered by critics who attacked Flaubert for his failure to incorporate a moral indictment in his novel, Baudelaire stated his view of the relationship of art and morality: "A true work of art need not contain an indictment. The logic of the work satisfies all the claims of morality, and it is for the reader to draw his conclusions from the conclusion" (*OC*, II:81–82). Flaubert may have remembered these very words when many years later (1876) he wrote: "The reader is an idiot or the book is false from the point of view of exactitude if the reader does not draw from it the morality which he should find there."[54]

Deeply pessimistic, both Baudelaire and Flaubert gave vent to their disillusionment with life in their superb use of irony. "Two fundamental literary qualities: irony and supernaturalism," the poet wrote in his *Journaux intimes* (*OC*, I:658). In the case of the poet, who had the capacity to look at himself with a stern and ruthless eye, irony took the form of mockery—especially the merciless mockery of himself. ("Hypocrite lecteur, mon frère, mon semblable.") The most intense feelings are often fused with irony, as Alison Fairlie has observed: "Baudelaire discovers how to make the reader share a feeling the more strongly because of the violent, sardonic, and lucid self-criticism which ironically underscores it."[55]

In Flaubert, irony is likewise fused with point of view and becomes an integral, inseparable part of both the form and substance of the novel. In *Madame Bovary* it is present everywhere: in the choice of an image or an adjective, in the juxtaposition of scenes, in the clichés that make up the dialogue, in the various points of view from which characters are seen by others. The very situation on which the novel is based is ironical; it could not be otherwise since it was based on Flaubert's own view of life. As Benjamin Bart points out, "It is Flaubert's reiterated contention in his letters that life is hateful, farcical, grotesque; that it consists of ignominy and stupidity. It is so hideous that the only way to stand it is to avoid it and to look upon the human race as "une vaste association de crétins et de canailles."⁵⁶ It is hardly strange that the novel reflects that view, though there are moments when Flaubert seems to forget his distaste for his characters and to show, almost in spite of himself, sympathy and even pity for the plight of both Emma and Charles.

Finally, both authors, despite their emphasis on impersonality and objectivity, became more personally involved in their work than their theories would lead us to believe. "The artist must no more appear in his work than does God in nature," Flaubert stated somewhat pontifically in 1875.⁵⁷ And of his novel *Madame Bovary* he wrote more specifically, "I wish that in my book . . . there not appear a single reflection of the author."⁵⁸ He boasted in a letter written on March 18, 1857, that "the story is entirely invented; I have put nothing of my feelings or of my life into it."⁵⁹

Yet at times at least he was apparently conscious of his personal involvement, for to Louise Colet he frankly admitted: "The more personal you are, the weaker you will be . . . I have always erred in that respect, I have always put myself into all that I have done."⁶⁰ At another time, Flaubert is reported to have said, "Madame Bovary, c'est moi," and though the story, according to René Wellek, is undoubtedly apocryphal ("it cannot be traced further than 1909"), its basic truth is confirmed by his admission to Louise Colet that "the heart I studied was mine."⁶¹

Baudelaire also insisted on the "voluntary impersonality" (*Corr.*, I:523) of his poetry, though in reality he succeeded no better than Flaubert in detaching himself from his work. One has only to remember his confession to Ancelle in a moment of desperation at the end of his life: "Must I tell you, you who have not guessed it any more than the others, that in this *atrocious* book [*Les Fleurs du Mal*] I have put all *my heart,* all *my love,* all *my religion* (travestied), all *my hate?* It is true that I shall write the contrary, that I shall swear by all the gods that it is a book of *pure* art, of *mimicry,* of *virtuosity;* and I shall be lying like a trooper" (*OC,* II:610).

It can be said of Baudelaire what Victor Brombert has said of Flaubert. All his works "betray his intimate dreams and obsessions" not in the form of "banal autobiographical transpositions, but rather of transmutations and revelations through his favorite themes."[62]

Like the novelist, Baudelaire often found life hideous and unbearable. Yet paradoxical as it may seem, both writers showed themselves capable in real life of genuine compassion and even self-sacrifice for those they loved.

It is hardly surprising that Flaubert and Baudelaire are both present in their works. How else could they have understood the hearts and minds of others without the self-knowledge that gave them the necessary insight? Where they differed from the Romanticists was in their ability to disguise their involvement and to avoid effusive self-confessions and self-revelations.

Considering the affinities that link Baudelaire and Flaubert, it is far from strange that the poet-critic's review of *Madame Bovary* remains one of the best critical studies ever done of the book. That Baudelaire understood and interpreted the author's intention perfectly is attested by Flaubert himself. Delighted by the subtlety and penetration of the critic's analysis, he wrote and paid him the highest of compliments: "You have entered into the arcana of the work as if my brain were yours" (*PLB,* p. 153).

Baudelaire was the first to realize that Flaubert had put much of himself into the heroine of his novel. What he didn't say and perhaps didn't fully recognize was that there was also much of himself in her character. After all, the very theme of the novel— the disparity between reality and an unattainable ideal—was not only the underlying theme of *Les Fleurs du Mal* but also the cause of much of the poet's—and of Flaubert's—own personal torment.

True, Emma, deprived of the genius and intelligence of a mature Flaubert and Baudelaire, sought an ideal that was tawdry and cheap, an ideal based on the foolish Romantic novels which she, like the author and critic, had secretly devoured during her school days. Yet despite all this Baudelaire maintained with a certain amount of exaggeration that, unlike the adulterous heroines of most novels, Emma "was pursuing the Ideal," or what she naively believed to be the "Ideal" (OC, II:84).

His contention that Emma was endowed with what he calls "virile qualities" was intended to exclude her from the ordinary woman whose unflattering portrait he drew in his *Journaux intimes* with the brutal frankness and scabrous language that often characterized him in moments of exasperation. In his *Journaux intimes* he maintains—to quote some of his milder comments—that woman is a "pure animal," guided by instinct and by her "natural" appetites—"unable to separate body from soul," "the complete opposite of the dandy" (OC, I:677, 699).[63]

Man, on the other hand, Baudelaire believed, possesses both spirituality as well as animality. Only man is capable of revery and is guided by imagination. Only man is able to escape the ugly reality of the human condition by transforming himself, through the discipline of self-purification, into the work of art known as the dandy.[64]

If Emma, in Baudelaire's view, had "all the attractions of a virile soul in a charming feminine body," it was mainly because of her imagination, "that supreme and despotic faculty, replacing the heart, or what is called the heart [an ironic euphemism for sensuality] . . . which generally dominates in a woman, as in an animal" (OC, II:81, 82). It was also, as we shall see, the result of a dandyism which, in her case, even Baudelaire admitted was mainly material.

Emma's imagination alone was an indication of her superiority—her longing to escape her drab, bourgeois surroundings and to enjoy, like Flaubert and Baudelaire, the exotic beauty of distant lands and far-off seas. In such poems as "Parfum exotique" or "La Chevelure," Baudelaire associates love with the beauty of remembered places—of ebony seas and warm, tropical ports. In them, Jeanne becomes a mere abstraction—a means to an end, a way of evoking dreams of the distant past. In

Emma's dreams, love is likewise associated with the enchantment of far-off places. Her dreams of a honeymoon are visions of strange and beautiful lands—of Swiss chalets, the perfume of lemon trees, carriage rides on steep mountain paths, the roar of distant waterfalls mingling with the tinkling of goats' bells and the song of the postilion. The imaginary lover, dressed in black velvet with ruffled cuffs, is only a part of the picturesque scene. Later on in the novel, about to elope with Rodolphe, Emma's dream is almost the same as that in which she had conjured up the honeymoon, and—strangely enough—the man she loves with such complete abandon (never once is he mentioned by name) remains as much an abstraction as the imaginary husband of her earlier dreams.

When, deserted by Rodolphe, Emma turns to Léon, her almost frantic sensuality seems to be a last desperate attempt to realize the love which she had tried to imagine from the books she had read. Though "she was as disgusted with him as he was tired of her" and though "she found in adultery all the platitudes of marriage," she did not dare admit it to herself.[65] Just as Baudelaire transformed Jeanne—half paralyzed, her beauty gone, ill from drugs and alcohol—into the "belle visiteuse . . . noire et lumineuse" of "Un Fantôme," so Emma in her letters to Léon transformed her pusillanimous lover into "another man, a phantom made of the most beautiful things she had read . . . ," a vague figure living in "a misty blue land where silken ladders hang swaying from balconies" (III, 6). Léon—like Rodolphe, like Jeanne—had become only another abstraction, necessary to maintain her dreams.

When Rodolphe refused to come to her aid and lend her the money she so desperately needed, Emma's dream world suddenly collapsed. In a state of shock, she suddenly realized that she had never been loved in the grand romantic manner, as she had liked to believe. For Emma, life was no longer worth living; unlike either Flaubert or Baudelaire, she had nothing to fall back on. As the author himself notes in one of his rare comments, "she lacked a sound enough intelligence to apply herself to anything at all" (II, 4). For Emma, there was nothing more in life. The only action that conformed to what was left of her dreams was to commit suicide, much like the romantic heroines of the novels on which she had been nourished. Stereotyped as was her act, to Emma it was dictated by what Baudelaire had elsewhere described as "the sophisms of her imagination"—an imagination that had motivated and determined her behavior throughout the novel.

Of perhaps even greater significance than the imagination which the poet-critic had recognized in Emma was her dandyism. Like the dandy of Baudelaire, Emma adopted an artificial self—but a self borrowed unfortunately from the sentimental novels and pictures that she had adored as a young girl. Though aware of the mediocrity and falsity of the model on which she had patterned herself, Baudelaire was, nevertheless, moved by her attempt to live the role which in her ignorance she had chosen. "The Dandy must aspire to be sublime without interruption, he must live and sleep before a mirror," the poet-critic had written in his *Journaux intimes* (*OC,* I:678). Of no one was the description more true than of Emma, who continued to play her role to the very end.

As a young girl, after her mother's death, her efforts to assume a Lamartinian melancholy left her "inwardly pleased to feel that she had attained at the first attempt that rare ideal of an ethereal life never achieved by *ordinary* souls" (my italics) (I, 6). After the ball at the Château de Vaubyessard, dazzled by the elegance and luxury she had known only in books, Emma renounced once and for all the stifling reality which surrounded her and determined to live her dreams. Like Baudelaire's dandy, she literally lived before a mirror, admiring her reflected self in the many roles she adopted to impress Léon, whether that of a virtuous wife, a devoted mother inspired by the Sachette of Victor Hugo's *Notre Dame de Paris,* or a romantic heroine dreaming over some book left lying in her lap. Even her emotional response after her surrender to Rodolphe reveals the importance she attached to playing the role she had chosen. Studying her reflection in the mirror, she thought only of the fact that she was finally about to realize her dream. In her long silent soliloquy Rodolphe's name is never mentioned. "I have a lover, I have a lover," she repeats, remembering the heroines of the books she had read and the happiness for which she had longed in vain. "She herself was becoming a very real part of her imaginary creations," Flaubert himself commented on one of the few occasions in which the narrator's voice is heard (II, 9).

Nowhere does Emma reveal more clearly the traits of the Baudelairean dandy than in the final pages of the novel: her rejection of Lheureux's advances to whom she had gone for money ("I am to be pitied, not bought"), her refusal to confess her guilt to Charles—though she knew he would end by forgiving her—for she could not bear "the weight of his magnanimity" (III, 7). After all, the role she had been playing depended on her belief that her husband's inferiority justified her attempt to find a love more beautiful than that which he could offer her.

Finally, as she lay dying, Emma called for a mirror and gazed at her image until great tears rolled down her cheeks. "Vivre et dormir devant un miroir," Baudelaire had written. Emma had done both, living and even dying before a mirror in the naive belief that she was realizing an ideal which seemed to her if not "sublime," at least eminently worthy of her aspirations.

If Baudelaire was moved by Emma's tragedy, there was good reason, for he too as a youth had been equally prodigal and foolish in his efforts to live the life of the dandy. He too had borrowed money, signed promissory notes, and even attempted suicide. But Baudelaire's dandyism had become more and more spiritual. Older and wiser, he was tormented not only by a lack of material success but by his failure to achieve moral perfection—to become "a hero and a saint *for oneself*," as he wrote in his *Journaux intimes* (OC, I:695). Emma would never have understood the final lines of "Un Voyage à Cythère"—"Ah, Lord, give me the strength to contemplate my heart and my body without loathing."

What Emma could have understood, however, and what she shared equally with the poet, was a desperate desire to escape—for Baudelaire, "anywhere out of this world," for Emma, anywhere filled with beauty and romance. And for both came the inevitable realization that escape could be found only in death itself.

Throughout the novel, Baudelaire must have noted parallels between Flaubert's heroine and himself: Emma's anguish and illness after having been jilted by Rodolphe, his own anger and grief at Jeanne's infidelity; Emma's effort to confide in the obtuse village priest, Bournisien, Baudelaire's disgust at the uncomprehending priest who had burned his copy of *Les Fleurs du Mal* in a fit of moral outrage; Emma's nostalgic memories of her convent days, the sight of the good sisters bent over their prie-dieux, the tall candlesticks on the altar, the gentle face of the Virgin; Baudelaire's nostalgic yearning for the innocence and happiness of his lost youth, for "le vert paradis des amours enfantines"; Emma's thoughts of the small farmhouse where she had grown up, her recall of the young colts galloping and galloping and of the bees striking against the windowpanes "like bouncing balls of gold" (II, 10), Baudelaire's memories of the small white house in Neuilly with the evening sun shining on the frugal cloth which covered the dinner table where he sat alone with his widowed mother.

Over and over on reading the novel, Baudelaire must have relived his own past and sympathized with the unhappy Emma. But where she, with her narcissism and egoism and her limited intelligence, had neither the capability nor the desire to change, he, at least, had the genius that allowed him to transform the spiritual loneliness of his tragic life into the triumph of his magnificent verse.[66]

Madame Bovary was the only novel that Baudelaire was to discuss formally, but five years later, after the publication of *Salammbô* in 1862, he aptly and incisively characterized the grandiose novel in a letter to his friend and publisher, Poulet-Malassis (December 13, 1862): "What Flaubert has done, he alone was able to do. Entirely too much bric-a-brac, but a great deal of splendor, epic, historic, political, even animal" (*Corr.*, II:271).

Flaubert for his part had great respect for Baudelaire's art and was outraged when, after the publication of *Les Fleurs du*

Mal, the poet was charged by the court with having offended public morals and was fined 300 francs and obliged to suppress six of his poems. Flaubert, who had narrowly escaped a similar fate and had even suggested a line of defense for Baudelaire's lawyer, was well aware of the power and originality of Baudelaire's verse. "You have found the means to rejuvenate Romanticism," he wrote from his retreat in Croisset. "You are like no one (which is the first of all virtues)" (*PLB,* p. 150).

In what follows it becomes clear that the author of *Madame Bovary* recognized in Baudelaire the very traits that he himself possessed and that he had attributed to Emma: "Ah! you really understand the dreariness of life!" Then in a final perceptive paragraph he adds what may well be said of Flaubert himself: "What I like above all in your book is that art comes first. And then you sing the flesh without loving it, in a sad and detached way that appeals to me. You are as resistant as marble and as penetrating as a London fog" (*PLB,* p. 150).

To *Les Paradis artificiels,* which Baudelaire had sent him in 1860, Flaubert had only one objection: "You have insisted (and on several occasions) a little too much (?) on an *Evil Spirit.* One perceives here and there a sort of Catholic leavening" (*PLB,* p. 155).

Baudelaire's answer to Flaubert's criticism (June 26, 1860) was typical and reveals the depth of his belief in an evil force seeking to control man's destiny: "I was struck by your observation and, after plumbing very sincerely the depths of my past reveries, I realized that I have always been obsessed by the impossibility of accounting for some of man's sudden acts and thoughts except by the hypothesis of the intervention of an evil force outside himself. That is a tremendous admission for which I won't blush even with the whole 19th century standing against me" (*Corr.,* II:53).

GEORGE SAND

Unlike Flaubert, Baudelaire had the greatest scorn and contempt for George Sand, with whom he had only a brief correspondence. Flaubert's affection for "la bonne dame de Nohant" was deep and sincere. He had wept bitterly at her funeral and, after her death, warmly praised her in a letter to a friend: "One had only to know her, as I knew her, to realize how much there was that was feminine in that great man, the immense depths of tenderness there were in that genius."[67]

Baudelaire's many ill-tempered and virulent comments made in the privacy of his *Journaux intimes* were at the opposite end of the pole. "She is stupid, she is ungainly, she is garrulous. Her ideas on morality have the same depth of judgment and delicacy of feeling as those of a janitress or kept woman. . . . I can't think of that stupid creature without a kind of shudder of disgust. If I met her, I couldn't keep from throwing a basin of holy water in her face" (*OC*, I:686–87).

Understandably, Sand's "famous flowing style so dear to the bourgeoisie" and her "social and moral ideas" were anathema to the author of *Les Fleurs du Mal* (". . . she claims that a good Christian does not believe in Hell. She has good reason to wish to abolish Hell" [*OC*, I:687]).

Yet there had been a time when Baudelaire thought more kindly of the author of *Lélia*. In his 1852 essay on Poe he had even referred to her as "a very great and justly famous writer," though he had qualified his praise by his restrictions about her facile style, which, he maintained, revealed, like that of all women, an "exuberant rapidity" ("she dashes off her masterpieces as if she were writing letters") (*OC*, II:283).

It is generally known that Baudelaire's hostility to the novelist dated from a misunderstanding regarding the actress Marie Daubrun, with whom he was in love. On August 14, 1855, the poet had written Sand asking her aid in obtaining a role for Marie in her play *Maître Favilla*. The role was given to someone else despite Sand's intervention, and Baudelaire, who believed that the novelist had made no effort to comply with his request, became incensed and was never able to forget what he believed to be her treachery.

The poet's hostility was exacerbated by a number of other factors—among them, envy of Sand's fame and success, despite what he considered her lack of artistry; her ideas pertaining to social and moral problems; and finally, her rejection of any belief in Hell and original sin.

In a provocative article entitled "Baudelaire et George Sand," Léon Cellier points out that, ironically, the poet owed a great deal to Sand's influence, whether or not he was actually aware of it. Cellier, like other scholars—including Antoine Adam and Jean Pommier—has noted the marked resemblances that are to be found in reading *Les Fleurs du Mal* and Sand's *Lélia, Lettres d'un voyageur, Les Sept Cordes de la lyre,* and *Consuelo.* Cellier even maintains that no one was more responsible than Sand for making spleen one of the discoveries of Romanticism and that *Lettres d'un voyageur* could well bear the subtitle *Spleen et Idéal.*[68]

Cellier agrees with J. Prévost, A. Fongaro, and M. Milner that Baudelaire's conception of Satan in his definition of beauty and in his poem "Les Litanies de Satan" owes much to the influence of George Sand. We have already noted that in his definition of beauty, Baudelaire had written: " It would be difficult for me not to conclude that the most perfect type of virile Beauty is *Satan*—in the manner of Milton" (*OC,* I:658). There is little doubt that Baudelaire's idea of Satan was completely Miltonic, but it seems quite possible that he arrived at that conception indirectly through the influence of George Sand. Quoting Fongaro, who maintains that "if Baudelaire had been sincere, . . . he would have written 'Satan in the manner of George Sand,'" Cellier adds, "For there is no doubt that Baudelaire owes much of his conception of Satan to *Consuelo,* as J. Prévost has pointed out. . . ."[69]

Cellier likewise refers to Max Milner, who has shown that from *Lélia* to *Consuelo* the figure of Satan becomes "more diverse and complex" and that he is presented as "the most beautiful of immortals after God." As Lucifer in the novel *Consuelo,* Satan is even transformed into "the incarnation of the democratic ideal" and consequently as "the justification of revolt."[70] Here, no doubt, Sand's Miltonic conception of Satan merged with the religious and revolutionary influence of Proudhon and resulted in Baudelaire's poem in which suffering and oppressed mankind turn away from the cruel, inhuman God of Proudhon and seek the pity of a Romantic and idealized Lucifer.

DUMAS PÈRE AND BALZAC

Of the other novelists of this time, Baudelaire knew—though only slightly—and thought highly of Alexandre Dumas père. As late as 1865 he admitted to Sainte-Beuve the fascination he felt for his washbuckling novels and dramas. In Brussels, where Dumas had come on a visit, Baudelaire was incensed when, as he wrote the famous *lundiste* (March 30, 1865), he saw the Belgians making fun of the novelist while forming a line to shake his hand.

Of all the novelists of the ninteenth century Baudelaire seems to have admired Balzac the most. The page that he devotes to the author of *La Comédie humaine* in his essay on Gautier is not only a great tribute in itself but is one of the most perceptive pages ever to have been written on the famous novelist. Like Philarète Chasles, he attributed Balzac's greatness to his visionary power rather than to his power of observation and, in so doing, inspired much of the criticism that has been written since that time. Moreover, there is little doubt that Balzac's novels, which dealt so effectively with modern subjects, not only did much to stimulate Baudelaire's ideas of modernity but also were one of the determining factors that prompted him to write *Les Tableaux parisiens*.

YOUNG WRITERS

Baudelaire was also acquainted with many of the lesser luminaries of his day—with critics, publishers, minor writers too numerous to mention. And to young aspiring writers, like Léon Cladel, Villiers de l'Isle-Adam, and Catulle Mendès, he was unfailingly generous and unselfish in his aid. He not only wrote a review (1861) of Cladel's *Les Martyrs ridicules* that afterward served as a preface to the novel itself but also helped in editing the style. The impoverished and eccentric Villiers de l'Isle-Adam, who seems to have met Baudelaire in 1859 and who shared the poet's enthusiasm for the music of Wagner, set to music three of his poems: "Le Vin de l'assassin," "La Mort des amants," and "Recueillement." In timid and deferential letters he poured out his high esteem for *Les Fleurs du Mal* ("Sooner or later its humanity and greatness will have to be recognized") and told of his wish to produce a study of the Master (*PLB,* p. 389).

The young, ambitious Catulle Mendès, who, like Cladel and Villiers de l'Isle-Adam, was an ardent admirer of the author of *Les Fleurs du Mal,* did what he could to encourage the ill and embittered poet. After coming to Paris from Bordeaux, he founded the *Revue fantaisiste,* an ill-fated journal that lasted less than a year, in which he published works of Baudelaire and his friends. Later, while Baudelaire was in Brussels, he wrote urging him to contribute any verses he might wish to *Le Parnasse contemporain, recueil de vers nouveaux,* which he was founding with L. X. Ricard. It was Mendès who suggested the title *Les Nouvelles Fleurs du Mal* for the group of poems sent him by Baudelaire. One of the poet's last letters, written at his dictation, was to express his approval of the title and to call attention to several slight mistakes in the proof that had been sent him.

It was also Mendès who, late one night in Paris, encountered Baudelaire at the Gare du Nord at the time when the poet, in desperation, made a quick trip to Paris from Brussels in an effort to settle an urgent financial matter involving the rights to three volumes of his works. Seeing Baudelaire haggard and unkempt and suspecting that he had little or no money, Mendès invited him to his lodging. That evening, lying fully clothed on the *canapé,* Baudelaire, after pretending to read, began to talk. He confided bitterly to his astounded young friend the pathetically small amount of money he had earned in a lifetime—15,892 francs and 60 centimes. Then, in a long monologue, occasionally broken by moments of silence, he began to speak—of Manet and of Wagner, of Banville, Vigny and Leconte de Lisle, and finally of Gérard de Nerval, who, he kept insisting almost hysterically, had not killed himself. Suddenly he ceased talking. Some time later, Mendès heard a deep muffled sob. The next morning he awoke to find Baudelaire gone; on the corner of the table there was a note saying only, "A bientôt."[71]

In the last years of his life Baudelaire had younger disciples whom he never met personally but who, filled with enthusiasm for the originality and power of his verse, hailed him as their "Master." Before the poet went to Brussels, the young Stéphane Mallarmé is said to have gone to Paris in the hope of meeting him. One day he saw Baudelaire looking at some books in a stall along the Seine but was too shy to speak or to introduce himself. In February 1865 he published in *L'Artiste* a prose poem in which he evoked the impression made on him by *Les Fleurs du Mal.*

On November 16 and 30 and December 23, 1865, Verlaine published in *L'Art* a series of highly laudatory articles in which he analyzed perceptively and sympathetically the poetry of *Les Fleurs du Mal.* Knowing how much it would mean to his mother, the poet forwarded to her two of the three articles which had been sent to him and in a letter (March 5, 1866) remarked: "There is talent among these young people; but how much nonsense! what exaggerations and what youthful infatuation! For some years I have been noticing here and there imitations and tendencies which alarmed me. I know nothing more compromising than imitators and I like nothing so much as to be alone. But that is not possible; and it seems that *the Baudelaire school* exists" (*Corr.,* II:625).

AUGUSTE POULET-MALASSIS AND CHARLES ASSELINEAU

Among lesser known figures, none were more closely associated with Baudelaire than Auguste Poulet-Malassis and Charles Asselineau. Though their names are scarcely known except by specialists in nineteenth-century literature, their influence on the author of *Les Fleurs du Mal* was obviously as great—if not greater—than that of the most distinguished men of his day. Highly intelligent, erudite, and knowledgeable both in contemporary literature and art as well as in that of the past, they offered him critical suggestions and advice, served as a sounding board for his ideas, and encouraged him in every way possible.

Of even greater importance, however, were the companionship and warm friendship that they never failed to offer the poet, especially in his moments of greatest need. Without their understanding and help, whether psychological or material, Baudelaire might not have had the wherewithal to publish what he did or the courage to continue his struggle in the face of increasingly difficult problems that at times drove him almost to the point of suicide.

Malassis, who shared in the poet's pleasures as well as in his misfortunes, played an especially important part in Baudelaire's literary life. His father in Alençon owned one of the oldest presses in the country, and Auguste, while still quite young, developed a deep interest in printing as well as research. His study at the École des Chartes was interrupted in 1848 by the revolution when, during the June insurrection, the young student, a convinced Socialist, began to publish a subversive paper, *L'Aimable Faubourien, journal de la canaille.* Arrested and imprisoned for carrying a gun, he was released through the help of influential friends and permitted to return to his studies.

Gradually he lost interest in school, became a member of Bohemia, and after the death of his father in 1852 returned to Alençon to take over the business, which he shared with his brother-in-law de Broise. While there he printed the *Journal d'Alençon,* in which he included articles by his literary friends, and beautiful editions of Banville, Baudelaire, Leconte de Lisle, Gautier, Sainte-Beuve, Asselineau, Champfleury and others.

Temperamentally, Malassis was more a man of letters than a businessman. One of the persons who reformed the art of typography in nineteenth-century France, he published books that today have become rarities sought by bibliophiles everywhere. His wit, culture, and charm, his brilliant conversation and sense of humor, his loyalty and generosity endeared him to his friends, who affectionately called him by such soubriquets as "Coco Mal Perché" or "le pullens male sedens." His lack of business acumen and the fact that he often published his friends' books at a loss annoyed and upset his more practical partner and led to serious financial difficulties for the firm.

Malassis's friendship with Baudelaire did not help the situation. Both were constantly in debt and had devised the most complex schemes of borrowing and reborrowing from each other to avoid paying their bills on the same day. The publication of *Les Fleurs du Mal* (1857) by Malassis only made matters worse. The long delay in the printing, caused mainly by Baudelaire's procrastination and meticulous proof-correcting, added to the expense of the publication, and the condemnation of the volume by the court proved disastrous. Baudelaire was fined 300 francs; Poulet-Malassis and de Broise 100 francs each. Six poems were to be banned and deleted from further copies sold. Interestingly enough, the judgment lasted until 1949, when it was reversed by the courts and Baudelaire was finally completely vindicated.

Malassis continued to be dogged by ill luck. The fine and the loss of the whole edition of *Les Fleurs du Mal* were followed by fines and lawsuits for other publications frowned on by the government. Baudelaire's brochure on Gautier was a financial failure, even though it sold for only one franc. *Les Paradis artificiels,* published in 1860, sold poorly, and the second edition of *Les Fleurs du Mal* (1861) scarcely did better. Baudelaire was deeply in debt to Malassis, and his friend was badly in need of repayment.

In 1861, de Broise withdrew from the partnership and became the sole owner of the press at Alençon, where the contract for the *Journal d'Alençon* in addition to other work assured him of financial security. Malassis took over the bookshop which the two had established in Paris. Imprisoned for debt in 1863, he decided after his month's stay in prison to go to Belgium, where, in addition to publishing rare and erotic books as well as political pamphlets attacking the Empire, he brought out Baudelaire's *Les Epaves* (1866).

Seven months after Malassis's departure for Belgium, Baudelaire joined him in Brussels (April 1864), hoping to be able to find a publisher for his complete works and to give a series of lectures. Unfortunately, the lectures proved a fiasco and the poet's hopes of finding a publisher failed to materialize. In the meantime, Malassis was again in serious financial straits, and Baudelaire found himself unable to pay the 5,000 francs that he had owed him since 1862. When Malassis threatened to sell the rights to the published works which the poet had given him as a mortgage, Baudelaire, in a hasty trip to Paris and Honfleur, tried desperately to obtain the necessary funds and finally mustered 2,000 francs, thanks to the assistance of his mother and also to that of Manet. The remaining 3,000 francs were not repaid until 1868, a year after the poet's death.

Despite his many problems, Malassis never lost his courage or his love of life. It was in his company and in that of the artist Félicien Rops that the poet found his greatest pleasure during his self-imposed exile in Belgium. In writing to Sainte-Beuve (March 30, 1865), he expressed his amazement at Malassis's "courage, activity, and incorrigible gaiety" as well as at his remarkable erudition in matters of books and prints (*Corr.,* II:491). And on a photo taken by the Belgian photographer Neyt, Baudelaire wrote the following tribute to his friend: "To my friend Auguste Malassis, the sole being whose laughter has lessened my sadness in Belgium."

When Baudelaire became ill, Malassis kept his friends in Paris informed of his condition and did his best to cheer the ill and discouraged poet. After Baudelaire's return to Paris in the company of Arthur Stevens, Malassis stayed on in Belgium until the amnesty of August 15, 1869. The last years of his life were devoted to scholarly and bibliographical publications.

Baudelaire's acquaintance with Asselineau began in 1845, when he was introduced to him by the painter Deroy at an exhibition in the Louvre. After 1850 the two became inseparable friends. Writer, bibliophile, and, during the last years of his life, director of the Bibliothèque Mazarine, Asselineau was known for his self-effacing nature, his sensitive mind, and his critical judgment.

Passionately fond of poetry, he was the devoted friend of a

host of writers and artists and always stood ready to encourage and aid them in moments of need. It was he who brought the desperately ill Banville to the nursing home at Bellevue when the poet was on the point of death, he whom Nerval sought out shortly before his suicide and who was asked to go to the morgue to identify the body, he to whom Baudelaire could always turn, whether for financial aid, for literary advice, or for help of any kind. Asselineau was the one who suggested adding what is now the third stanza of "L'Albatros" and who, in 1857, was persuaded to "take into protective custody" copies of *Les Fleurs du Mal,* when it became evident in July of that year that prosecution was imminent.

In his turn, Baudelaire assisted his friend with the preface to *La Double Vie* and afterward wrote a flattering review that appeared in *L'Artiste.* Moreover, in 1862 he composed the poem "Le Coucher du soleil romantique," intended as an epilogue for a book that was to be published by Asselineau: *Mélanges tirés d'une petite bibliothèque romantique.* For the same volume Banville wrote "L'Aube romantique," which was to serve as a prologue. The book did not appear until 1867.

During Baudelaire's last illness Asselineau stood by until the end and made most of the arrangements for his care. After the poet's death, he sent out the announcements to the literary world and, with Banville, pronounced one of the funeral orations at the grave. His voice choked with emotion, he strove to reveal the Baudelaire who had hidden his real self beneath the mask of "ironic reserve" which he had created for himself. "I can only pity those who were deceived by it," he concluded.[72] Later, with the help of Banville, he edited the posthumous edition (1868–70) of Baudelaire's works. In 1868 he published a moving biography of the poet.

MARQUIS DE CUSTINE

"You reflect like a faithful mirror the spirit of a sick society and time," the Marquis de Custine wrote the author of *Les Fleurs du Mal* in August 1857 (*PLB,* p. 109). Baudelaire, who had the greatest respect for the intelligence of the marquis and who saw in him the embodiment of the dandy, had sent him a complimentary copy of his volume of verse. Although Custine was one of the few who supported Baudelaire at the time of his prosecution, the comment in his gracious and dignified letter was intended to be frankly critical. The wealthy marquis, a man of letters in his own right and a friend and patron of the Romanticists in 1830, was among those who had failed to note how Baudelaire had succeeded in transforming ugliness into beauty—how, in fact, he had carried out in practice the very theory that he had suggested in his essay on Gautier: "It is one of the prodigious privileges of Art that the horrible, artistically expressed, becomes beauty . . ." (*OC,* II:123).

Yet in one respect Custine's observation was perfectly correct. The poems of *Les Fleurs du Mal,* like everything else Baudelaire wrote, were indeed a mirror of his time, for they were written by one who knew every aspect of his age.

So lively had been the poet's interest in all that went on around him, so much energy had he devoted, especially in his earlier years, to seeking pleasure—aesthetic, intellectual, and social—so many hours had he spent in talking and discussing problems with painters, musicians, and men of letters that he often seemed to have been neglecting his own career. Although he frequently blamed himself for what he called his idleness, in time he came to realize that the hours he thought wasted had proved as much an advantage as a hindrance. In his *Journaux intimes* he noted: "It was partly through leisure that I grew. To my great detriment, since leisure without fortune increases debts. But to my great profit so far as sensibility, meditation, and the possibility of dandyism and dilettantism were concerned" (*OC,* I:697).

Baudelaire was right. Despite his lack of productivity, his ideas had been growing and maturing and he had become more and more the product of his day. "I am a part of everyone; everyone is a part of me," he wrote in his *Journaux intimes* (*OC,* I:651). The many aspects and problems of nineteenth-century life—aesthetic and metaphysical, social, political, and psychological—that faced the men and women he knew or observed became the "substantific marrow" both of his poetry and prose and gave them a richness and significance they would have lacked had he been less a man of his age. "Almost all our originality comes from the stamp that *time* imprints on our feeling," Baudelaire wrote in *Le Peintre de la vie moderne* (OC, I:696), and it cannot be denied that Baudelaire's originality and the impact of his prose and poetry stem in large degree from this very fact.

Moreover, Baudelaire seems to have a special appeal for the twentieth-century reader, whose problems and dilemmas are not unlike those of the nineteenth century. "The impulse to self-destruction," wrote Henri Peyre in 1957, "the obsession with death and the absurd, the delights and, even more, the cerebral torments of eroticism, the horror and pride alternately taken in man's fate and, most of all, the lucid view of man in his self-inflicted pangs, 'la conscience dans le mal,' all those accessories of modern man as the literatures of several countries portray him today are already present in Baudelaire. Poetry, with him, rivalled the novel in density and in riches. We read *Les Fleurs du Mal* at fifty with the same sense of reward as when we discovered them in our adolescence."[73] Not only Baudelaire's poetry but his prose and in particular his critical essays too have retained their appeal and timeliness for the twentieth-century reader; the subjects they treat and the ideas they express seem as pertinent today as at the moment they were written.

If Baudelaire offers us a keen and penetrating insight into a whole period, it is largely because he was so completely a man of his time. Fortunately, for the reader of today, his work has lost none of its relevance and appeal and has made its author a man not only of his own time but of ours as well.

Notes

CHAPTER 1

1 David Kelley, *Baudelaire: Salon de 1846* (Oxford: Clarendon Press, 1975), p. ix.

2 At the request of Eugène Crépet, who was writing the "Etude biographique," which he placed at the beginning of the *Oeuvres posthumes* of 1887, Prarond wrote a long letter in which he furnished Crépet with much valuable information about Baudelaire's early years. For the letter in question, see Claude Pichois, *Etudes et Témoignages* (Neuchâtel: A la Baconnière, 1967), pp. 12–36.

3 See Jean Ziegler, "Emile Deroy et L'Esthétique de Baudelaire," *Gazette des Beaux-Arts* (May–June, 1976), pp. 153–60.

4 *Diderot: Sur l'art et les artistes,* edited and introduced by Jean Seznec for the Miroirs de l'Art series (Paris: Hermann, 1967), p. 12.

5 Ziegler, "Emile Deroy et L'Esthétique de Baudelaire," p. 155.

6 *Baudelaire et Asselineau,* ed. Crépet and Pichois (Paris: Nizet, 1953), p. 168.

7 René M. Galand, "Baudelaire et la Fontaine de Jouvence," *Bulletin Baudelairien,* vol. 2, no. 1 (1966), p. 6. *See also* his discussion in his book *Baudelaire: Poétiques et Poésie* (Paris: Nizet, 1969), p. 41.

8 Kelley, *Baudelaire: Salon de 1846,* p. 44.

9 Ziegler, "Emile Deroy et L'Esthétique de Baudelaire," p. 154.

10 The above material comes mainly from Ziegler, p. 155.

11 *Baudelaire et Asselineau,* p. 69.

12 Ibid.

13 Ibid., p. 71.

14 Various dates have been assigned the composition of the poem, but Pichois argues convincingly that it was written between 1845 and 1846. OC, I:998.

15 Kelley, *Baudelaire: Salon de 1846,* p. 109.

16 Frances Suzman Jowell, *Thoré-Bürger and the Art of the Past* (New York: Garland Publishing, Inc., 1977), p. 357, n. 29.

17 It is believed that Balzac himself did not formulate Frenhofer's views but that he had the help of someone who had a greater understanding of art than he. *See* Jerrold Lane, "Art Criticism and the Authorship of the *Chef-*

d'Oeuvre inconnu: A Preliminary Study," in *The Artist and the Writer in France, Essays in honour of Jean Seznec*, eds. Francis Haskell, Anthony Levi, and Robert Shackleton (Oxford: Clarendon Press, 1974), pp. 86–99.

18 Jowell, *Thoré-Bürger*, pp. 77–78.

19 *Baudelaire et Asselineau*, p. 75.

20 Jowell, *Thoré-Bürger*, p. 158.

21 Kelley, *Bandelaire: Salon de 1846*, p. 109.

22 Baudelaire himself guessed that it was about 1845 when he met Delacroix for the first time, but Armand Moss argues convincingly that the meeting took place in 1846. See Moss, *Baudelaire et Delacroix* (Paris: Nizet, 1973), p. 39.

23 Lloyd James Austin, "Baudelaire et Delacroix," *Baudelaire, Actes du colloque de Nice* (25–27 May 1967), Annales de la Faculté des Lettres et Sciences Humaines de Nice, 1968, p. 18.

24 Moss, *Baudelaire et Delacroix*, p. 32.

25 A comment made by Delacroix in his *Journal* (August 30, 1859) about modern poetry may well give us a clue to his private opinion of *Les Fleurs du Mal*: "One should have Boileau under one's pillow; he delights and purifies: he makes us love the beautiful and the honest, whereas our moderns breathe only acrid fumes, sometimes fatal to the soul, and lead our imagination astray with fanciful images." *Journal d'Eugène Delacroix*, 3 vols., ed. A. Joubin (Paris: Plon, 1932), 3:231.

26 Quoted from Austin, "Baudelaire et Delacroix," p. 18.

27 See Delacroix, *Journal*, 3:270, 289–90.

28 Alan Bowness is one of those who accept the 1848 dating: "When he moved into the Parisian literary Bohemia in 1848 Courbet portrayed his new friends—Champfleury, Baudelaire, Trapadoux." See Bowness, "Courbet's Proudhon," *The Burlington Magazine* (March 1978), p. 123.

29 Alan Bowness, "Courbet and Baudelaire," *Gazette des Beaux-Arts* (December, 1977), p. 194.

30 Ibid.

31 Ibid., p. 196.

32 Champfleury, "In Defense of the Funeral at Ornans," in *Courbet in Perspective*, ed. Petra Ten-Doesschate Chu (Englewood Cliffs: Prentice-Hall, 1977), p. 72.

33 Jowell, *Thoré-Bürger*, p. 152.

34 Bowness, "The Painter's Studio," in *Courbet in Perspective*, pp. 135–36.

35 Delacroix, *Journal*, 2:363–64.

36 The distinguished art historian Francis Haskell has recently questioned the authenticity of the painting. See "Baudelaire at the Petit Palais," *The Burlington Magazine* (March, 1969), p. 173.

37 Bowness, "Courbet and Baudelaire," p. 199.

38 Champfleury, *Souvenirs et portraits de jeunesse* (Paris: Dentu, 1872), p. 188.

39   Joseph C. Sloane, *Paul Marc Joseph Chenavard* (Chapel Hill: The University of North Carolina Press, 1962), p. 162.

40   Chenavard was also a good friend of Delacroix, who loved to talk and argue with the philosopher from Lyons despite the differences in their aesthetic beliefs and in their art. According to Baudelaire, Delacroix in his last hours expressed the desire to shake the hand of his friendly adversary (*OC*, II:766).

41   Margaret Gilman, *The Idea of Poetry in France* (Cambridge: Harvard University Press, 1958), p. 269.

42   Sloane, *Chenavard*, p. 187; idem, *Iconographie de Charles Baudelaire* (Geneva: Pierre Cailler, 1960), pp. 216–17.

43   Maurice Rheims, *Nineteenth Century Sculpture* (New York: Abrams, Inc., 1977), p. 48, n. 57; p. 108.

44   Ibid., p. 45, n. 10.

45   Baudelaire, *Les Fleurs du Mal*, ed. Jean Pommier and Claude Pichois (Paris: Club des Librairies de France, 1959), pp. 488–89.

46   Jowell, *Thoré-Bürger*, p. 50.

47   Rheims, *Nineteenth Century Sculpture*, p. 48.

48   Francis Hyslop, "Baudelaire and Michelangelo," *Les Bonnes Feuilles*, vol. 4, nos. 1 & 2 (Spring, 1975), pp. 19–31.

49   Jowell, *Thoré-Bürger*, p. 52.

50   Oliver W. Larkin, *Daumier: Man of his Time* (New York: McGraw-Hill, 1966), p. 91.

51   Jean Adhémar, *Honoré Daumier* (Paris: 1954), p. 32.

52   Larkin, *Daumier: Man of his Time*, p. 149.

53   Baudelaire also mentions Meryon in *Peintres et Aquafortistes* and in *L'Eau-Forte est à la mode*. In 1858, Boissard had published in *Le Siècle* a glowing article on Meryon, whose prints he had just discovered. The article may have influenced Baudelaire; at least, both stress the mystery and poetic quality of Meryon's work. *See* Jean Ziegler, "Baudelaire et Meryon," *Bulletin Baudelairien*, vol. 2, no. 1 (Summer, 1975), pp. 3–14.

54   Charles Meryon, *Prints and Drawings*, Catalogue by James D. Burke (New Haven: Yale University Press, 1974), p. 69.

55   Lois Boe Hyslop and Francis Hyslop, "Baudelaire and Manet: A Re-Appraisal," in *Baudelaire as a Love Poet and Other Essays*, ed. Lois Boe Hyslop (University Park and London: The Pennsylvania State University Press, 1969), pp. 87–130.

56   Antonin Proust, *Edouard Manet* (Paris: H. Laurens, 1913), p. 22.

57   Ibid.

58   Ibid., p. 35.

59   Quoted from George Mauner, *Manet, Peintre-Philosophe* (University Park and London: The Pennsylvania State University Press, 1975), p. 159. Mauner has reversed the usual interpretation of Manet. According to him, Manet—far from being just an eye and a hand—was a philosophical artist

whose work contains a rich symbolic content, some of it related directly to Baudelaire's writings. Mauner stresses Baudelaire's emphasis on the transitory and eternal elements of beauty and insists that "modernity and its relationship to the eternal is the basis of all his [Manet's] major works of the 1860s, and of many after that."

60 Anne Coffin Hanson, *Manet and the Modern Tradition* (New Haven: Yale University Press, 1977), p. 54.

61 Ibid., p. 55, n. 3.

62 Proust, *Edouard Manet*, p. 39.

63 Both Mauner, *Manet, Peintre-Philosophe* (p. 61), and Hanson, *Manet and the Modern Tradition* (p. 67), agree with Nils Sandblad, who has convincingly demonstrated that the paintings were done in 1862.

64 Nils Sandblad, *Manet, Three Studies in Artistic Conception* (Lund: C. W. K. Gleerup, 1954), p. 32.

65 Jean Adhémar, "Baudelaire, critique d'art," *Revue des Sciences Humaines* (Jan.–Mar., 1958), p. 118.

66 Hyslop and Hyslop, "Baudelaire and Manet: A Re-Appraisal," pp. 101–02.

67 A. Tabarant, *Manet et ses oeuvres* (Paris: Gallimard, 1947), p. 132.

68 Mauner, *Manet, Peintre-Philosophe*, p. 120.

69 Diderot, *Salons*, 4 vols., ed. Jean Seznec and Jean Adhémar (Oxford: Clarendon Press, 1957–67), 3:94.

70 George Heard Hamilton, *Manet and his Critics* (New York: W. W. Norton & Co., 1969), p. 153.

71 John Rewald, *The History of Impressionism* (New York: Doubleday, 1961), pp. 86 and 198.

72 Proust, *Edouard Manet*, pp. 90–91.

73 Paul Jamot, George Wildenstein, and M-L. Bataille, *Manet*, 2 vols. (Paris: Beaux-Arts, 1932), 1:102.

74 Ibid.

75 Etienne Moreau-Nélaton, *Manet raconté par lui-même*, 2 vols. (Paris: Laurens, 1926), 2:96.

76 Paul Haesaerts, *Histoire de la Peinture moderne en Flandre* (Brussels: Les Editions de l'Arcade, 1959), pp. 60–61.

77 Jacques Crépet, *Propos sur Baudelaire*, comp. Claude Pichois (Paris: Mercure de France, 1957), pp. 90–94.

78 Charles Baudelaire, Correspondance générale, 6 vols. ed. Jacques Crépet (Paris: Conard, 1948), 4:305–06, n. 2.

CHAPTER 2

1 Lloyd James Austin, *L'Univers poétique de Baudelaire* (Paris, 1956), p. 272.

2 Pommier, *Dans les chemins de Baudelaire* (Paris: Corti, 1945), p. 316. *See also* Antoine Adam in his edition of *Les Fleurs du Mal* (Paris: Garnier,

1961), p. 269. The problem has been discussed in detail in my article "Baudelaire's *Elévation* and E. T. A. Hoffmann," *The French Review* (April, 1973), pp. 951-59.

3   E. T. A. Hoffmann, *Kreisleriana*, trans. Albert Beguin (Paris: Editions Fourcade, 1931), p. 34. The translation of Hoffmann known by Baudelaire may have been that of Loève-Veimars, though other translations, notably those of Théodore Toussenel and of H. Egmont, were available.

4   Baudelaire even owned a lithograph of Hoffmann done by Lemud which hung on a wall of his apartment in the Hôtel Pimodan. See Cl. Pichois, "Sur Baudelaire et Hoffmann," *Revue de littérature comparée* 27 (1953):98-99.

5   *Kreisleriana,* p. 30.

6   *Baudelaire et Asselineau,* ed. Crépet and Pichois (Paris: Nizet, 1953), p. 157.

7   Ibid., p. 175.

8   Charles Baudelaire, *Edgar Allan Poe: Sa vie et ses ouvrages,* ed. W. T. Bandy (Toronto and Buffalo: University of Toronto Press, 1973), p. xviii.

9   Léon Guichard, *La Musique et les lettres en France au temps du Wagnérisme* (Paris: Presses Universitaires de France, 1963), p. 264, n. 10.

10   Ibid., p. 16.

11   Ibid., p. 28.

12   Ibid., p. 29.

13   *Realism and Tradition in Art, Sources and Documents 1848-1900,* ed. Linda Nochlin (Englewood Cliffs: Prentice-Hall, 1966), p. 38.

14   Guichard, *La Musique en France,* p. 30.

15   Ibid., p. 262, no. 56. In 1869, after attending a performance of *Rienzi* at the Théâtre lyrique, Gautier seems to have forgotten all his reservations and, contradicting much of what he had written in 1857, showed himself an ardent and enthusiastic Wagnerite. Although his daughter had undoubtedly done much to influence her father, it is significant that *Rienzi* was far more traditional than *Tannhäuser* and closer to the type of opera to which Gautier was accustomed.

16   Reyer himself had published an account of the opera in the *Courrier de Paris* on September 29, 1857.

17   Guichard, *La Musique en France,* p. 18.

18   Ibid., p. 268, n. 62.

19   Ibid., p. 37.

20   Richard Wagner, *My Life,* authorized translation from the German (New York: Dodd, Mead, and Co., 1953), p. 730.

21   Ibid., pp. 730-31.

22   Guichard, *La Musique en France,* p. 268, n. 52.

23   Wagner, *My Life,* p. 780.

24   W. T. Bandy, "Baudelaire and Liszt," *Modern Language Notes* (December, 1938), p. 585.

25   Wagner, *My Life*, p. 780.

26   Charles Baudelaire, *L'Art romantique*, ed. Jacques Crépet (Paris: Conard, 1925), p. 512. *Baudelaire et Asselineau*, p. 185.

27   Baudelaire was also planning to write *Un drame sur les Bohémiens* and, in his unfinished sketch for the libretto of an opera *La Fin de Don Juan* (1852 or 1853), intended to have one of the scenes take place in a gypsy camp in the mountains. At the end of the sketch, Don Juan seems to voice Baudelaire's sentiments in his remarks: "I would almost wager that they have elements of happiness that I don't know. . . . That strange race has for me the charm of the unknown" (*OC*, I:628).

28   Charles Baudelaire, *Petits Poëmes en Prose*, ed. Robert Kopp (Paris: Corti, 1969), pp. 309–10.

CHAPTER 3

1   For an account of Baudelaire's political activity in 1848, *see* Jules Mouquet and W. T. Bandy, *Baudelaire en 1848* (Paris: Emil-Paul frères, 1946).

2   Eugène Crépet, *Baudelaire. Etude Biographique*. Review by Jacques Crépet (Paris, 1907), p. 79.

3   Marcel Ruff, *Etudes baudelairiennes* III (Neuchâtel: A la Baconnière, 1973), p. 212.

4   Léon Cellier, *L'Epopée romantique* (Paris: P.U.F., 1954), p. 104.

5   Claude Pichois, *Baudelaire. Etudes et Témoignages* (Neuchâtel: A la Baconnière, 1967), p. 107.

6   Ibid., p. 101.

7   Ibid., pp. 101, 103.

8   Mouquet and Bandy, *Baudelaire en 1848*, p. 239.

9   Pichois, *Baudelaire. Etudes etTémoignages*, p. 117.

10   T. G. Clark, *The Absolute Bourgeois* (Connecticut: New York Graphic Society, 1973), p. 166.

11   Ibid., pp. 207–08, n. 100.

12   Gerstle Mack, *Gustave Courbet* (New York: Knopf, 1951), p. 57.

13   Champfleury, *Souvenirs et portraits de jeunesse* (Paris: Dentu, 1872), p. 188.

14   Ibid., p. 191.

15   Ibid., p. 298.

16   Clark, *The Absolute Bourgeois*, p. 163.

17   Eugène Delacroix, *Journal*, ed. André Joubin (Paris: Plon, 1932), 1:258.

18   Charles Baudelaire, *Correspondance générale*, ed. J. Crépet and Cl. Pichois (Paris: Conard, 1949), 5:201, n. 3.

19   Mack, *Gustave Courbet*, p. 70.

20   Baudelaire, *Les Fleurs du Mal*, ed. Crépet and Blin (Paris: Corti, 1942), p. 546.

21   René Galand, *Baudelaire, Poétiques et Poésies* (Paris: Nizet, 1969), p. 453;
     Clark, p. 167. Clark also suggests that the tone and argument of "Le Renie-
     ment de Saint Pierre" owes everything to the *Philosophie de la misère*. I
     had reached this conclusion independently several years before reading
     Clark.

22   Baudelaire, *Les Fleurs du Mal,* ed. Antoine Adam (Paris: Garnier, 1961), p.
     420.

23   Alison Fairlie, *Leconte de Lisle's Poems on the Barbarian Races* (Cam-
     bridge: University Press, 1947), p. 263.

24   P.-J. Proudhon, *Carnets* (Paris: Marcel Rivière, 1961), 2:272.

25   Proudhon's confinement to prison was not excessively strict. He was
     allowed to receive visitors, read any books that he wished, write articles,
     and even circulate freely in the city on occasion. In December 1849, while
     still in prison, he obtained a leave and permission to marry. See comments of
     Théodore Ruyssen in *POC,* IV:49–50.

26   *Carnets,* 3:286–87.

27   Charles Baudelaire, *Les Fleurs du Mal,* ed. J. Crépet (Paris: Conard, 1922),
     p. 475, and also Crépet and Blin (Paris: Corti, 1942), p. 511. Pichois
     likewise cites the passage in the Pléiade 1975 edition of the *Oeuvres com-
     plètes,* 1:1081.

28   Baudelaire, *Les Fleurs du Mal,* ed. Antoine Adam (Paris: Garnier, 1961), p.
     144.

29   Adam, p. 423.

30   Mario Praz, *The Romantic Agony* (New York: Meridian Books, 1956), p.
     56.

31   Cited from Praz, p. 57.

32   Chateaubriand, *Le Génie du Christianisme,* pt. 2, 4:9.

33   Jules Troubat, *Champfleury, Courbet, Max Buchon* (Paris: Lucien Duc,
     1900), p. 109.

CHAPTER 4

1   Edmond and Jules Goncourt, *Journal* (Paris: Flammarion, Fasquelle,
     1935–1936), 1:141–42.

2   Ernest Raynaud, *Baudelaire et la religion du dandysme* (Paris: *Mercure de
     France,* 1918), p. 46.

3   Théophile Gautier, *Salon de 1841,* cited from M. C. Spencer, *The Art Criti-
     cism of Théophile Gautier* (Genève: Droz, 1969), p. 17.

4   Georges Poulet, *Etudes sur le Temps Humain* (Paris: Plon, 1950), p. 305.

5   Joanna Richardson, *Théophile Gautier, His Life and His Times* (London:
     Max Reinhardt, 1958), p. 298.

6   Théophile Gautier, *Les Jeunes-France: romans goguenards* (Paris: Charpen-
     tier, 1883), pp. 194–95.

7   Poulet, *Etudes sur le Temps Humain,* p. 278.

8   *Baudelaire et Asselineau,* ed. Crépet and Pichois (Paris: Nizet, 1953), p. 151.

9   André Coeuroy, *L'Esprit français et Wagner* (Paris: Gallimard, 1965), p. 173.

10 W. T. Bandy and Cl. Pichois, *Baudelaire devant ses contemporains* (Monaco: Editions du Rocher, 1957), pp. 138-39.

11 Cited from Pichois, *Oeuvres complètes* (Paris: Gallimard, 1976), p. 1161.

12 Bradford R. Collins, "Manet's *Luncheon in the Studio:* An Homage to Baudelaire," *Art Journal* (Winter, 1978), pp. 107-13.

13 For the most thorough and up-to-date study of the relationship of Poe and Baudelaire, see W. T. Bandy's critical edition of Baudelaire's first and longest essay on Poe (1852), *Charles Baudelaire—Edgar Allan Poe: Sa vie et ses ouvrages* (Toronto: University of Toronto Press, 1973).

14 Jacques Petit, "Baudelaire et Barbey d'Aurevilly," *Revue d'Histoire Littéraire de la France* (April–June, 1967), p. 62.

15 Armand B. Chartier, *Barbey d'Aurevilly* (Boston: Twayne Press, 1977), p. 29.

16 Ellen Moers, *The Dandy* (New York: Viking Press, 1960), p. 282. For Baudelaire's highly original conception of dandyism, see his chapter on the subject in his essay *Le Peintre de la vie moderne.*

17 Chartier, *Barbey d'Aurevilly,* p. 56.

18 Petit, "Baudelaire et Barbey," p. 68.

19 Ibid.

20 W. T. Bandy, *Baudelaire Judged by his Contemporaries* (New York: Institute of French Studies, Columbia University, 1933), p. 97, n. 187.

21 *Baudelaire et Asselineau,* p. 219.

22 James S. Patty, "Baudelaire et Babou," *Revue d'Histoire Littéraire de la France* (April–June, 1967), p. 40.

23 Ibid., p. 44.

24 Norman Barlow, *Sainte-Beuve to Baudelaire* (Durham: Duke University Press, 1964), p. 171.

25 Bandy and Pichois, *Baudelaire devant ses contemporains,* p. 187.

26 Gérald Antoine and Claude Pichois, "Sainte-Beuve, juge de Stendhal et de Baudelaire," *Revue des Sciences Humaines* (Jan.–March, 1957), pp. 29-31.

27 Ibid., p. 26.

28 Ibid.

29 Ibid., p. 28.

30 Henri Peyre, *Connaissance de Baudelaire* (Paris: Corti, 1951), p. 27.

31 Pichois, *Baudelaire, Etudes et temoignages* (Neuchâtel: A la Baconnière, 1967), p. 19.

32 Ibid.

33 It is often forgotten that the flattering essay of 1861 was concerned only with Hugo the poet and was based on *Les Contemplations* and *La Légende*

des siècles, as Baudelaire carefully reminds us in the opening paragraph of his essay on *Les Misérables.*

34 Armand Fraisse, one of the best critics of his time according to Cl. and V. Pichois, continues to be more or less obscure largely because he stayed in Lyons, where his work remains hidden in *Le Salut public* of that city. See Cl. and V. Pichois, *Armand Fraisse sur Baudelaire* (Gembloux: Duculat, 1973).

35 In his poem entitled "Plein Ciel," belonging to *La Légende des siècles,* Hugo actually envisions the balloon as the savior of mankind.

36 See Margaret Gilman, *Baudelaire the Critic* (New York, 1943), pp. 191-93; Crépet, *Correspondance générale* (Paris: Conard, 1949), 5:13, n. 1.

37 For a more detailed discussion of Baudelaire's review of *Les Misérables,* see my article "Baudelaire on *Les Misérables,*" *The French Review* (October, 1967), pp. 23-29.

38 Quoted from Léon Cellier, *Baudelaire et Hugo* (Paris: Corti, 1970), p. 201.

39 For Barbey d'Aurevilly's judgment of *Les Misérables, see* G. Corbière-Gille, *Barbey d'Aurevilly, critique littéraire* (Paris: Minard, 1962) and J. Petit, *Barbey d'Aurevilly critique* (Paris: Belles-Lettres, 1963). *Le Compère Mathieu* was written by Henri de Laurens (1719-97) in the libertine spirit of the eighteenth century.

40 Cellier, *Baudelaire et Hugo,* p. 200.

41 Crépet, *Correspondance générale,* pp. 40-41, n. 1.

42 Letter cited by Crépet in his notes to *Les Misérables, l'Art Romantique* (Paris: Conard, 1925), pp. 560-61.

43 Asselineau has suggested that the poet wrote his review of *Les Misérables* "to answer certain treacherous lies" (Eugène Crépet, *Baudelaire,* p. 301). In an explanatory note Crépet concludes that Asselineau was referring to an article, published in *Le Figaro,* June 11, 1858, in which Jean Rousseau had accused Baudelaire of loudly proclaiming in the Divan Lepeletier, "Hugo, what's that?" The argument appears very dubious in view of the fact that the accusation had been made in 1858 and that Baudelaire had already had an opportunity to praise Hugo's poetry not only in his 1859 essay on Gautier but also in his highly laudatory essay on Hugo in 1861.

44 Asselineau's comment on *Les Misérables (see* n. 43) and, in particular, his use of the word "dexterité" would seem to confirm this theory: "Certainly he admired Victor Hugo. He has given public evidence of that in many an article, more particularly the essay in the *Poètes français* of E. Crépet. He even insisted, in order to answer certain treacherous lies, upon doing a review for a newspaper of *Les Misérables* in which he showed all his skill; for, basically, the book with its moral outrageousness, its leaden paradoxes, irritated him immensely" (Crépet, *Baudelaire,* p. 301).

45 In recent years, two distinguished critics have taken exception to the view that Baudelaire's review was hypocritical. The late Jean Pommier in 1967 hazarded the opinion, without further explanation, that the article was not

as much an attempt at flattery as might appear. *See* Pommier, "Baudelaire et Hugo," *Revue des Sciences Humaines* (July–Sept., 1967), fasc. 127, pp. 345–46. In 1970, in his volume *Baudelaire et Hugo,* Léon Cellier generously approved my opinion and quoted extensively from the article in *The French Review (see* n. 37). For Cellier's book, *see* n. 38.

46   In his letter of May 24 to Madame Meurice, Baudelaire was not referring, as is usually believed, to Hugo in speaking of "le célèbre _____" who lectured him for two hours. Scholars have suggested that the blank space stood for "cuckold" or another derogatory term. Cellier is the first to point out that Baudelaire could not have meant Hugo, since the latter was in Guernsey at the time. *See* his *Baudelaire et Hugo,* p. 241.

47   Cellier, *Baudelaire et Hugo,* p. 263.

48   Ibid., p. 258.

49   Ibid., p. 259.

50   Ibid., p. 265.

51   Flaubert, *Correspondance* (Paris: Conard, 1926–33), 3:249.

52   Ibid., 3:320.

53   Ibid., 7:285.

54   Ibid., 7:285.

55   Alison Fairlie, *Baudelaire: Les Fleurs du Mal* (London: Edward Arnold, 1960), p. 16.

56   B. F. Bart, "Madame Bovary after a Century," in *Madame Bovary and the Critics, A Collection of Essays,* ed. B. F. Bart (New York: New York University Press, 1966), p. 196.

57   Flaubert, *Correspondance,* 7:280.

58   Ibid., 2:365.

59   Ibid., 4:164.

60   Ibid., 2:461.

61   René Wellek, *A History of Modern Criticism: 1750–1950,* 4 vols. (New Haven and London: Yale University Press, 1965), 2:9; Flaubert, 2:457.

62   Victor Bromberg, *Flaubert par lui-même* (Paris: Editions du Seuil, 1971), p. 5.

63   Baudelaire's attitude toward women was often ambiguous. In certain poems or in letters sent either to Madame Sabatier or to Marie Daubrun he could be as sentimental or as prone to idealization as a Lamartine. To his older friend, Madame Meurice, he always showed the greatest respect and affection. At other times, depending on his mood, he saw woman, and especially the young girl, as the "bel animal" of Joseph de Maistre. In his chapter on women in *Le Peintre de la vie moderne,* he describes woman as "a kind of idol, stupid but dazzling, enchanting, who holds wills and destinies suspended on her glance" (*OC,* II:713).

64   For Baudelaire's ideas on dandyism see his chapter "Le Dandy" and "Eloge du maquillage" in his essay *Le Peintre de la vie moderne.* In addition, the

Journaux intimes contain numerous comments both on women and on the dandy.

65 Flaubert, *Madame Bovary,* bk. III, chap. 6. All references to *Madame Bovary* are contained within the text and cited according to book and chapter.

66 For a more detailed discussion of the relationship between Baudelaire and Madame Bovary, see my article "Baudelaire: Madame Bovary, c'est moi" in the *Kentucky Romance Quarterly* 20, no. 3 (1973):343–58.

67 Benjamin Bart, *Flaubert* (Syracuse: Syracuse University Press, 1967), p. 658.

68 Cellier, "Baudelaire et George Sand," *Revue d'Histoire Littéraire de la France* (April–June, 1967), pp. 15–35.

69 Ibid., p. 28.

70 Ibid.

71 Bandy and Pichois, *Baudelaire devant ses contemporains,* pp. 157–62.

72 *Baudelaire et Asselineau,* p. 252.

73 Henri Peyre, *The Centennial Celebration of Baudelaire's* Les Fleurs du Mal (Austin: University of Texas Press, 1958), p. xiv.

Index

DATE DUE

WITHDRAWN

DEMCO 38-297